D0554443

BASIC CONCEPTS IN MUSIC EDUCATION, II

BASIC CONCEPTS IN MUSIC EDUCATION, II

Richard J. Colwell, editor

UNIVERSITY PRESS OF COLORADO

Copyright © 1991 by the University Press of Colorado
P.O. Box 849
Niwot, Colorado 80544

All rights reserved.

The University Press of Colorado is a cooperative publishing enterprise supported, in part, by Adams State College, Colorado State University, Fort Lewis College, Mesa State College, Metropolitan State College of Denver, University of Colorado, University of Northern Colorado, University of Southern Colorado, and Western State College.

Library of Congress Cataloging-in-Publication Data

Basic concepts in music education, II / edited by Richard J. Colwell.
   p.   cm.
   Includes index.
   ISBN 0-87081-228-9
   1. Music — Instruction and study.   I. Colwell, Richard.
MT1.B33   1991
780'.7 — dc20   91-18068
                                                                              CIP
                                                                              MN

The paper used in this publication meets the minimum requirements of the American National Standard for Information Sciences—Permanence of Paper for Printed Library Materials. ANSI Z39.48–1984
∞

10 9 8 7 6 5 4 3 2 1

Contents

Contents

Part II: Music in the Schools

Contributors

Eunice Boardman (née **Meske**), Director of Graduate Studies in Music Education, University of Illinois, Urbana-Champaign

Wayne Bowman, Professor of Music and Chairman of Music Education, Brandon University, Brandon, Manitoba, Canada

Allen P. Britton, Dean Emeritus, School of Music, University of Michigan, Ann Arbor

Harry S. Broudy, Professor Emeritus of Philosophy of Education, University of Illinois, Urbana-Champaign

Clifton A. Burmeister, John W. Beattie Professor of Music 1952–1978, Northwestern University, Evanston, Illinois

Richard J. Colwell, Chairman of Music Education, Boston University

Robert Ehle, Professor of Music Theory and Composition, Graduate Coordinator of the School of Music, and Director of the Electronic Music Lab, University of Northern Colorado, Greeley

Charles Fowler, Director of National Cultural Resources, Inc., Washington, D.C., and former Editor of the *Music Educators Journal*

Richard M. Graham, Music Therapist, Indiana Mental Health System; Professor of Music and Head, Music Education and Music Therapy, University of Georgia, Athens

Foster McMurray, Professor Emeritus of Philosophy of Education, University of Illinois, Urbana-Champaign

James L. Mursell, Former Professor of Music Education, Teachers College, Columbia University, New York City

G. David Peters, Professor of Music Education and Director of the Illinois Technology-Based Instruction Project, University of Illinois, Urbana-Champaign

Contributors

Bennett Reimer, John W. Beattie Professor of Music, Chairman of Music Education, and Director, Center for the Study of Education and the Musical Experience, Northwestern University, Evanston, Illinois

Marilyn P. Zimmerman, Professor of Music, University of Illinois, Urbana-Champaign

Preface

Basic Concepts in Music Education, I, was originally published as the *Fifty-seventh Yearbook of the National Society for the Study of Education, Part I.* Thurber Madison was the chairman of the committee that obtained approval of the proposal for the yearbook in February 1956. The book appeared in 1958. Approval of this revised edition was obtained in 1988, and the book will appear in 1991.

The first yearbook on music education appeared in 1936 as the *Thirty-fifth Yearbook of the National Society for the Study of Education,* the idea for the yearbook originating with the board of directors of the society. The 1958 yearbook was suggested by the Music Educators National Conference and approved by the society. Despite steady sales of the yearbook over a twenty-five–year period, the society decided not to continue publishing yearbooks in music education after 1958.

The yearbook has been fundamental to the education of so many music educators in this century that it seemed important that the publication be continued. I contacted the living authors of the 1958 version, and they unanimously agreed that the yearbook should be continued and offered their cooperation in continuing the tradition. The University Press of Colorado undertook the publishing responsibilities; the resulting product you have before you.

Because several of the authors from the first edition are still living, the appropriate format seemed to be to continue the thrust of the 1958 book with suggestions about how the concepts for music education have changed in nearly thirty-five years. In Part I, Charles Fowler has written the lead chapter, replacing Thurber Madison's work, "The Need for New Concepts in Music Education." Chapter 2 is Foster McMurray's original chapter followed by his elaboration of the ideas that he originally presented. In Chapter 3, Harry S. Broudy makes very few alterations to his original chapter: he found that the concepts underlying a philosophy of music education have not changed in thirty-five years and cannot be expected to change over much longer periods. Wayne Bowman comments on the chapter originally authored by George McKay, and Bennett Reimer does the same for James L. Mursell's work (included in this volume). Both authors have added many

new insights to the original work. Marilyn P. Zimmerman's thinking replaces that of Louis Thorpe, and Part I is completed by Allen P. Britton's
fresh new chapter, which replaces his contribution to the first edition.

In this new edition, we have not made such a clear distinction between
Part I, "Disciplinary Backgrounds," and Part II, "Music in the Schools." The
two are more closely related as we approach the twenty-first century. Leading off Part II, Clifton A. Burmeister takes up where he left off in 1956,
finding much the same and much that has changed in the teaching of general
education. A composer and theorist, Robert Ehle has written the next chapter. Ehle is an individual who has been able to connect aesthetics and
criticism with the creative activities of the student and musician. Functional
music has become of greater importance to all teachers during the past
thirty-five years, and Richard M. Graham has written a chapter that clearly
puts functional music into perspective for all music educators. G. David
Peters adds a chapter on technology, and I have written the chapter on
evaluation, finding that this field has gone through three stages since Charles
Leonhard's original chapter but that the use of evaluation and the thinking of
music teachers about evaluation has changed little. The book is brought to a
close with a message for the teacher of teachers. Eunice Boardman
demonstrates the extent to which that field has changed since Oleta Benn
provided us with her message and guidelines for the beginner in the mid-
1950s.

The basic concepts of the profession should not change — and they
have not. It is important that we have this new book, which so vividly
portrays the consistency and the adaptations in a discipline that is as basic to
our culture as is music education.

RICHARD J. COLWELL
EDITOR

BASIC CONCEPTS IN MUSIC EDUCATION, II

Part I

Disciplinary Backgrounds

1

Finding the Way to Be Basic: Music Education in the 1990s and Beyond

Charles Fowler

As music educators entering the 1990s and looking ahead to the first decades of the twenty-first century, we must take stock of our present circumstances and the issues that plague us. Thirty years ago, Thurber Madison began Chapter 1 of *Basic Concepts in Music Education, I,* by justifying the need for new concepts in light of the well-recognized successes of the field. Today the situation appears to be quite different: the troubled waters of music education make the need for new concepts imperative.

This volume reverberates from the earlier work, but it resounds with its own perceptions born of the convictions and wisdom of some of today's outstanding leaders and scholars. Unlike the earlier work, in which the writers were surefooted and offered clear-cut solutions from a score of perspectives, some of them conflicting, the writers in this volume raise as many questions as they answer. Wayne Bowman admits that music is a complex business without many "pat, easy answers," and the quandaries raised by the other authors seem to prove his point. Foster McMurray discusses whether music is "a special privilege of a social and economic elite" or whether it belongs to all in equal measure. McMurray is one of four writers of the original volume who appear again here. Bennett Reimer asks whether "only certain *kinds* of expressiveness are good." Does music education embrace all music or only the so-called classical Western tradition? Robert Ehle ponders how the field should deal with the culture question. Pass it on, yes, he says, but *what* should be passed on?

Both Allen Britton and Clifton Burmeister explore the conflict between the emphasis on performance for the few and general music for the many. The problems of exceptional children, mainstreaming, and special education are examined by Richard Graham, and the complex maze of learning theories and their possible application to music teaching are studied by Marilyn Zimmerman. Eunice Boardman questions what the future music teacher needs to know, David Peters describes the status of technology, and Richard Colwell surveys an area rife with controversy — what we should do about evaluation and assessment in music education.

Our footing today is obviously less certain than it was three decades ago. The authors of this volume offer ways of thinking about the study of music given the dilemmas we face and the difficult choices and decisions that must be made. Music education: What is it? Why does it exist? Where is it headed? These questions permeate the pages of this book. They help to give focus and unity to the material, but the pervasive organizing principle is the general quest to find ways to make the study of music more effective and more highly valued.

Ferment that boils from uncertainty often leads to significant change. The seeds of change brew heartily in many of these treatises. At this juncture, music education appears to be on the precipice, edging its way cautiously through some fundamental adjustments. Let us acknowledge at the outset that no reader will agree with all of this book or, perhaps, even all of any one author. These thoughtful probings offer points of view based on research, logic, observations from experience, and gut-level belief and intuition. Some authors attempt to hold the ground, others to reach forward. There is disagreement here that calls for the reader to make choices. From these individual decisions will emerge the concepts that will guide practice in the future.

The task of this chapter is to set the stage, just as Madison set it in the preceding volume. In spite of the success Madison claimed for music education, he questioned whether this public acclamation was "necessarily an indication that the ultimate objectives of music education had been met" (p. 12). He raised concerns for higher standards, for balanced programs, for a realistic relation to national culture, and for adopting concepts from other fields "at the expense of legitimate values of music education" (p. 28) — all issues that haunt us today. But I choose to start where Madison left off, with "concern for the future conceptual framework of music education" (p. 29). Music educators, he said, "have always operated within the framework of general education and will continue to do so," but as education adjusts to changes in our culture, the arts themselves "can be affected" and "might well reflect such changes" (p. 28).

Necessarily, music education operates within the contexts of society and education, and it is in these contexts that the conceptual framework of music education takes shape.

THE CONTEXT OF THE ARTS IN AMERICAN SOCIETY

During the past thirty years, while arts programs have been steadily eroding in many public schools, particularly those in cities, the arts in society first flourished extraordinarily and then started to decline in the 1980s. National trends show that even our finest arts institutions are facing severe financial problems. The most recent Harris Poll found that attendance at arts events has declined 12 percent since 1984.[1] Lack of sufficient audiences has caused several orchestras to disband (Miami, New Orleans, Oklahoma, Oakland, Denver) and is threatening the existence of a number of others. Museum attendance is down, and the proportion of Americans who read serious contemporary literature is dwindling.

Lack of public support is causing many opera companies to shorten their seasons, scale back productions, and hire fewer big-name stars. Ballet and theatre companies are fighting to find enough season subscribers to sustain themselves. Some have succumbed: the Dallas Ballet, the Boston Shakespeare Company, the Hartman Theatre Company of Stanford, Connecticut, and the Alaska Repertory Company, among others. The serious music publishing industry in the United States is almost defunct.[2] To compound matters, some members of the U.S. Congress continue to mount periodic and determined campaigns to discontinue the National Endowment for the Arts.

LACK OF PUBLIC SUPPORT

A 1989 Post-ABC poll revealed that federal aid to public television and radio and assistance to the arts are not highly valued in the United States. Fewer than one out of five respondents favored higher spending for these areas. The U.S. value system seems to be turning its back on the arts, certainly in their classical forms. Part of the explanation for this decline is that older audiences for the arts have simply not been replaced. According to a Survey of Public Participation in the Arts, conducted by the National Endowment for the Arts in 1985, 53 percent of the citizens polled said "no" when asked if they had had lessons or classes in music when they were in school, and 80 percent said they had never studied music appreciation. Music appreciation courses were likely to have been taken only in college.[3]

We know from these studies that audiences for music consist of the better-educated segment of society. These are the people who support the symphony orchestras and who, we might presume, support the study of music in public schools. But there is a vast public who are unschooled in music and may be relatively indifferent to such values. When difficult choices have to be made in the hard-pressed world of school finance — say, whether to hire a reading specialist or another instrumental music teacher — priorities tend to favor the former.

The excellence of home sound systems may make concertgoing less necessary for some music lovers today. But the fact that they no longer offer their support in the form of ticket purchases to attend live performances is crippling. William Bolcom hypothesizes that people have come to eschew concerted activity, that "crowds *have* often become ugly in a way that wasn't true a short time ago."[4] Others would have us believe that the lack of audiences is due to the anarchy of today's art, detached as much of it is from public purpose, meaning, and understanding. Certainly the fact that art has gone its private way has not helped it in the marketplace. Nor does it serve the interest of the marketer, in this case the opera companies and symphony orchestras who try to relate to the twentieth century and look like they belong to it by occasionally performing works so socially defiant that they offend their conservative patrons. But the artist's anarchy, as damaging as it is to the vibrancy of these institutions, is not the crux of the problem. What we must remember is that when subscription seasons were sold out, the new music then was no more or less hospitable to the public.

CULTURAL UPHEAVAL

What we are facing is cultural upheaval. Our values are in flux. As public taste increasingly seems to embrace the sensational, the commercial, and the gross, aesthetic quality is being trashed in favor of the expedient — fast food, the quick fix, and easy entertainment. The world of America looking toward the new millennium is an increasingly barbaric place with slaughter on the streets, drugs perverting lives in almost every family, and constant revelations of deceit and crime in high places. It seems to be growing cruder and more insensitive. The fine arts are fundamentally at odds with these conditions.

In creating curricula in music, we must review and renew the notion that it is the responsibility of the school to pass on the cultural heritage — all of it — to the younger generation. And we must weigh this responsibility in the clear light of the revolution apparently going on in our culture among a public that revels in pop and exhibits little interest in the classics. Perhaps they are exhibiting, by default, the lack of alternatives the schools have taught them. What we do not give students teaches them something, too: that studying music is just for the bright and talented, that it is not really important, and that one can be considered educated without having any musical understanding.

THE EFFECTS ON MUSIC EDUCATION

The present condition and circumstances of classical music in American society should alarm colleges, universities, and conservatories that continue to churn out musicians for a drastically shrinking job market. It should cause them to take more serious interest in and responsibility for arts education in the public schools. Their future and the future of the arts are linked irrevocably to the fortunes of arts education in the total pre-collegiate educational curriculum.

They should be aware, too, that Western classical music is just part of the musical culture of Americans. Music education must encompass the whole cloth, not just part of it. Thurber Madison expressed concern "to bring the field [of music education] into a more realistic relation to the total social and cultural scene of life" (p. 25). He spoke of "the wide differences in musical tastes of our population and the greatly expanded nature of our national culture," and declared that "the music of minority groups should be given more attention."

Unless the United States can become more socially conscious and culturally responsible, the cultures of our minorities and majorities may be lost. Classical music as we have known it may continue to dissipate to be replaced by a more egalitarian, popular form, one that does not require an educational infrastructure to sustain itself. That decimation could extend to blues, gospel, and jazz — particularly the latter, which has become a classic American form today. When any part of a nation's cultural heritage is obliterated, everyone loses. Commercial forms of musical culture perpetuate themselves. The rest of our music heritage has to be nurtured to be preserved. This fact of life impinges on the entire music and music education world.

There is some good news in all this. Our artistic culture is such a precious part of us that even the threatened loss of any of it arouses our sense of preservation. With the incursion of technology and science overrunning our humanity and our humaneness, we need the arts more, not less. This threat has brought the embattled arts and arts education enterprises closer together. The two appear to be locked in a synergistic dependency much like science and science education. Arts and arts education enterprises

7

are beginning to recognize that they are interlocking and interdependent components of the same universe.

Increasingly, the arts and arts education embrace to survive. For symphony orchestras, opera companies, and chamber music groups (including jazz), music education is the long-term solution. Consequently, the National Endowment for the Arts and the state arts agencies have begun to pay increasing attention to the infrastructure of education. Similarly, arts education looks increasingly to arts organizations for their support and assistance. There is increasing awareness that without music in the schools, the less commercial and therefore more fragile forms of it will not ultimately survive in society.

There is other good news. After the antiaesthetic 1980s, we may be due for a turnaround: a more humanitarian wave may wash over American society. John Naisbitt and Patricia Aburdene, the authors of *Megatrends 2000*, see the declines of the recent decade as temporary. They say that "during the 1990s the arts will gradually replace sports as society's leisure activity." They predict "a modern renaissance in the visual arts, poetry, dance, theater, and music throughout the developed world . . . in stark contrast with the recent industrial era, where the military was the model and sports was the metaphor."[5] The emphasis on high-tech, the authors say, has created an imbalance that has to be corrected. We will have to regain our sense of meaning by reexamining our humanity. The sciences do not tell us what it means to be human. The arts do.

THE CONTEXT OF EDUCATION

In 1957, the year prior to the publication of *Basic Concepts*, our response to the Russian launching of *Sputnik* was a massive ($1 billion) federal mobilization of education to meet the pressing demands of national security and to keep our competitive economic edge in math and science. This conscription of education to serve the nation's political and economic agenda set a precedent for a policy that remains in effect today. In 1983, the National Commission on Excellence in Education issued the report *A Nation at Risk: The Imperative for Educational Reform*, which again tied education directly to our ability to compete in world markets and to regain "our once unchallenged preeminence in commerce, industry, science, and technological innovation."[6]

THE EFFECTS OF EDUCATIONAL REFORM

What are the major educational concerns described in *A Nation at Risk?* The report states that "average achievement of high school students on most standardized tests is now lower than 26 years ago when Sputnik was launched." Declines are noted specifically in reading, writing, and comprehension, in mathematics, and in science.[7] Now the challenge is the new "Information Age." Again the federal government has taken action to redefine education along totally utilitarian lines and to sell science and math to the American people as the panaceas of the future. In 1990, President Bush called for renewed emphasis on science and mathematics education.

The successive waves of back-to-basics educational reform during the past thirty years have seriously eroded the stature of music in the schools. Across the country, particularly in many of the largest cities, programs of music instruction at the elementary level have been reduced to ineffectuality. Where educational priorities favor a compulsive curriculum of reading, math, and science, music and the other arts are eliminated or consigned to the periphery. Many large-city school systems, among them Baltimore, Boston, Chicago, Los Angeles, New York, Philadelphia, and Seattle, no longer hire enough music specialists at the elementary level to provide even a minimal program, and elementary teachers pressured by increased testing do not have the time, the inclination, or the expertise to replace the lost instruction.

Pressures and priorities at the secondary level are similar. During the 1980s, credit requirements in the "five new basics" — English, mathematics, science, social studies, and computer science — were increased for high school graduation, threatening to eliminate the time for electives in music and other arts. The new basics elbowed the arts to the sidelines. In some states, bands, choruses, and orchestras were headed for extinction. A number of states reacted to the situation by establishing requirements in the arts for high school graduation, effectively preventing their demise. In states like Florida that had a six-period day, most school districts extended the day to seven periods, once again providing time for electives.

But support for the arts is relatively soft. Only nine of the thirty-one states that have established graduation requirements actually mandate some arts for every high school student. Eight of the thirty-one states require study of the arts for only the college-bound. Fourteen states require credit in the fine arts or other subjects, which means that students can still graduate without any arts. Nineteen other states do not require the arts at all for high school graduation. This means that in forty-one states, students today can be given a high school diploma and called educated without any study in the arts.

9

THE ECONOMIC IMPERATIVE

Exacerbating the situation is the further conscription of education to serve the interest of the corporate and business sectors. Corporate executives frequently complain about the quality of our educational system, and usually with good cause. AT&T says it spends $6 million a year to educate 14,000 employees in basic reading and math. American Express claims it spends more than $10 million a year to teach its employees to do their jobs competently. Other corporations have been forced to engage seriously with education. The report of the Committee for Economic Development, which represents most of the major corporations in the United States, states that "our schools stand accused of failing the nation's children and leaving the economy vulnerable to better-educated and more highly trained international competitors."[8]

Business wants a work force that can function, and it wants education to make students employable.[9] But few in the corporate sector see any relationship between the very practical outcomes they seek from education and what students learn from studying the arts.[10] This shortsightedness further reduces the importance of arts education. By underestimating the educational potential of the arts for every student, corporate leaders further relegate the arts to the educational periphery. So, in developing new curricula in music, we have to take into account and address those very practical matters that make students productive citizens.

TESTING

As wave after wave of reform and demands for "back-to-basics" have washed over our school systems, accountability and testing have increased commensurately. These tests breed attitudes and conditions that are not hospitable to the arts. In effect, they dictate to school administrators, faculty, parents, and students what is important. Consequently, the resources of the schools are funneled accordingly. These tests define education: what is tested is what is taught and valued.

In general, the arts are not in this picture: the Scholastic Aptitude Test deals with reading comprehension and mathematics. In a very real sense, this test defines the mind as being primarily an instrument of verbal and mathematical intelligence. Because education has become the handmaiden of these tests, schools actually delimit intelligence. To a large extent, where these tests become the engines of education, schools stop addressing the rest of the human mind.

Although music education exists in this context, we do not have to accept being a victim of it. Educational testing itself is constantly undergoing evaluation. Its failure to serve the needs of general education as a whole, including an education in the arts, can be made known. Then, too, improved evaluation and assessment in music could be a gateway to develop more effective programs and teaching and to increase the status of music in education.

THE NEW GOAL: TO BECOME BASIC

The unrelenting pressure on schools to serve corporate and commercial needs has established an elite core of subjects in American schools that are labeled "the basics." These are the subjects that every student must master. The arts are seldom included in this core. What we must come to realize is that, in establishing that hierarchy, we have not just shut out the arts: we have also closed the schools to certain students who would choose means other than those that are linguistic and mathematical to express themselves, relate to the world, and excel. If students do not fit the linguistic/mathematical pattern today, they are apt to find it difficult to be successful in most public schools.

COMMANDING MORE THAN MARGINAL STATUS

In many of today's schools, there is too little opportunity for certain students to explore the world through other forms of intelligence — musical, spatial, bodily/kinesthetic, and the personal intelligences of knowing oneself and others — as Howard Gardner has framed them.[11] This is one of the reasons that students rebel and drop out. Were Edison and Ford great readers? Was Beethoven good at addition? Was Picasso a great speller? Was Balanchine a master of English? These humans changed the world, but not from minds based on linguistic or mathematical intelligence.

What apparently is lacking is the empowerment of music and the other arts to command anything more than marginal status in the public educational system. By the early 1980s, budgetary restraints and pressures to emphasize basic subjects caused schools to allow arts instruction to languish. In 1985, the Getty Center for Education in the Arts issued a review of art education that found it lacking in substance and standards and generally not seen as vital to a child's education.[12] The Center launched a nationwide effort to make art education more academic with the thought that increased rigor and a broader curriculum encompassing aesthetics, art history, and art criticism as well as the development of the skills of production would alter perceptions of art education and establish it as a basic. The reasoning: If art

11

education is to be accepted as an academic subject, it must look and act like one. The model of the artist that had long held center stage in the teaching and learning of art was supplemented by the models of the aesthetician, historian, and critic. Acquisition of knowledge replaced creative endeavor as the emphasis.

Will being more academic bring greater educational respectability? These efforts are still underway, causing considerable ferment in art education. The Center has begun to make overtures in music education, and it remains to be seen what influences and changes this outside agency will bring to the field.

The possible shallowness of some music education programs was a concern three decades ago. Madison spoke of "the conflict between recreational and education concepts" (p. 20). Today, we might speak of the conflict between entertainment and substantive education. The period from 1958 (when *Basic Concepts, I* was published) to 1990 roughly corresponds to the beginning of the television age and the birth of the technological society. We as music educators must be cautious that our concentration on performing does not result in the public equating music education with the frivolous world of TV and entertainment and not with the technological future that has become the serious business of education. We must find ways to make clear connections between music education and national educational priorities.

During the 1980s, the National Endowment for the Arts (NEA) asserted new interest and commitment to arts education. Heretofore, the NEA had limited its involvement in education almost exclusively to supporting artists in schools. But the arts establishment found it increasingly in its interest to do something to counter the effects of curtailments that have hampered and diminished arts education programs in many public school systems. These programs constitute the infrastructure that educates the artists and audiences that are the lifeblood of the nation's professional arts organizations. A vast knowledgeable public is needed to sustain the country's cultural enterprises. Indeed, for arts organizations the goal of arts education is clear and simple: to develop new audiences. What is important, seemingly, is not what the arts can contribute to the individual but what the individual can contribute to the arts. Even so, the entry of the NEA into mainline, curriculum-based arts education is an acknowledgment of the difficulties faced by the field and the crisis brewing.

In 1988 at the behest of Congress the NEA issued a report on arts education that states flatly that "basic arts education does not exist in the United States today."[13] The report defines basic arts education as a curriculum that provides all students, not only the gifted and talented, with knowledge of, and skills in, the arts. In light of their penchant to concentrate on performance programs for the talented, music educators would find it difficult to take issue with this assessment. This bias for performance probably contributes to the perception that music education is more devoted to entertainment than to serious learning. When skill becomes an end in itself, knowledge of music is often given little attention.

Why does music not command greater educational esteem? Clearly some of the reasons are outside the control of the field; that is, compromising the larger purposes of education in the interest of serving the narrow goal of employability, overloading the curriculum by intensifying academic requirements and testing in the interest of guaranteeing our economic future, and creating a bare-bones, so-called "no-frills" curriculum by underfinancing local school systems in the interest of saving taxes. But some of the reasons are in our court completely. Why is the educational importance of music underestimated? Why are we continually on the defensive, continually having to justify our existence?

DEFINING WHAT IS BASIC

The curriculum of American schools stresses a core of common learnings — a broad set of knowledges and understandings that are important to every citizen. What is this basic curriculum? Ernest L. Boyer gives this answer: "Broadly defined, it is a study of those consequential ideas, experiences, and traditions common to all of us by virtue of our membership in the human family at a particular moment in history."[14] These common learnings teach the next generation about their human heritage. If the arts are part of this heritage — and who could argue sensibly that they are not? — then they should be included in these common learnings. They should be basic. They should be required of all.

If our current situation was as simple as this logic suggests, music and the other arts would now have the status of science and mathematics in American schools. In truth, it should be that simple, but reality and practice intercede. In visual arts, all that creative play with crayons and paint with little emphasis on the development of technique, understanding of aesthetic principles, or knowledge of art history has been viewed as inconsequential. In music, particularly in the high school, all that concentration on skill development for the select students in band and chorus has been recognized for what it so often is — not an education in the musical heritage but a perfecting of performance. Our educational practices in the arts have betrayed us. In music the goal has not been education through performance so much as performance as an end in itself. The goal has not been to teach all students their musical heritage but rather to teach production to the talented. We have been remarkably effective at achieving the latter and outrageously negligent at providing the former.

13

Some would have us believe that performance and appreciation are at odds, that we must choose one or the other, and that those who speak for one are necessarily the enemy of the other. Thirty years ago, Madison noted that "the school music program appears to be administered on the assumption that the *performance* of music is the means through which most appreciation is developed" (p. 24). Performance remains one of the most essential means of learning about music. With the artist as model, in this case the performer, learning by doing has been a central strength of music education. If we have been negligent, it is in ignoring the model of artist as composer. Being creative is another vibrant way for students to acquire musical understanding. Clearly, to be basic, music education does not have to become academic in the staid meaning of that term. We do not have to give up one of our strongest cards—that music is refreshingly dynamic *because* of the different way in which it is taught and learned. Performance, let us hope, is here to stay, and creating music will be accorded ever greater emphasis in the years ahead. Both should be important components of any general music study.

Today, the attempt to make music basic is the galvanizing goal of music education. Surely music curricula cannot be limited to just skill development for the talented and achieve this status. As soon as we harness our energies behind the belief that music education is part of general education, that music education is basic education, we have to accept the idea that music is a worthy study for *every* student. If music is basic, it is no different than math or science. No person can be truly educated without some understanding of it.

We do not need more and better music education to create more and better musicians or music educators. We need more and better music education to produce better-educated human beings, citizens who will value and evolve a worthy American civilization. If music is going to be accepted as a basic part of the curriculum, it must be taught so that it makes people better educated. This concept recognizes that a certain amount of performance is a necessary part of how we develop musical perception. But is performance the goal, or is performance a means of serving other more important ends?

A GENERAL CURRICULUM FOR ALL

We have made a serious error in music education. For many years we have put most of our energies into educating the gifted and the talented. In this sense, we have consigned ourselves to vocational or career education. In doing this, we have compounded the problems of music in American society. We have assumed responsibility for developing new musicians and music teachers but not the new audiences necessary to sustain them. What good is it to develop and spawn new artists if we do not develop an understanding and supportive public? The two go hand in hand. Where is the greater need — for more musicians or for more public interest in music? If we are going to have symphony orchestras and opera companies in the future, we have to educate people to value these forms and attend performances of them. We cannot assume that these audiences somehow hatch on their own. They have to be nurtured. Are we nurturing them sufficiently through our performing groups and through our efforts in general education?

Schools have an obligation to pass the musical heritage on to every child. These windows on the world that touch our spirit and enlighten and enliven our lives are not private domains, and we have no right to make them so. They are part of our basic human heritage. If music education does not take on the responsibility of passing a basic understanding and knowledge of our musical heritage on to the new generation, we have failed fundamentally.

But there is another compelling reason for music teachers to take on responsibility for general music education: we cannot afford to have any enemies in the arts. We must face the fact that it is the people whom we do not reach in music that end up being unsupportive members of Congress, state legislators, mayors, school board members, school administrators, curriculum coordinators, classroom teachers, and parents. Paradoxically, these are the people who often make the rules and set the policies about the arts in spite of, and even because of, their scant knowledge of them.

That ignorance comes back to haunt us as music educators. We victimize ourselves when we deny people a music education, and the indifference returns in the form of curtailments, slashed budgets, and lack of general support for music education programs; in insufficient audiences for live music performances; financial problems for community musical groups; and attacks on the National Endowment for the Arts. If we cannot afford to have such enemies, we must not only educate every student in music but also fight for the right to do so. From this perspective, providing a general musical education to every student is the focus and goal of music education, and our performing groups are a specialized component of it. This realignment in no way reduces the importance of performance or performing groups. On the contrary — making performance a central means to attain this outcome places it squarely in the context of general education. It establishes it as a part of basic education, a status that evades it at present.

If we want music to be basic, we have to teach it as a basic. We will have to strike a better balance between skill development and the acquisition of knowledge. We will have to recognize creativity as an essential tool for developing musical thought and understanding. We will have to provide courses for all students — not just the talented. We will have to combine directing with real teaching on every level.

WHAT MAKES MUSIC BASIC?

The case for music education is as strong as, perhaps stronger than, it has ever been. Even a cursory reading of Bennett Reimer's *A Philosophy of Music Education*[15] should assure anyone that we are on very firm ground. Basing our educational approach to music in the schools on the aesthetic philosophy of absolute expressionism is basing our practice on the solid foundations of the integrity of music as an art. But translating what we know about the art form into an educational rationale is not easy. Staking our claim that music education is basic education on aesthetic philosophy poses difficulties. The question, as Reimer reminds us, is "how to balance philosophical honesty with practical efficacy."[16] Considering the fact that the curriculum of American schools is justified in largely utilitarian terms, that is excellent advice.

Given the fact that it is the practical (pragmatic) viewpoint of the public and most school administrators and board members that determines what is important in the curriculum, it behooves us to show them in precisely those terms why music is basic. From a pragmatic perspective, music education provides the human family with at least three fundamental and unique functions. These practical and useful functions of music education are true to the nature of music as an art form. In this sense, they represent a meeting and melding of aesthetic and instrumental values. All three can be applied across the other art forms as well, though with somewhat different emphases and interpretations. Because they are indigenous to the arts, music and music teaching do not have to be distorted to teach for these outcomes. These functions could serve as a conceptual framework for music education, providing the foundations and focus of the curriculum and the substantiation for music being included in basic education. They are concepts that could set our course in the years ahead. For the purpose of this overview, "concepts" are defined as those underlying truths that can serve as a rationale for establishing the place of music education in the schools, for formulating its curriculum, and for guiding our actions and advocacy efforts. If, as Harry Broudy suggests, general education should be thought of "as the cultivation of *capacities* for realizing value,"[17] then these functions should lie at the center of education in music.

1. The study of music provides an essential part of the foundation for humane civilization by encouraging all students to cultivate and refine their sensibilities.

At its best, arts education opens the door to learning. It awakens our eyes, our ears, our feelings, our minds. Encounters with the arts invite us to explore worlds of meaning that lie right next to the curtain that the old Persian proverb says has never been drawn aside — Rembrandt showing us the soul of his subjects; Mozart showing us the beauty of order; Shakespeare showing us the triumph of the human spirit over adversity. Such insights help students to break through the mathematical, factual, "you name it," and "memorize-this" confines of public education. By intensifying the relationship between our senses and the world around us, the arts quicken our curiosity about the mysteries of the intuitive and imaginative worlds that beckon us beyond the simplistic right and wrong litanies that prevail in so many American classrooms. They put us in touch with our inner being, our real selves. Beeb Salzer, a professor of theatre design at San Diego State University, explains it this way: "The arts play a special role in a society such as ours, which is founded on a linear rationality and humanism. They offer a permissible contact with the irrational, the emotional, and the mysterious forces that logic cannot explain."[18]

One's feelings and spirit are part of the cognitive process, but education seldom accords them the attention they deserve. We need to educate the emotive part of our being so that we have clearer perceptions of those fundamental human states that have so much to do with interpersonal relations — love, hate, anxiety, hope, and a host of other feelings. Music is a way we give concrete representation to these inner mental states. Susanne Langer called this process the "*objectification* of subjective life."[19] Just as science captures and represents parts of the world in scientific terms, the arts capture and represent parts of the world in artistic terms. Music expresses a unique realm inexpressible by any other means.

Through music education, students develop their musical intelligence. In defining human cognition, musical intelligence is recognized as one of our autonomous intelligences.[20] The fact that humans can think sound and rhythms and organize them into patterns and forms to give representation to our sentient life is a unique capacity. It permits us to capture, record, store, and share perceptions about our emotive life that might otherwise escape us. Even Stravinsky, recanting his earlier statement to the contrary, stated that "a composer works in the embodiment of his feelings and, of course [music] may be considered as expressing or symbolizing them."[21] Music puts us in touch with our feelings and spirit as they relate to their ideal expressive embodiments in the musical works of the ages. Beethoven's "Ode to Joy" from his Ninth Symphony comes to mind as a prime example of the apotheosis of such expression and a reason our musical heritage is so important.

Should schools provide access to music study because it is a basic intelligence? Gardner points out: "Whereas, in the case of language, there is considerable emphasis in the school on further linguistic attainments, music occupies a relatively low niche in our culture, and so musical illiteracy is acceptable."[22] As an intellectual faculty, musical intelligence has been neglected with little seeming consequence. Or has it?

17

There are many indications that the failure of schools to cultivate and refine the sensibilities of their students has had adverse effects upon the younger generation. Drugs, crime, hostility, indifference, and insensitivity run rampant in schools that do not provide sufficient instruction in the arts.[23] In the process of overselling science, mathematics, and technology as the salvation of commerce, schools have denied students something more precious — access to their inner beings and their personal spirit. Music speaks through and to a different sensory system than any other subject — that of auditory perception. As Elliot Eisner has pointed out, when we deny children access to a major expressive mode such as music, we deprive them of "the meanings that the making of music makes possible."[24] The result is a form of human deprivation. Without attending to the human spirit, schools tend to turn out insensitive citizens who lack compassion — people whose macho aggressiveness is not tempered by the controlling forces of sensitivity and caring about others. Many of today's schools, devoid of the arts, are cultivating a generation of modern-day barbarians. American society is the victim.

In teaching us to be receptive to our own and other's intuitions, insights, and feelings, the arts teach us something even more valuable: how to be empathetic. Scholastic Aptitude Tests do not measure the heart. Let us always remember that intelligence can be used to deceive and to cheat; it can be used self-servingly as a tool of greed; it can be used cruelly and with indifference; it can cause others to suffer and even to die. Some of Einstein's most important discoveries, born of great intelligence, were put to destructive use. In contrast, empathy intercedes; it reigns in such uses of intelligence. If we have empathy, we can assume another person's point of view. We can put ourselves in their shoes. To the degree that the arts create empathy, they develop a sense of humane responsibility and are a vitally important part of our moral education. Without empathy, we have no compassion for other human beings.

The arts teach children sympathy. They allow children to perceive themselves in relation to other human beings, who also fear, suffer, love, fail, and triumph. That is learning to react and to interact and to project one's own personality into the life of another, and that is basic education.

2. The study of music provides an essential part of the foundation for humane civilization by establishing a basic relationship between the individual and the cultural heritage of the human family.

As advancing systems for travel and communication bring the peoples of the world closer, understanding human differences becomes increasingly important. The foundations for peace between peoples depends on intracultural respect and exchange. Recognizing our interdependence as peoples is the backbone of commerce in today's world. By building relationships between the individual and the community we assure the stability of our communal society.

American society today is a microcosm of the entire world. Our multiculturalism is an American fact of life, and music is one of the most pervasive and persuasive ways we express it. Immigrant populations are challenging schools to find new ways to study cultural differences and to build bridges between cultures. Music provides a fundamental way to understand our own and other people's humanness. We neglect such enlightenment at our own peril. Schools that do not provide sufficent education in music are not investing youth in the tradition of community values that unite the society. Nor are they providing a basis to study and appreciate or, at the very least, to understand the values of other societies.

Because music is an expression of the beings that create it, it reflects their thinking and values as well as the social milieu from which it originates. Even if it is not the overt intent of the composer, the music we listen to tends to define who we are and give us identity as a social group. Because it reflects identity, music also provides the basis for understanding identity. Music is a basic way that humans express the individuality of their social character. Tribal music evokes the soul of the tribe, just as many different kinds of music represent the cultural mix of the United States. African-, Asian-, European-, Hispanic-, and Native-American music define the multicultural makeup of American society. This is why the country from which a piece of music originates can often be distinguished by sound alone. Recognizing this characteristic of music, nineteenth-century composers made nationalism an aesthetic movement. The blue notes that Gershwin and Copland introduced into their music are distinctively American because they emanate from African-American musical traditions.

In his opening chapter of *Basic Concepts, I,* Madison speaks of the success of music educators and the "universal and highly varied appeal of music itself to children and youth" (p. 4). Today, the appeal of music to youth remains intense, albeit for commercial music. Our youth are the targets of a multimillion-dollar industry. Television and radio broadcasting, pop concerts and recordings, and the ever-present portable cassette player have made music ubiquitous and diverse for youth — without help from schools. Black, white, and Hispanic pop of an incredible variety exist; there is something for every taste. This is music in the vernacular — music that deliberately uses everday "language" and is tailored to readily appeal and communicate.

Like any of the many genres of music, some of this commercial music is fine by any standard, some is merely good, and much of it is vacuous and ephemeral. Harry Broudy has asked: "Do public school pupils in a democratic society need 'fine' art or will the popular brands do just as well?"[25] It is the pervasiveness and command of this music — its capacity to saturate and satiate — that poses the challenge for music education. Our youth must be given opportunity to access the full range of music that is their rich heritage, not just one form or style, however varied by new releases.

The diversity of music in the world is a richness we share with the human family. The greatest gift one people can give to another is to share its culture, and one of the most revealing ways to do this is through music. If we are not to be a country of many insular groups, we must establish cultural connections. Music provides a way to do this by establishing understanding across our many distinguishable artistic legacies. Music teaches respect for the genius of human musical invention; the characteristics that distinguish cultural styles are marvels of human creation. One cannot be moved by the zeal of gospel music without respecting the humanity that created it. To share musical creations across cultures is to share our deepest values. Recognizing our similarities and understanding our differences gives us a base to establish cultural cohesiveness and respect, two vitally important values in a shrinking world in which technology seems to doggedly deny our humanness.

Music provides us with another important connection with our communal heritage: it enables us to express the ceremonies of our lives. Music is a fundamental way we express the tragedy of war, the triumph over adversity, consolation in death, our reverence for God, the meaning and value of peace, harmony, and love — universal human states that express the values held by society. The feelings of patriotism and victory, of hope and dignity, of community pride and solidarity are all given clear expression in music. A culture's imprint, its sense of celebrating its own life-style, is inherent in its music.

The extent to which school performing groups, particularly high school bands, have expressed civic homogeneity is the extent to which they have been valued by the community. A high school band marching in a Fourth of July parade celebrates its town's patriotism and hope for the continuity of life tomorrow. Perhaps no group personifies this aspect more than the Harlan (Kentucky) Boys Choir that sang at President George Bush's Inaugural Ceremony in Washington, D.C., in January 1989. The members of this choir are young men from a coal-mining town in the Appalachian Mountains known for its history of labor violence. Cat Stacey, owner of Cat's Beauty Shop in Harlan, called the choir's performance "one of the highlights of my life. A cold chill just goes through you to hear them." The choir's director, David Davies, said of the students, "[They] represent normal everyday children. We want music to be important to their lives, but not [be] their whole lives." These students are not studying music to become musicians.

They are learning that music is a basic way that a society expresses its character and the values it believes in. The people of Harlan support music as a symbol of their indelible community spirit — their pride in who they are. These performers are learning how to communicate — how to "speak" to and for their community — and music is valued in the schools accordingly.

Many of our high school graduates have difficulty communicating because they have not been introduced to many of the *tools* of communication. All the art forms are means of expression and communication, even though the emphasis in arts education has been largely on the former. But each of the arts functions as an important and unique communication system, and education in the arts is primarily a search for meaning.

The arts are forms of thought every bit as potent in what they convey as mathematical and scientific symbols. They are the ways in which human beings "talk" to themselves and to each other. They are the languages of civilization through which we express our fears, anxieties, curiosities, hungers, discoveries, and hopes. (I have borrowed some of the ideas and language here from my book, *Can We Rescue the Arts for America's Children?* [New York: American Council for the Arts, 1988]). The arts are modes of communication that give us access to the stored wisdom of the ages. Most important, they are the ways we give form to our ideas and imagination so that they can be shared with others.

The arts are nothing if they are not responsive to people. To think of the various art forms as systems of communication is vastly different from thinking of them as self-expression, a kind of self-indulgence that can be socially irresponsible and, therefore, little regarded. Arts that communicate put us in touch with others; they reach out to embrace people. They are of the people, by the people, and for the people. Communication shuts down the ivory towers. It makes our symphony orchestras and other presentation arts enterprises responsive to the public, something they sometimes forget. And it makes our arts programs in schools touch everyone. It means that when we use the arts for expressive purposes — when we create in music — our intent is to convey to others. That assures connections between people, all kinds of people, and those connections are fundamentally important. They are part of basic education.

3. The study of music provides an essential part of the foundation for humane civilization by furnishing students with a crucial aesthetic metaphor of what life at its best might be.

Corporate America is deeply concerned about the failure of schools in making people employable, particularly because of their inability to read, write, and compute. But the schools' relationship to employability should extend much further. Paul E. Burke, a member of the Commission on

Standards for School Mathematics (of the National Council of Teachers of Mathematics) says, "To be educated, you need to know various habits of thought. There is a mathematical approach that works in some situations. But kids have been exposed to that for eight years before high school. And it's not the only approach. Art and history also involve certain habits of thought that are worth acquiring."[26] And he might have added music.

America suffers from a loss of quality in craftsmanship and design. The U.S. automotive industry lost its competitive edge to workers in other countries who can produce a product of quality and reliability. Quality is produced by people who care about what they are doing. The arts teach that kind of caring. They teach us to live up to something. They teach us craftsmanship.

In the process of musical creation — whether it is in the form of composing or performing — students learn how to pursue and try to realize an ideal. They are confronted by, and attempt to live up to, a standard. In the process of creating, they inevitably compare their product at any given moment with an image — in this case an aural image — of what they are striving for. They learn to be self-critical, to apply a standard to their own efforts and make the necessary changes to achieve it. And in their pursuit they learn perseverance — how to work and achieve over the long term.

For a society to have an effective work force, it is essential that it turn out citizens who recognize and respect good craftsmanship, who care about detail and are committed to an artistic result, and who have the ability to judge their own efforts by the highest standards and make corrections accordingly. Music is a celebration of that kind of perfection, that kind of excellence. It is one of the basic ways we learn to release our positive energies toward an aesthetic result. It is one of the essential ways we acquire the habit of thinking aesthetically.

Music provides students with an aesthetic frame of reference that has broad applicability; individuals who are educated musically think differently because of it. Music study transforms the self, providing an aesthetic value orientation. Ideally, the aesthetics of music become the aesthetics of life. Through the study of music we recognize the beauty of order. We understand the striving for perfection. We appreciate how all the elements — the details — make the expressive whole and how important those details are. These conceptual understandings are not discarded when the student leaves the music classroom — these understandings emerge in other settings and are applied there.

The aesthetic awareness we learn through the study of music becomes a way we relate to the world. Personal taste and the expression of it are basic elements of the human condition. Aesthetic considerations are essential to the satisfactory conduct of society and empower us to create our own best state of existence. When the aesthetic component is ignored, we denigrate life: we dehumanize our environments, bombard people with ugliness, and deprive people of the comforts and satisfactions they need for their psychological well-being. Aesthetics is a natural and important part of our encounter with life. It is the way we bring our sensual and rational being to terms with the world around us.

Conflict between the rational and the emotional human impulses is ages old. Somehow each generation learns how to reconcile these conflicting extremes — the opposition of thought and feeling — to bring harmony to our fractured nature. Friedrich Schiller (1759–1805) pointed out in his *Letters on the Aesthetic Education of Man* that these two opposing drives are both important and should be preserved, that neither should be sacrificed to the other. He saw the answer in the development of a nature both sensuous and rational. The arts permit this reconciliation because in them the sensuous and the rational are combined.

If schools do not provide students with sufficient education in the arts, they deny students opportunities that would enable them to think and operate with an aesthetic frame of reference. The important point here is the significant transfer of aesthetic understanding from music to other realms of life. The quality of aesthetic thought, expectations, and satisfactions learned through music study, applied across the board, can make a substantial difference in the quality of life. That is why the arts are not the domain of only the privileged, the rich, or the talented, but belong to all. The life of every citizen can be enhanced by acquiring an understanding of music. Quality of life and quality of workmanship are concepts that are of fundamental value to American society. They are basic education.

These concepts of music as a means of cultivating and refining our sensibilities, of establishing a basic relationship between the individual and the cultural heritage of the human family, and of furnishing students with a crucial aesthetic metaphor of what life at its best might be constitute basic education at its finest. These goals derive directly from the indigenous nature of music itself. We do not have to distort music and misuse it to achieve these very practical outcomes. But we do have to establish our curricula with these outcomes in mind if we want to claim and achieve them.

RECOMMENDATIONS

Improving the status of music education in today's schools will require simultaneous efforts on two fronts — education and music education. The field will have to support and work to implement some fundamental changes in overall educational policy in the nation at the same time that it institutes its own internal reforms. Outward change will require inward change.

POLICIES IN EDUCATION

Persuading schools to budget and provide arts instruction for K–12 as part of basic education will require some substantial alterations in the way educational leaders think about the arts. I suggest the following general recommendations for educational policy as a start:

1. All American children should be afforded access to their cultural heritage as a right of citizenship. One of the irrefutable responsibilities of schools in the United States is to pass on the cultural heritage to the next generation. That heritage includes music and the other arts.
2. The arts should be recognized and valued as vast resources for teaching youth how to function effectively in the world. These resources complement and balance learnings in science, technology, and other subjects.
3. Equality of educational opportunity is as important in cultural subjects as in any other. Every American citizen is endowed with the fundamental right to develop his or her artistic talents and knowledge and should be provided equivalent basic opportunities to do so.
4. The arts constitute a curriculum equivalent in importance to the sciences and social studies and deserve equivalent educational treatment and resources, including study that is formal and in-depth.
5. The arts, like any major area of accumulated perception and insight, should be taught by persons who have understanding, skill, knowledge, and commitment. School systems have an obligation to provide such expertise in the arts to their students on the same basis as other subjects and to offer instructional programs of substance, expectation, and verified quality.

POLICIES IN MUSIC EDUCATION

The greatest impetus for making music basic must come from within. We cannot ask for educational reform without considering our own reform in the process. The profession cannot simply declare music basic;[27] that status must be earned. New strategies and policies can help to nudge us along in this direction, but concerted efforts and willingness to change will be required. To establish music as basic, we will have to refocus curricular goals, alter the content of learning, and improve music teaching. To make music basic, the field will have to make the following basic changes:

1. Recognize that music education serves the interests of music in American society and that both music and music education can and should be

mobilized to work as allies.

2. Formulate the music curriculum on the basis of the practical value of music study for every child and the well-being of American society; in other words, develop a curriculum that treats music as basic education.

3. View the musical heritage of Americans as multicultural and the focus of the curriculum as transcultural.

4. Treat music as part of a comprehensive arts curriculum so that its stature is enhanced by its position within a major branch of knowledge in the same way that biology, chemistry, and physics luxuriate under the generic banner of "science."

5. Make the acquisition of general musical understanding central to music education whether the means is through performance, creativity, or through general courses of other kinds.

6. Find the musical means to evaluate and assess students, teachers, and programs to assure high curricular standards, quality of learning achievement, and methodological effectiveness.

These extraordinary times call for extraordinary changes. We must be willing to reason anew, to rethink our goals, and to meet challenges head on. That is what this book and the chapters that follow are all about. Thirty years ago, Thurber Madison observed that "over the years, through successful promotion and planning, the music-education program has developed to the place where, today, it is in reality an established part of the program of the nation's schools" (p. 18). Can we make that same claim, unequivocally and without reservation, today? The new concepts we establish, the agenda we set, and the new modes of operation we adopt for music education must unify and ignite our energies and send us into the new millennium with renewed convictions about the role and value of music in American schools.

NOTES

1. *Americans and the Arts V: Highlights From a Nationwide Survey of Public Opinion,* conducted by the National Research Center of the Arts, an affiliate of Louis Harris and Associates, Inc. (New York: American Council for the Arts, 1988), p. 12.

2. William Bolcom, "Trouble in the Music World," *Musical America,* March 1990 (Vol. 110, No. 2), p. 20.

3. These figures cited in *Toward Civilization: A Report on Arts Education* (Washington, D.C.: National Endowment for the Arts, 1988), p. 33.

4. Bolcom, *op. cit.,* p. 21.

5. John Naisbitt and Patricia Aburdene, *Megatrends 2000: Ten New Directions for the 1990's* (New York: Morrow, 1990), pp. 62–63.

6. The National Commission on Excellence in Education, *A Nation at Risk: The Imperative for Educational Reform* (Washington, D.C.: U.S. Government Printing Office, 1983), p. 5.

7. *Ibid.* See pp. 8 and 9.

8. *Investing in Our Children: Business and the Public Schools* (New York: Committee for Economic Development, 1985), p. 2.

9. *Ibid.,* p. 17.

10. The Committee acknowledges that the arts, which it calls nonacademic extracurricular activities, are worthwhile for "certain students." Even though the Committee admits that "music, drama, and art develop an appreciation of aesthetics and cultural awareness and require discipline and teamwork," it suggests that eligibility for participation be based on "a desired level of academic competence." See *ibid.,* pp. 21 and 22.

11. Howard Gardner, *Frames of Mind: The Theory of Multiple Intelligences* (New York: Basic Books, 1983).

12. *Beyond Creating: The Place for Art in America's Schools* (Los Angeles, California: The Getty Center for Education in the Arts, 1985), pp. 2–6.

13. *Toward Civilization, op. cit.,* p. 13.

14. Ernest L. Boyer, *High School: A Report on Secondary Education in America* (New York: Harper & Row, 1983), p. 95.

15. Bennett Reimer, *A Philosophy of Music Education,* second edition (Englewood Cliffs, New Jersey: Prentice-Hall, 1989).

16. *Ibid.,* p. 10

17. See p. 83 in this volume.

18. Beeb Salzer, "Teaching Design in a World Without Design," *Theatre Design & Techonology,* Winter 1989, pp. 64–65.

19. Susanne Langer, *Problems of Art* (New York: Scribners, 1957), p. 9.

20. Gardner, *op. cit.,* pp. 99–127.

21. Robert Craft and Igor Stravinsky, *Expositions and Developments* (London: Faber & Faber, 1962), pp. 101–102

22. Gardner, *op. cit.,* p. 109.

23. Judith Hanna (ed.), *Dropout Prevention: Literacy and the Performing and Visual Arts* (Washington, D.C.: U.S. Department of Education, Office of Research and Improvement, 1991).

24. Elliot W. Eisner, *Cognition and Curriculum: A Basis for Deciding What to Teach* (New York: Longman, 1982), p. 55.

25. Harry S. Broudy, "Praise May Not Be Enough," Chapter 4, Charles Fowler (ed.), *The Crane Symposium: Toward an Understanding of the Teaching and Learning of Music Performance* (New York: Potsdam College), p. 39.

26. As quoted by William Raspberry in "Math Isn't for Everyone," *The Washington Post,* March 15, 1989, p. A23.

27. In 1984, the Music Educators National Conference made the policy pronouncement that "by 1990 every student, K–12, shall have access to music instruction in school, and the curriculum of every elementary and secondary school, public or private, shall include a balanced, comprehensive, and sequential program of music instruction taught by qualified teachers," but merely saying it does not make it so.

2

Part 1: Pragmatism in Music Education

Foster Mcmurray

Pragmatism is well established in the foundations of modern education. Historically, this fact may be attributed to the influence of John Dewey and his many followers. Nevertheless, the ideas to be presented in this essay, although typically pragmatic, are not those of Dewey, and in some places they might seem at odds with the Dewey influence. This raises a question about the relation of philosophy to education and to music education.

PHILOSOPHY AS A RESOURCE FOR MUSIC EDUCATORS

Educators are inclined to assume without question that, when they are searching for basic concepts of their profession, they should turn to philosophy. This reflects the esteem in which philosophy is held. It also reflects an opinion that, for any complex human enterprise, there must be a set of fundamental ideas, some of them philosophic in nature, which are said to "underlie" the professional or practical activity. Perhaps this opinion is so widely shared because it seems so obviously reasonable. It would seem that the attitudes we take toward education must reflect our beliefs about what kind of world it is we inhabit and, also, our more specific beliefs about what is real, what is most to be valued, and what it means for human conduct to know the world as it really is. Since beliefs of that kind are peculiarly the province of philosophy, it is philosophy which provides our most basic

Part 1 of Chapter 2 originally published in *Basic Concepts in Music Education, I*, Nelson B. Henry, editor, 1958. Reprinted with permission from the National Society for the Study of understandings. Those who think of philosophy as related in this way to education and, therefore, to music education might be surprised to learn that among philosophers themselves the relationship is not so clear. Some philosophers would deny any contribution at all of philosophy to the professions and their doctrines. Others would find no relationship save the use of a philosophic method shared in common. Still others would say that the solution to a philosophic problem cannot, by itself, provide a solution to problems in education.

Philosophic assertions, being empirical in their reference, make claim to be true of anyone's experience in a common world. They have, therefore, an element of prediction implicit in what they affirm, which makes them at least potentially verifiable by that same test of experience which science employs. In what way, then, are philosophic assertions different from those of the empirical sciences? According to the originator of pragmatism, and still the most authoritative source for the meaning of that name, ". . . philosophy, which deals with positive truth, . . . contents itself with observations such as come within the range of every man's normal experience, and for the most part in every waking hour of his life."[1] What a philosopher does, in his assertions, is to try to give clear expression to the way all of us read or interpret our common experiences. But when we use a roughly workable set of beliefs about how to read the meaning of our experiences, we are sometimes led astray by their crudeness. Hence, what philosophic method can accomplish is a critical refinement of what we seem to have found true or useful in our approach to experience.

A SHORT INTRODUCTION TO PRAGMATISM

Having employed the term "pragmatism" frequently in the discussion of philosophy as a resource for music educators, it is appropriate to give a brief definition at this point. The injunction to define terms at the onset is not such good advice as those who are prone to give it might think. What a term means is whatever is done with it throughout the length of discourse, and nothing short of every idea in which its meaning plays a part can be said to have established its definition. That statement is itself a part of pragmatism.

It is often said that pragmatism is a doctrine, holding truth to be determined by what works. Thus, it might be said that a statement can be found true only when and as it is found workable in action; indeed, in *practical* action. It is also said that a pragmatist in education is one who believes only in learning by doing. To deny any truth in these popular conceptions would be almost as erroneous as to accept them for fair representations. As a matter of fact, a pragmatist might accept the above definitions as a reasonably satisfactory starting point if he could then go on to define further what he means by "workable in action," or by "practical." But what most people would mean by these expressions in popular discourse would be a gross misrepresentation of pragmatism, a long way indeed from the truth.

In a way not too common among scholars in philosophy, pragmatism may be described most honestly and accurately in a form which Charles Sanders Peirce evolved in the mature years of his life, some time after he had given the new kind of philosophy a first publication. In this connection, a slight reference to history is helpful. Early in the last quarter of the nineteenth century Peirce expressed his original insight of pragmatism, which took the form of an intellectually applied test to clarify the meaning of any complex idea. To determine whether an idea has meaning, and if so, what that meaning really is, ask yourself what differences in your experiences would conceivably come about if the idea were true. The total of such conceivable differences is the entire meaning of the idea. Although it has been said that this test is itself in need of clarification — several different interpretations may be found for it — nevertheless this brief introduction of pragmatism took hold immediately in the popular work of other philosophers, some of whom expanded pragmatism with success, even a fashionable success.

It was William James who made pragmatism synonymous in the minds of many with practicalism, with the doctrine that an idea is true to the extent that it "works." Peirce himself was not too happy about these further developments. About twenty years later he returned to the explicit consideration of pragmatism as enunciated in his original treatise and thereafter tried to give it a somewhat different set of meanings than those with which it was more recently identified. It is generally recognized that his more mature considerations have had less general influence than his earlier work and its elaboration by other philosophers. Dewey,[2] the most latterly influential of the pragmatists, suggested that his (Dewey's) theory of knowledge is quite similar to Peirce's but with some important differences. At the present time, the Harvard philosopher, C. I. Lewis, seems closer in many ways to Peirce's own pragmatism than most others have been. The central concepts to be presented here are typical of the doctrines of both Peirce and Lewis.

The positive content or conclusions of pragmatic inquiry may be described as a clarification of what it means to act intelligently. To act intelligently is (a) to act deliberately, with awareness of justified intent; (b) to act in the light of consequences foreseen; (c) to control one's immediate feelings and desires in their effect upon conduct by consideration of longer range desires and goals. Hence, pragmatism is a theory about human action as guided by cognition of consequences, a theory of deliberate or rational self-control, of intellectually achieved continuity in behavior.

As theory of knowledge, a central claim of pragmatism is that the principal function of knowledge is to guide action. This does not mean merely that the importance to human beings of knowledge is its usefulness when applied to the control of conduct. That idea by itself is an evaluation which the man in the street might be inclined to accept as obvious. Anyone who feels that there are other and possibly higher values in our possession of knowledge could at least agree to allow a pragmatist his own personal opinion. But the pragmatic claim is not simply an expression of preferred value. It is a claim that to know anything about a stable characteristic of our world is to know how that aspect of a world would be experienced, how it would "feel" and, therefore, at the same time, to know how one ought to control his own relationship to such a state of affairs; that is, how one ought to comport himself.

Any statement representing something to be true is, in what it says, more truly expressed in the form, "In such and such state of affairs, then do so and so, or expect such and such." If this pragmatic claim is true, then it means that to know something to be true of our world is to be predisposed by that knowledge alone to act in ways appropriate to the known situation. Thus, to know that a stove is hot is to know that it will produce a painful burn if touched and that, under any usual circumstance, touching the stove is to be avoided. Or it means that if one is uncomfortably cold, then one ought to stand closer to the stove. And so on for many other possibilities of conduct.

From this it should be evident that knowing and valuing are held to be intimately allied. As a matter of fact, pragmatists are rigorous advocates of what is called a "cognitive" (as opposed to "emotive") theory of value, meaning a theory which asserts that value judgements are a kind of knowledge, different, not in kind but only in certain details of complexity, from judgments of facts.

A pragmatist need not be pushed into the position of saying that we can prove by empirical evidence the truth of a statement about what is ultimately right for everyone. "Valuation is always a matter of empirical knowledge. But what is right and what is just can never be determined by empirical facts alone."[3] When a pragmatist agrees to this, he is not surrendering his value theory. He would say that those who deny cognitive status to value beliefs are looking at the issues in a mistaken way. They are contending that in order to have knowledge of what is good or right or beautiful, we would have to know for certain the truth of an ultimate moral claim upon everyone. Since we cannot know the latter, they say, then we cannot know anything about what is good. In putting the matter in this light they are avoiding those familiar facts of common experience which are most relevant to the major issue in value theory.

This preliminary sketch of pragmatism would be incomplete if nothing should be written about the term "practical," which has featured so prominently in public perceptions of this philosophic movement. It was, of course, Peirce who introduced the consideration of practicability as an essential part of pragmatism. The usual meanings of practicability, however, are not what pragmatists have in mind. In usual discourse, the term is synonymous with anything which can be used to achieve an end or to realize a desire of that kind most directly related to basic needs, such as food, clothing, and shelter. It is opposite, in usual meanings, to theoretical and aesthetic. The peculiar sense in which pragmatists employ the term is one which includes purely theoretical concerns and is compatible with an insistence that scientists must not be motivated in the research by merely practical concerns — "practical" being used in the customary sense. For example, John Dewey maintained that:

> The attainment of knowledge of some things is necessarily involved in common sense inquiries, but it occurs for the sake of settlement of some issue of use and enjoyment, and not, as in scientific inquiry, for its own sake. In the latter, there is no *direct* involvement of human beings in the *immediate* environment — a fact which carries with it the ground of distinguishing the theoretical from the practical.[4]

And Peirce declared that:

> . . . in philosophy, touching as it does upon matters which are, and ought to be, sacred to us, the investigator who does not stand aloof from all intent to make practical applications will not only obstruct the advance of the pure science, but, what is infinitely worse, he will endanger his own moral integrity and that of his readers.[5]

Here we have pragmatists using the common parlance in the usual way and actively supporting the values of theoretical as against practical inquiry.

What, then, could Peirce have meant when he defined the pragmatic maxim in such terminology as: "Consider what effects, that might conceivably have practical bearings, we conceive the object of our conception to have. Then our conception of these effects is the whole of our conception of the object."[6] His own effort to clarify is as follows:

> . . . all reasonings turn upon the idea that if one exerts certain kinds of volition, one will undergo in return certain compulsory perceptions. Now this

sort of consideration, namely, that certain lines of conduct will entail certain kinds of inevitable experiences is what is called a "practical consideration." Hence is justified the maxim, belief in which constitutes pragmatism.[7]

From this explanation it is possible to see that the research work of a pure scientist involves "practical" considerations of the same general kind as would characterize the intellectual behavior of a businessman or a farmer, even though the work of the scientist is not at all practical in the usual sense.

AIMS OF MUSIC EDUCATION

In recent years music educators have felt that now is the time to establish music firmly in the school curriculum, to gain increased acceptance of the idea that music should be an essential part of general education for everyone. Achievement of this ambition requires an expanded range of communication between music educators and all other educators, plus the interested public. For it is only by a wider sharing of ideas that changes can occur. To achieve this, a very sensible approach has been used, of which this yearbook [*Basic Concepts, I*] is typical. The approach is one of placing ideas about the values of music education in a broader context of ideas about education in general and of building relationships between the intellectual resources of music educators and a wider domain of theory and doctrine. This is surely advisable, even necessary. Nevertheless there are difficulties inherent in an operation of that kind.

One such difficulty is that our contemporary materials in philosophy, in educational theory, and in psychology are not unified. They are, on the contrary, at theoretical odds. A danger implicit in this situation is the possibility that deeper thinking about the background of music education will become entangled in the dialectic disputes of systematic schools of thought in disciplines other than the discipline of music education itself. Among music educators there are many conflicts in opinion that have their locus directly in ideas about music teaching. Probing deeper into our common possession of theoretical resources could have the effect of widening and deepening the arena of dispute rather than of helping build a unified perspective about the whys and hows of music education. If this should happen, conflicts of opinion might become more difficult than ever to resolve, since music educators would now have taken on the unresolved issues of other disciplines in addition to their own. The competence of specialists in one field to aid in resolving the conflicts of specialists in other fields is surely less than their competence to work toward solid intellectual background for their own.

These remarks are a preliminary to consideration of what happens when music educators seek to justify their claim for music as part of general education.

First, it should be admitted frankly that no one with a strong interest in this endeavor would question seriously his belief that music does belong prominently in general education. When he looks for "justification" of that conviction, he is not trying to convince either himself or others that he is right in holding the values he holds. He is trying to show how his own specialized role in schoolwork fits in with the various contributions of all other specialists to produce a well-rounded educative product. One knows that it does, somehow, but still it is difficult to be sure just how it happens and how to make more sure than before that it happens effectively. Hence, the search to clarify objectives.

Those who have been concerned with this enterprise have been attempting to state a set of aims for education, which are well established in the minds of all educators, and then to subsume the aims of music education under these more universal ones. They have tried to show that what all of us everywhere hope to achieve in general education will be achieved better when it is recognized that music has a contribution too. This procedure is understandable and, let us say, proper. But there are two ways of doing it, one of them better than the other. Unfortunately, the poorer of these approaches is more typical in contemporary literature of music education.

The poorer of the two approaches is to take, as general aims of education, a list of specified outcomes, the whole sum of which is deemed an adequate description of what a well-educated person is; and then to claim that learning in music can also contribute, along with other kinds of learning, to the achievement of these specified objectives. Thus, there are the well-known seven cardinal aims of secondary education, including good citizenship, health, vocational ability, and the others. At the present time it is popular to place citizenship at the head of the list of recognized values; and so, perhaps inevitably, we sometimes hear that above all else, music contributes most to citizenship.[8] But it is also claimed that education in music contributes to health, to recreational and spiritual activities in the home and community, that it gives people an enjoyable avenue to group memberships and group spirits, helps to build self-confidence and poise, gives vocational and avocational skills, contributes to self-discipline, and so on. To each specifically described outcome, music makes a contribution.

A reader may wonder why a pragmatist should want to direct adverse criticism against this way of claiming importance for music education. It is

certainly true, is it not, that skills and appreciations taught by music specialists do help to accomplish these various objectives? Or that, where they do
so only in part or poorly, the possibility is there, waiting to be realized by
more widely directed effort? If, for example, a music teacher sees his
responsibilities in this light, he could surely teach the music of other nations
and other cultures, and thereby help develop a sense of tolerant understanding and world citizenship. And he could easily use instrumental or choral
groups to build effective habits of group participation and group loyalty. Or
develop patriotism through love for nationalistic music. Or give therapy to
emotionally disturbed children. Obviously, these are real possibilities and,
undeniably, they may contribute to the goals of general education. Then,
what could be bad about such claims for music education?

What is at least potentially bad about this way of thinking is that it
conceives music as an instrument to the realization of nonmusical values. It
recognizes nothing distinctive and unique in music experience itself and
claims for music only that it helps pupils develop other talents and learnings.
When music specialists stake their claim for support from the educational
world upon their service to nonmusical outcomes, they are in the fragile
position of all those who say, "me too." We say it is a fragile position
because it offers no reason for supposing that a musical education is a direct
and effective means for achieving such a variety of specific goals.

Suppose that one is interested in education for citizenship as a central
objective for teaching. In that case, one might suppose that instruction in
civic issues, in the ideals and institutions of democracy, and in other forms
of knowledge pertaining directly to citizenship would be a more suitable and
directly effective means to the goal than the less directly effective outcomes
of experiences with music. However high a value for growth in music one
might care to posit, it would be difficult, perhaps even absurd, to claim that
intimacy with music is one of the most effective of educational means to
growth in good citizenship. It is indeed reasonable to claim that musical
learning contributes to making a person "well-balanced" or "well-rounded"
in personality, and that a balanced person is more likely than not to be a good
citizen. And yet it is entirely possible that a person of great skill and taste in
music might not be either well balanced or a good citizen. These observations do not mean that music cannot contribute to the particular goal in
question, but they *do* mean that we cannot show a direct and reliable route
from music to citizenship. If our minds are clearly focused on so particular
an outcome, then we are likely to regard music as a very minor means. The
danger to music education is that, by claiming contribution to a variety of
specific and nonmusical outcomes, music educators will unintentionally
give support to the feeling that music is an unessential frill.

To generalize the argument, we might put it this way: To urge a place for music in general education on the grounds that it contributes instrumentally to an array of popular and specific objectives is to promote philistinism; that is, to promote the kind of attitude which uses music to achieve a snobbish social status, approval of the "right" people, or favor with the boss.

In this situation an odd trick of contemporary history may be noted. Pragmatism is often confused with a closely related doctrine advocated by John Dewey and properly called "instrumentalism." An unintended outcome of Dewey's influence is the belief, now widespread, that to make a case for music in this manner — that is, by claiming its instrumental contribution to a list of nonmusical objectives — is the modern or "progressive" approach to educational thought. Although it is true that Dewey was an instrumentalist, his position on educational aims was in opposition to the way of thinking described in this discussion. For it was Dewey who argued that we should accept no aims of a sort external to the educative process.

The pragmatist would hold that to aim at such external goals as good citizenship is to direct educational process toward many particulars of behavior which in their general texture spell out the meaning of good citizenship. And this means that we should have to *impose* our own beliefs, concerning what makes anyone a good citizen, upon new generations. If we are not prepared to say that a good citizen does this rather than that, believes this way rather than that way, for a wide range of behavior patterns, then we could never know how to educate a youngster toward the achievement of it. If we put ourselves in this position, we are then taking an attitude toward the meaning of democracy that makes it scarcely distinguishable from totalitarianism. In recognition of this, Dewey had argued that the aim of education is nothing else than growth leading to more growth. The democratic aim is to encourage those kinds of learning that show promise of increased capacity for further learning, that is, further learning just as further learning and not toward such external goals as can be described specifically in noneducational terms. Unfortunately, this pragmatic concept of educational aims has been as unacceptable to many modern educators as to the traditionalists.

Rather than claim for music a part in specific outcomes, there is a significant alternative. The alternative is to find a broadly generalized statement of what is to be aimed for in general education and then to show in what manner education in music may be subsumed under the universal.

As indicated in preceding discussion, a pragmatist is one who tries to give expression to a common human intent. If he succeeds in formulating a statement of educational aims, his success is a measure of how well he has put into words what all of us hope to achieve through schooling. As a preliminary effort in that direction, it may be suggested that three considerations together determine the nature of educational aims. First, we realize that a primary purpose of schooling is to perpetuate an accumulated cultural heritage by doing what is often called "passing it on" to new generations. By this expression we seem to mean that we encourage new generations to convert our public culture into a personal possession. Second, we hope that the personal possession of culture will be of benefit to those who acquire it. We hope, that is, that having learned what is to be learned through schooling, each person will thereafter behave in a way different from what his behavior would otherwise have been, and different in a positive direction. Third, because we believe in democracy, we take a special attitude toward the first and second which marks a departure from the more ancient heritage of ideas about schooling. Concerning the transmission of culture, we no longer believe, as in older societies, that culture is to imprison new generations within a rigid mold from the past. Concerning the second, we no longer believe that the personal benefit of culture acquired in formal schooling is one of setting the educated apart from the mass of mankind in a "cultivated" elite, marked by special manners and special ways of talking, and destined to rule an uneducated majority. This third and democratic consideration has not yet been perceived by many, even among those who profess to believe in democracy, and for all of us its full meaning has yet to be discovered. Nevertheless, it is already institutionalized in America.

The outcome of these three considerations may be expressed in the following manner. *The aim of general education is to use our accumulated knowledge, values, and skills to acquaint everyone with those more subtle forces in his world which influence his life, with the hope that, if he learns of their existence and their force, he can control his relations with environment to gain more of good and less of preventable bad outcomes.* This is, of course, a typically pragmatic statement. It reflects the characteristic pragmatic features of emphasis upon the use of knowledge to guide behavior and of emphasis upon the inseparable relations of cognitive with ethical and aesthetic judgments. But if it should have any claim to truth as an expression of educational aim, then it has this claim, not because it stands or falls with pragmatism as a philosophic system, but only because it clarifies what all of us would mean.

A key to the full intent of the preceding definition is the word *subtle.* Why should the school be limited, in its communications, to that which is subtle? The answer, in general, is that we do not need a formal school to communicate that which is obvious or so prominently observable within the environments that one need only to live within it to perceive it. In primitive societies, where so many of the most potent environmental powers and forces are not understood, there is no need for formal schools, not because they lack a rich culture but because it attaches to the obvious, the observable, and the directly active, even when wooing the unseen powers. Even in our present civilization, those kinds of knowledge that are most immediately necessary to daily existence are not taught in schools. It is the upper level of cultural resources, not the basic common sense, that we communicate in school.

By translation from the universal aim of general education, the aim of music education may be explained in this way. *It is: to help everyone to further awareness of patterns of sound as an aesthetic component in the world of experience; to increase each person's capacity to control the availability of aesthetic richness through music; and to transform the public musical culture into a recognized part of each person's environment.* This definition has several parts, each of which might be explained further.

If music education has a significant part in education for everyone, then it has this part, first, because patterns of sound are a prominent part of everyone's world and, second, because whatever is most immediately evident in producing or in hearing sounds is a relatively small part of what is potentially there. Music education is justified because, when the more refined portions of our musical culture are communicated, the person to whom they are communicated will find in music what he would not have been able to find otherwise, thereby expanding his environment and increasing his power to find a good life through deliberate guidance of his behavior and its outcomes. In a world where patterns of sound are omnipresent, he will have increased power to control what happens to him musically, and to make the aesthetic quality of his experience less a matter of mere accident. This is an important kind of contribution to anyone's general education, and it respects the values of musical experience as something other than minor instrumentalities to nonmusical goals.

A pragmatist is particularly sensitive to the possibility that very broad generalizations about ultimate aims will verge upon rhetoric of vague feelings, so vague that, when the temporary emotion subsides, practical conduct is left without a clearly understood sense of direction. The preceding paragraph, for example, if it should have any practical value, has it to whatever degree its ideas, when entertained, could promote a sense of integrity in music education. A sense of integrity is a practical matter, making differences in conduct. There are further meanings of a practical sort to be found in the position suggested. One of these is an answer to a question that must be faced by all music teachers.

The question is this: Does good music-teaching necessarily terminate in each pupil finding within himself a new and strong appreciation for music — a marked liking for it, that is, and a determination to hear it and to perform it as a steady part of subsequent living? Should a teacher aim at getting pupils to *like* music very much, and should he judge his relative success by how much additional liking he helps to create? There is, of course, a natural tendency to think so; but is this attitude of wanting other people to share one's own enthusiasms justified?

The answer provided by pragmatism is not a simple *yes* or *no,* but it is, nevertheless, clear-cut and decisive. To explain, it might be simplest to say: No. A music teacher should neither attempt nor expect to teach his pupils a new and stronger liking for music. In his contribution to a pupil's general education, at least, this strengthening of positive appreciation is no part of his job. A teacher's job is only to show his pupils what is to be found in music when obstacles to perception are removed and when the learned capacity to attend and to hear has been developed. If, when a pupil has truly learned to hear more of what is potentially there, he does not value highly the new content, then that evaluation is his own rightful concern and no one else's.

With good reason, we suppose that a positive emotional response to music is universal among human beings. As will be pointed out below, an aesthetic judgment is, in effect, a prediction that anyone whatsoever will be able to find in a given piece of music a specifiable degree or quality of aesthetic response. Hence, it is likely that good teaching will, in fact, produce in pupils a stronger liking for music. Nevertheless, this close relationship is not an essential part of criteria for judging the success of music education. The difficulties in realizing this are further complicated by the fact that an important part of a music teacher's task is to remove popular prejudices and negative biases against serious music. They are a hindrance to perception and may prevent a pupil from finding in music the many elements which are perceivable by an educated listener. A teacher's task is to help pupils become sensitive to the less obvious, the less immediately evident, qualities which only training can bring into experienced awareness. A culturally induced dislike for some kinds of music is a form of blindness; so long as it exists it makes those who suffer from it, in effect, noneducable. But if, after removing culturated bias, a pupil's response is then not one of strong liking, this fact must be accepted as perfectly compatible with good education.

A further aspect of pragmatic aims suggests that an essential part of music's contribution to general education is to acquaint pupils with the body of literature which has been accumulating in and about music for many centuries. This is justified because this body of literature is itself a part of the world to which everyone's eyes should be opened. To remain ignorant of anything of common human interest is to live in an unnecessarily restricted environment and to enjoy, less than to the utmost, power to control life and its consequences deliberately. To be brought into acquaintance with a body of literature is to have expanded one's capacity to use intelligence in the pursuit of a good life. Everyone ought to know, for example, that the late quartets of Beethoven are thought to be among the best of musical compositions. It should be noted that what is called for by this aim is a purely *cognitive* outcome. To know that learned opinion in the musical world accords certain status to composers and their various works is to know a useful *fact*. That is different from knowing the music itself, and different from having come to share, in one's own aesthetic feelings, the common consent. The last-named outcome is actually unnecessary for satisfaction of our educational task, whereas the cognitive outcome is central.

PERFORMANCE SKILLS

Music teachers are usually classified in a special category within the school, wherein their educational services are thought to be available mainly to those who have already found a special interest in learning a particular skill. In this situation there is a force tending to keep music education in a special niche, as something like an added luxury or a nice decoration. There is nothing distinctively pragmatic that could tell how to change the situation. But within the meaning of democracy, at least one idea appears relevant.

Equality of opportunity, as many are fond of saying, does not mean opportunity for everyone to be just like everyone else. It means equal chance for every person to find the avenues of growth and training that will effect a stable compromise between individuality of taste and talent, on one hand, and socially allowed or usable division of labor, on the other. For educational institutions this ideal makes necessary a diversified program, a theory now widely accepted. But when a modern school offers such diversity of opportunity as our complex society can well support, there are traditionalists in educational thought who appeal to the honored ideal of a common general education and make the appeal in a way to suggest that a diversity of offerings is a threat to the meaning and the spirit of general education. Criticisms of that kind offer a challenging problem for educational theorists. For music educators the basic problem comes out as a problem of finding the right place for instrumental and vocal instruction within the total school program. Granted that the problem is usually settled for a practicing teacher by the growing number of demands for instrumental instruction and for performing groups, the problem of criticism and that of a faltering sense of direction remain unsolved.

There are at least two important reasons why some measure of instruction in performance skills in music should be included within everyone's formal education. In the first place, no one can be said to have discovered whether or not he has talent or liking for musical performance unless he has tried it. In the second place, it seems probable that learning to hear music in its full reality is made easier of accomplishment if accompanied by training in the making of music. Both of these reasons are well known to everyone in music, so that the mere mention will suffice. But further issues are broached.

Consider the ideal of self-discovery. How much training and practice is required before a person may be said to have discovered his degree of interest and talent? This is partly an empirical question, to which a philosopher has no answer. But, there is also involved here a problem of analysis, where philosophic technique is more at home. It may be assumed that, in general music class, a pupil learns a little of how to play simple melodies on a simplified instrument. For example, he might learn to enjoy the exercise of his little training and to feel that he might have some talent for further exploitation. Whether he does have any further talent can be discovered only if he goes further in training. And if he secured further training, and if he continues to make progress with enjoyment and satisfaction, he has learned that he has that much talent. Yet, unless the speed of his learning is obviously extraordinary, he has still not learned how much farther he could or should go in musical training. Each further stage offers a new and untried gamble, a predicament which continues even after professional training. What does this fact mean of relevance to educational theory?

For one thing, it means that a small amount of simple instruction in performing skills is not really defensible on grounds that it leads to the discovery of each pupil's musical potential in performance. It would, indeed, be possible to argue that for some pupils there might be, otherwise, no opportunity at all to see what music-making is like; or that occasional, rare talents might be brought to light; but not that each pupil is able to discover his degree of talent.

A further meaning is that a modest ability to play or sing, such as might be expected to result from public school music-training, offers no insight, merely by itself, to the intensity and artistry of great professional performers. There is little or no reason to suppose that a youngster's performance on violin or piano prepares him to perceive the precision and the subtleties of interpretation which distinguish concert performance. These latter qualities are the product or final blossom of devotion to the aesthetic content of music. A concert artist's way of producing tones is his nearest approach to the physical creation of an artistic object, the ideal of which has already been created in his mind as a standard to guide performance. Before he can create a good sound, he must know what to listen for; he must have a *prior* ideal construct against which to measure his produced patterns of sound and such familiarity with the perfection of aesthetic content that he can tell how much of it he is realizing, and how much correction of the initial production is needed to bring the total to an acceptable level of realization. During the years of preparation, his ability to construct for himself an ideal of aesthetic content to be realized keeps changing and improving as his technique changes and improves. Nevertheless, this slowly forming ideal must always *precede* his capacity to realize it. If it did not, then he would not know in what direction to find improvement. In his practice, each effort must be listened to and judged for its quality; judgment, which is an intellectual act, depends upon having ideas, and the ideas, in addition to those about technique, must include ideas about ultimate aesthetic content. He must know what the composer intended or, at least, what the composer ought to have intended. To know this, he must know what music means. To be a first-rate performer is to be able to find or to understand the fullest range of meanings potential in music.

Now the point at issue here is this: If nonprofessional performers are to learn the full meaning of music, or to perceive the full aesthetic content, then there must be a great gap between their level of aesthetic insight and enjoyment on the one hand and their technical ability as performers on the other. It would be tragedy if the aesthetic insight and responsiveness of people were limited to their own personal command of instrumental or vocal technique. From this, the conclusion follows: To realize the aims of general education in music, we cannot rely upon instruction in performance skills per se as a means to full understanding of musical content. To teach sensitivity to aesthetic content, we must rely upon other educational experiences than those of performance. Whatever the values of musical performance might be, we must recognize that performance is not a *primary* means to development of aesthetic sensitivity.

The career of George Bernard Shaw is illustrative. Shaw was one of our greatest music critics, and as a critic he was always demanding perfect execution by concert performers. Perhaps because of his extraordinary love for music, he was easily pained by any departure from musical perfection. And yet, in his own playing at the piano, which he enjoyed with gusto, he played with more enthusiasm than with technical command. His frequent mistakes did not detract from his pleasure. At least one meaning which might be inferred from this example is that there must be a distinctive educational value, apart from the improvement of aesthetic sensitivity, for training in techniques of music-making.

INTEREST VS. PLEASURE

Several negative conclusions have emerged in the preceding discussion. One of them is that the aim of general education is not to create a strong liking for music, even though it is reasonable to suppose that with good instruction a stronger liking will often result. Another is that instrumental and vocal performance skills are not a principal means to the goal of increased sensitivity to the aesthetic qualities of music. Nevertheless, it is often supposed by music educators that in a general music class a teacher ought to include music-making and at least a minimum of instruction in instrumental and vocal technique, if only for the reason that making music has recreational value and, hence, contributes to greater interest in music.

There is certainly a measure of educational wisdom in this widespread belief. But how much, and for what reason, seems now to be obscure. That it is obscure should be evident from the fact that music educators cannot agree upon one very important question, namely, whether to bring any substantial amount of theory, or purely cognitive content, into general music classes, or whether, on the contrary, to limit theory so as not to destroy interest or endanger possible success. A particularly challenging result of this confusion is the present prominence of musical instruments that require very little knowledge or training to play. This might seem to be like trying to have one's cake and eat it, too. To make headway in clearing up our ideas, we would have to consider directly the difficult question of whether to concentrate primarily upon *enjoyment* of music or upon changes in pupil's *cognitions* of and about music.

Putting aside the question of enjoyment, it must be granted that a very first consideration is to keep alive the possibility of continuous change, learning, or growth in a pupil's experiences with music. If this does not occur, there is no good reason for music within an educational institution. Possibly it is for this reason that teachers are sometimes willing to do anything which promises further musical enjoyment and sometimes are hesitant to introduce a kind of instruction that might prove difficult and dull. Historically, this tendency to avoid difficult technical material is traced to the influence of pragmatism, for it was the progressives who believed in the importance of maintaining a high level of interest. But in this aspect of our most recent history there has been a serious misunderstanding. The heart of this misunderstanding is the result of having confused the word *liking* with what is meant by *interest,* a different kind of thing.

It is truly maintained by pragmatists that, if educational growth is to continue steadily, there must be a steadily maintained interest in the content of educational experiences. And it is further true that one kind of interest is positive pleasure or enjoyment. But it is equally true that a negative emotion like fear is also a form of interest. There are many complex patterns of emotional coloring in human experience, some of them so complex that one cannot say easily whether they are positive or negative, pleasant or unpleasant, in feeling tone. What pragmatists have been pointing to is that the presence of emotional coloring, or interest, is essential to good learning; but they have meant any kind of emotional response that is appropriate to situations encountered, no matter whether obviously pleasant or not. In fact, a mere feeling of pleasure is not the kind of interest that is most conducive to further growth.

The reason why pragmatists insist that good learning is present only when interest is also present is perhaps obvious. Learning is an activity which requires effort, at least as much effort as is needed to overcome inertia and to launch a learner upon a new course. For the most part, human beings are not ready to exert effort in new directions unless they are, in a sense, "forced" to it by their having found themselves somehow caught up in an event, in something going on, which challenges or threatens the possibility of getting or of keeping something already believed to be good. And that means, by definition, that people are ready to learn only when caught up in a situation of interest.

A distinctively pragmatic aspect of the argument is a claim that the experience of being interested is both cognitive and emotive together. To be interested is to have perceived a notion and to have used prior knowledge as a means of predicting possible directions and outcomes. In that respect, the occurrence of interest is a part of one's intellectual life. It is intellectual in the broadest sense, rather than in the narrowly limited sense in which the term is generally used. It signifies a combination of perception and conception, a putting to use of one's previous acquaintance with natural processes in order to foresee potentials, and also a putting to use of one's knowledge about the effects of natural processes upon one's immediate feelings or direct findings of good and bad. These are cognitive and intellectual processes. And it is these perceptions, predictions, and implicit judgments that precipitate an emotional tone, or a complex of emotional tones, appropriate to the nature of one's expectations and one's knowledge of what is found good or bad when it is directly experienced. Hence, emotional and intellectual life are inseparable.

Given this description of how interest is related to learning, then a question of more direct practical concern may be answered in its light. How do various kinds of content for a general music program contribute to keeping a high level of interest?

It is axiomatic that a teacher ought to begin with the already established interests of his pupils, with the intent that these previous interests might be expanded and modified to incorporate new interests. Although the principle is sound, it is usually taken to mean that a teacher ought to begin with music and with musical activities that are immediately enjoyed from the beginning. This could be simplified even further to mean that a teacher ought to find out what kinds of music his pupils like and then give them that kind of music.

But music perceived as already familiar, and as easy to hear with pleasure, is not a stimulant to growth in musical perception. It is simply an occasion for enjoyment.

To produce a kind of situation that holds promise of educational value is to offer an activity, either of listening or of singing or of creating musical sounds by instrument, in which there is a large element of what is familiar, but with something else that offers a point of conflict or of resistance to be overcome. There are many terms by which to describe the element of challenge and novelty: terms like *exotic, strange, piquant, alien,* but the trouble with them is that they suggest too much the merely bizarre, the strikingly outlandish. What is intended is something in the experience which pupils find unusual only in the sense that their previous experience had not led them to expect it, something which occasions a shock of nonrecognition and which, because it occurs in a context of what is felt to be familiar, seems to demand an understanding or an overcoming. For the most part, such occasions of the unexpected are not immediately liked; they have a tang that is not altogether pleasant, but they are also pungent and exciting. It is this element of the difficult to assimilate, the challenging, the not easily placed and readily disposed of, which creates interest. To be interested is to be aroused and ready to learn, and this condition, which is a kind of irritation one is eager to be free from, has no necessary connection with enjoyment.

There is good reason why the element of challenge should occur within a context which seems for the most part familiar. It is that when familiar music is heard or played or sung, a pupil finds an identity of his selfhood with what he has already learned to perceive. Then, when an unexpected irritant appears, or some difficulty in accepting a situation, or the sense of resistance encountered, a pupil feels that his own self has been challenged. He is made to feel, as it were, *personally* inadequate, with a result that, to restore his comfortable feeling of integrity, he must learn what it is that he now begins to feel he had been missing before. If, on the contrary, the entire experience is novel or interpreted as one having no relations of intimacy with him personally, then he feels no challenge to attend and to learn.

Throughout the history of music, composers have employed this same idea to tighten up and heighten the aesthetic effect of their music. More common even than innovations in form has been the use of sounds that seemed discordant or atonal, with the result that over generations of time a cultivated musical audience has come to hear harmony where earlier generations had been outraged. There was a time quite long ago when singing in thirds was thought to be too excitingly dissonant. Later, of course, it came to be heard as consonance and acceptable for use at almost any point.[9] In a recent Harvard lecture on aesthetics, Igor Stravinsky tells how, in his labors of composition, he refuses to accept the readily available and easy solution to each problem but searches further for that which offers a sense of resistance. The extraordinary cleanness of his music, never merely pretty or sentimental, shows the result.

For educational method, the general recommendation is to create and hold interest, which is more a matter of finding a resistance or a conflict than of finding pleasure. How then do musical activities, where pupils make music themselves, contribute an educationally useful level of interest? The answer depends upon what sort of content is to be taught. If the teacher's purpose is to teach appreciation for the aesthetic content of good music, then music-producing activities are not necessarily a good means. The kind of music produced through pupils' efforts is apt to be less rich in aesthetic content than music performed by professionals, either live or reproduced. If pupils should try in their performance to create aesthetically patterned sound of high order, they might quickly lose interest if they noted, as they should, the large gap between the musical result of their efforts and their own mature standards in listening.

There are ways, however, of building interest through pupil performance that do not involve the inept creation of music which is poor in quality. Performance on instruments can be used to teach facts from physics concerning how tones are produced, or to teach facts about orchestral coloring, or about types of intervals and their sounds, or about theory of composition or rules of harmony. Pupil activities involving the use of instruments and of singing in order to clarify theory, or as a means of lending a sense of reality to the intellectual and aesthetic *study* of music, are altogether different in educational intent and in theoretical justification from playing or singing indulged merely as an enjoyable sport. When pupils are encouraged to try their hand at producing musical sounds in an experimental attitude, then the level of interest is likely to be high and the learning good, no matter how unskilled the performance. At this point it is appropriate to recall the well-known emphasis upon experimentation which has characterized pragmatic theory.

When music-making activities are used in an experimental approach to the study of music, several conditions must be satisfied. To be experimental in producing musical sounds, a pupil would have to be guiding his activity by an idea he wanted to try. To have a guiding idea — a hunch, a guess, or a hypothesis — he must first have experienced something puzzling or doubtful or problematic. And to have found something problematic in his experience he must have been responding to something going on in his environment, something which caught his attention or which offered aliment to his purposes. In temporal sequence, therefore, what is desired first in an educative situation is a musical object in the pupil's environment, an object which captures attention; second, a sense of doubt or difficulty in responding to the musical object; third, a desire to remove the doubt or difficulty; fourth, a search for clues, for further observations, or for a way of taking hold of the problem; fifth, the discovery of a hunch, or the feeling of insight into a possible connection among events that might resolve the problem; sixth, an experimental effort of trying to act upon the hunch to see if it works; seventh, a noting of results to see what happens, and to see whether what happens confirms the hunch. This outline of an experimental learning situation is similar to John Dewey's famous five steps.[10]

During the past several decades, the import and interpretation of experimentalism has had unfortunate consequences. It has been supposed, for example, that these listed requirements of an experimental learning situation are to be taken as steps in a procedure of teaching. That is not true. They describe what happens in a pupil's experience, but not what a teacher should do to bring about such sequences. Following William H. Kilpatrick's lead, many teachers have felt that the best way to promote experimental learning is by getting pupils started on an interesting long-range activity or "project," such as preparing a program of Christmas music to be presented in the school auditorium two or three weeks hence. This is supposed to promote "purposeful learning" and "learning by doing." Without considering at all the merits of a project method, it should be noted that a great variety of teaching procedures, including even the use of lectures and demonstrations, could be compatible with pragmatic theory. It is not necessary to engage pupils *first* in purposeful activity.

A more thoroughly pragmatic approach is for a teacher to introduce a musical element deliberately, an element chosen for its power to secure attention and to arrange the presentation in a way that emphasizes the most striking parts of the musical whole and also those which are most difficult to assimilate. For example, a teacher might introduce a musical passage of marked rhythmic appeal and marked also by a change in time signature, thereby producing an odd sensation which pupils feel and yet would find difficult to describe or to duplicate technically. If the teacher asks what it was that had happened and offers an opportunity for pupils to try to duplicate the rhythmic pattern and to secure again the odd effect, then, to whatever extent the total situation has been dramatized, pupils will try to accept the problem and to solve it.

This simple example is offered for its contrast with more widely accepted ideals stemming from progressive education. It is an example in which the environmental situation is arranged and brought into existence as a deliberate pedagogic act and in which the novel or disturbing element is forced upon the attention of pupils. If this is done in a continuing atmosphere of pupils trying to learn more about the subtle forces in musical structure and in an atmosphere of freedom to act experimentally in trying for full realization and theoretical mastery of what had previously seemed hidden from perception, then the generally recognized requirements for experimental learning would have been satisfied. Furthermore, it is an example of pupils' activity in trying to produce musical effects not simply to enjoy playing or singing but to enjoy the sense of discovery and of intellectual grasp.

MUSIC THEORY IN GENERAL EDUCATION

At this point it becomes necessary to ask whether cognitive learning, or the study of what music teachers call "theory," should or should not play a part in everyone's general education.

It is undoubtedly true that a properly aesthetic response to music is an affair of immediate feelings rather than of intellectually formulated thoughts. To hear a concert or recital is to hear organized patterns of sound and to find that the quality of the listener's experience is good in its over-all effect. Having an aesthetic experience is a direct relation between perceiving sounds and a perceiver self, needing no intermediary of knowing and thinking. Hence, it is possible to be keenly responsive to music, and even highly discriminating in "taste," and yet be ignorant of musical theory.

Granted no necessary connection between cognitive and appreciative experience, it is important to consider what advantages can be claimed for knowing musical theory. For a pragmatist, a technical knowledge of music is useful when it serves to secure more of whatever one finds valuable in music. To take this position is to have realized that knowing what one likes is a form of knowledge similar to any other kind of knowledge: It is not easy to come by, it is not something had naturally and without study. To really know what one likes is to have *discovered* the truth. To learn what one likes is not different in effort required than to learn facts about other people and other aspects of the world. Contrary to popular belief in this matter, there is no special form of knowledge to which each person has direct access simply by looking within. We learn about ourselves in the same way that we learn about anything else. No one doubts that to learn the truth about things external to ourselves requires effort, study, and the use of technical resources. And yet, we easily mistake the nature of self-knowledge, supposing that the mere presence to ourselves of conscious awareness is a form of knowledge. Partly because of this common mistake, people might be said to know less about themselves than about almost anything else of prominence in the environment.

A simple example will clarify the matter. Almost everyone responds

47

positively to pleasing melody. Because of this, popular music relies almost entirely upon simple statement and reiteration of melody. The average person usually supposes that the simple, direct liking he feels for popular tunes of the day exhausts his capacity for musical enjoyment. He continues to suppose this even though he knows that after a few months of intense popularity a song becomes so tiresome that he wishes to be rid of it. Consistent with this failure of self-understanding, he supposes that in serious music there is only a bare minimum of melody, not enough to be pleasing. If this average person were to learn more about himself, he would learn that he likes, not only melody, but also a sufficient variety and complexity of melodic structure to keep from becoming surfeited with it. He would learn that the feelings of goodness he receives from melody can be secured even more readily from serious than from popular music; a fact which, prior to study of both himself and of music in interaction with each other, he had thought to be opposite. As a result of seeking to know more about his own responses to music, and to know more about what it is in music that he really finds most aesthetically satisfying, anyone whatsoever is increasing his power to command richness of aesthetic content.

In this process of self-discovery and of increased power to control an aesthetic environment, a knowledge of music theory can be quite useful, even granted that it is not absolutely essential. To come at once to the main point, a knowledge of musical structure, and of theory generally, is educationally useful because it *changes the objects perceived in music.* For example, anyone might listen to a dominant seventh and its inversions: listen, that is, to what a musician knows to be such. But what a person hears in his own private awareness may be almost anything. If a chord is explained and illustrated, compared in its emotional impact with other chords, and its uses in composition or orchestration are noted, then when a dominant seventh is played, it can be *heard* as what it is, funded with meanings and with a distinct and recognizable personality. What happens, as a result of cognition about music, is that music becomes heard as a different kind of thing than before.

The use of technical knowledge to change what can be heard in music is not, by itself, necessarily good in effect upon aesthetic sensitivity and critical judgment. Conceivably, a person might be well trained technically and yet blind aesthetically. But this consideration is not truly important. What is important is that a teacher shall convert sounds and rhythms into stimuli, into something heard with as much of the subtle and the intricate brought into awareness as possible. And the teaching of theory can help accomplish this end.

According to pragmatism, the sad effects of traditional ways in teaching music theory arise from having taught theory as materials to be mastered in themselves and as materials largely in the medium of special symbols. That is to say, knowledge about music is presented as an intrinsic goal, and learning theoretic materials in symbolic representations is perceived by pupils as their whole task. A nonpragmatist might wonder what could be wrong about that. If knowledge of music, its special vocabulary and its symbols, is something good for pupils to learn, then why not set pupils to learning it? Even if this viewpoint seems reasonable, there is an alternative that could repay serious consideration.

The alternative in teaching theoretical or cognitive materials is to introduce them within a situation of first-hand experience with the raw materials of sound. Procedurally, the idea is to begin with sounds, either musical or nonmusical; to introduce theory as an intellectual instrument for doing something to or with the original raw materials; to conclude with further experience of music, changed in some way by cognition. In short, the teacher should introduce theory as a means to reconstruct first-hand experiences. To illustrate what is intended, consider by contrast the traditional method of teaching musical notation in conjunction with solfeggio. The traditional procedure is one of introducing music notation as an object to be learned, such that after it has been mastered, through lengthy practice with sol-fa syllables, pupils may then at least enjoy the fruits of their labors. Specifically, the point of contrast is this: In traditional pedagogy, musical notation and solfeggio are presented as environmental objects to be mastered; in pragmatic procedures, it is musical sounds which are presented as environmental objects, symbols being introduced as a means to increase control over the production or the hearing of music. In the latter case, it is, more than in the former, a matter of gaining mastery over music theory as an intermediate instrument, rather than of gaining mastery over the instruments themselves. Pupils begin with singing and are shown how to improve the musical result by learning to interpret symbols. They come to perceive that the interpretations of symbols allows for precision in singing the right notes in the right time.

It is true, as critics of pragmatic theory are likely to point out, that at some point in acquiring musical skill, there must be intensive practice in sight-reading, scales, and the like. But intensive practice should be expected only *after* a desire and determination to acquire skill has already appeared. For those who have not yet expressed a special desire for special lessons in musical skills, or who never do so, the kind of knowledge to be expected in general musical education is *not* of that special kind which requires intensive practice. What belongs in general education is that kind of knowledge which is sometimes called "insight." Insight is learning characterized by intellectual grasp, or understanding, or the ability to perceive relations, and is different in kind from skills which require long habituation in muscular and eye co-ordinations.

To illustrate the idea involved here, the subject matters related to musical keys, such as physical relations in intervals between notes and melodic and harmonic relations within a system, are appropriate content for general musical education. But knowledge *about* keys is not the same thing as practice of scales, nor is it the same thing as having built in by long practice an automatic habit of performing the right notes for a given key. It is possible to learn intellectually about such relations as we designate by keys, to understand what a key signature does and why different signatures are used at different times, and what a change of key does to a pattern of sound, without the long practice essential to smooth performance. This is the kind of knowledge that belongs in general education. When it is communicated to pupils, it should be communicated in reference to organized tones directly experienced, in such a way that information about keys is perceived by pupils as offering them a means for understanding and ordering the subtle differences they begin more clearly to hear.

MUSIC AND EMOTION

Having minimized the importance of a merely pleasurable liking for music, and having considered with favor the values of musical knowledge, a pragmatist would find his task unfinished if he failed to recognize that aesthetic response to music is, after all, a matter of feeling. But what a pragmatist might say on this topic is not necessarily agreeable to those who perceive in music a parade of grand passions. It is a fact that many of the more elaborate, lengthy, or ambitious of musical works are ones which stir the emotions deeply. Granted that fact, it would be hasty to conclude that the ultimate value of music is its emotional impact. Possibly it is, but if that should turn out to be the case, then such an outcome would have to be established as the conclusion of an investigation to clarify our way of using words.

To begin such an investigation, one might ask himself whether it is really true that the quality of a musical experience is to be measured by degree of emotional involvement. There would seem to be many well-informed persons who think so. To read a music critic's description of, say, a Beethoven symphony is to be told about profound and exalted stirrings of the soul of such a magnitude that, if a listener were to experience all of it in an evening's concert, his heart and his tears would be wrung dry. Furthermore, it would appear that in each climax a new insight into the meaning of the universe is revealed. This kind of writing is characteristic of humanists in all the arts. It is claimed, for example, that Shakespeare in a short phrase was able to express more searching wisdom than lesser writers can communicate in many pages. And Plato, it is said, foresaw and communicated, in his random mentions, every good idea about education that has ever been thought of since, and more besides which we are not yet able to appreciate. Toward claims of that kind, a tendency to be skeptical might seem a proper antidote to the excesses of scholarly humanism.

Given an honest skepticism, a few pertinent observations will come to the fore with a fresh relevance. In the first place, professional musicians and conductors in serious performance are generally not carried away in the grip of strong emotions. If they were to indulge their feelings freely to every latent orgy of emotional richness, they would cease to perform in an acceptable manner. And yet, it is also true that performers and especially conductors must remain sensitive to complex patterns and to nuances of feeling. A similar observation is true of seasoned listeners. Unlike a neophyte, whose emotional responses are apt to be excessive, a veteran concert enthusiast is rarely moved to the more strident of emotions. But he values his musical listening much, and his capacity for refinement of feeling is used fully. How should this observation be interpreted?

It seems advisable to make a distinction in terms. A distinction, in this case, between emotion and feeling. Suppose we should agree to say that the more inclusive of the terms is *feeling* and that within the broader category of feelings are more specific kinds, the emotions, which are called by names such as joy, anger, sorrow, love. Thus, a preliminary basis for distinction is to say that any feeling which is clearly recognizable as belonging in a common category and, hence, as being easily named in words is that special kind of feeling properly called an emotion. This way of using terms accords roughly with ordinary speech. But the fact that some feelings are categorized as specific emotions is the outcome of a more fundamental fact.

Specifically named emotions are the kinds of feelings that attend certain kinds of events in experience, events characterized by the properties of a narrative: a beginning, a development of tensions and forces, leading to a conclusion which seems the logical outcome for human striving. For the death of a lovely woman, the attendant kind of emotion is sorrow. For achievement of a cherished goal after prolonged effort against odds, the appropriate emotion is either exultation or humble thankfulness. The non-emotional class of feelings, on the other hand, those which have no names, are distinguished from the emotions by their being less specifically related to types of dramatic event and to practical purposing. They are aroused, they attend our experiences from one moment to another as a shifting and blending but almost never ceasing accompaniment to the impact of sensory experience. If a person looks at a beautiful rose, and smells it, feelings will be there, possibly very pleasant ones, but ordinarily it would be impossible to say what kind of feeling is being experienced. In many ordinary situations, it would be impossible to say even whether one's feelings are pleasant or unpleasant. Neither this nor any other category seems to apply, if only because the question of categorization is irrelevant.

In contexts of this kind, philosophers are inclined to use the word *quality*. The quality of sensuous experience is registered in feelings. When objects at the center of attention are clearly related to specific purposes and plans, then the associated quality of the situation is likely to produce an emotion. But when there is no relation of sensuous content to any particular plan or goal, then the quality of such experience is a matter for feelings of the more general and amorphous kind. Although unemotional feelings are vague and often indescribable, they are not less important than emotions to the goodness of human living. If a person should be asked whether his life is a happy one, he would look for an answer to the general feeling of his day-by-day living rather than to the more specific emotions. A life could be judged good even though marked from time to time by unhappy or tragic emotions, provided that the pattern of daily feelings is generally favorable.

This distinction between feeling and emotion is especially useful in considering the relation between music and the emotions. There are occasions of some frequency in musical experience when namable emotions are aroused. Program music and theater music are the most familiar sources, for the obvious reason that a narrative, or related sequence of events, is part of the content. But most often it is the unemotional feelings which are the natural response to musical sensations. Indeed, it is not too much of exaggeration to say that the aesthetic value of music depends upon the general feelings which it arouses rather than upon emotions. For even the emotions, like joy and sorrow, which seem appropriate to some sequences in theater music, are not the real and original emotions of directly experienced events. If they were, we would not deliberately subject ourselves to tragic music but would rather avoid it, just as we try to avoid tragedy in our own lives. To speak more accurately, therefore, we ought to say that a joyful or sorrowful passage is one which arouses a kind of feeling appropriate to the perception of an artistically executed object of joy or sorrow, rather than one which stimulates joy or sorrow directly. The artistically objectified emotion is not the listener's emotion. It is the emotion of a protagonist in a story, and what the listener experiences is a less easily named feeling, similar to but not the same as the original joy or sorrow. For such reasons, it is more accurate to speak of musical experience as essentially an experience of feelings rather than of emotions.

There are reasons why this way of using terms is advisable. One reason is that teachers who understand it will avoid one of the more unpleasant practices among music critics, humanists in general, and teachers of music appreciation in particular: the practice, namely, of speaking about music in phrases meant to convey the outer extremes of unbridled emotionalism, thereby pushing away from music those who have not already cultivated a peculiar taste for that kind of wordy extravagance. Also to be avoided is the related practice, in teaching music through words, of trying to convert all music into program music in hopes that this will stimulate a flow of emotions appropriate to a narrative or a description. Finally, it is possible that if music teachers aim to stimulate only such feelings as are stimulated naturally by patterns of sound, with no admixture of literary material, then music will stand for itself and its own true quality. This would be the final advice from a pragmatist: Let music become known for its sounds and its felt qualities.

NOTES

1. *Collected Papers of Charles Sanders Peirce* Vol. I, Par. 241. Edited by Charles Hartshorne and Paul Weiss. Cambridge, Massachusetts: Harvard University Press, 1931.

2. John Dewey, *Logic,* New York: Henry Holt & Co., 1938, p. 9 n., et. seq.

3. C. I. Lewis, *Analysis of Knowledge and Valuation,* p. 554. La Salle, Illinois: Open Court Publishing Co., 1946, p. 554.

4. Dewey, *op. cit.,* p. 61.

5. *Collected Papers of Charles Sanders Peirce,* op. cit., Vol. I, Par. 241.

6. *Ibid.,* Vol. V, Par. 2.

7. *Ibid.,* Vol. V, Par. 9.

8. "At the risk of under-emphasizing many of the other important functions of music in the curriculum at all levels of education today, I believe I would put *education for citizenship* as its most important function." Benjamin C. Willis, "The Stake of Music in Education," in *Music in American Education* (Music Education Source Book Number Two), p. 3. Washington: Music Educators National Conference, 1955.

9. Henry Thomas Moore, "The Genetic Aspect of Consonance and Dissonance," *Psychological Monographs,* XVII, No. 2 (September, 1914).

10. John Dewey, *Democracy and Education,* New York: Macmillan Co., 1916, p. 176.

Part 2: Variations on a Pragmatic Theme

Foster McMurray

The history of educational concepts is a history dominated by philosophers. With few exceptions, the most creative and original agents of educational reform have been those who applied their philosophic habits of mind to creating educational theories. This state of affairs is sometimes taken to mean that whenever we seek new educational insight, we might best turn to systematic philosophy for its philosophic concepts — concepts that perhaps offer to inform us about the good, the true, and the beautiful — which are undeniably "basic." But this is a mistake. New insights about education are not drawn by logical implication from philosophic doctrine. Indeed, the typical academic philosopher, who is, after all, an educator as well as a philosopher, is almost certain to have reactionary thoughts about education. This person longs for a return to the kind of schooling that he or she imagines we used to have at some time — usually either the time of his or her own childhood or else that of Plato's childhood — in the past. We don't need new ideas, this philosopher thinks, because we already have the best; they are to be found in our traditions. This hidebound characteristic of most philosophers is not a function of their being philosophers, but rather of their being humanists. As for the great giants of educational doctrine, from the sophists to John Dewey, their singularity among humanists is testament to their originality and creativity. It is also testament to their dissatisfaction with education as they found it around them and to their taking seriously the need to think of new educational doctrine. Among philosophers, they are the singularly bold and creative exceptions.

These unkind remarks about philosophy and humanists may seem strange when one considers that they come from one whose assignment in these proceedings is to represent pragmatic philosophy. Is not pragmatism one of the philosophic schools, or systems? Because it is now more than 100 years old, is it not a part of the humanities?

If we should agree that pragmatism is a philosophy, this would be acceptable only if we note that it is unlike the more traditional philosophic systems like realism and idealism. Pragmatists, insofar as they are pragmatic, do not presume to tell the world about the nature of reality, or of truth and beauty. They set for themselves a more modest kind of goal. Rather than to elaborate a claim that reality *is* this or that kind of thing, and that truth is this or that great thing, a pragmatist tries to bring into clear conception the criteria that we have implicitly within our minds when we try to distinguish the real from the illusory, or the true from the false. A pragmatist assumes that all of us have such criteria already "there" in our minds, but in a form that is not altogether clear and not yet critically examined. To bring such criteria into conscious recognition and to seek an accurate and self-consistent accounting of what they require of us is a difficult business. And to have ventured a formulation of their contents is to make a trial of putting it in words. The results of philosophic thought are more or less temporary stopping places while we continue the search.

In political journalism, especially during the early part of George Bush's presidency, the adjective "pragmatic" occurs frequently. It is said of some politicians, nearly always with approval, that they are pragmatic, by which is meant that they are open to new ideas, not committed to a forever unchanging ideology. In this kind of ordinary parlance, to be pragmatic is to be able to continue to learn, and in the light of new experience to change one's mind toward a refined insight. This is not only good usage; it is also a fair and accurate reflection, on the commonsense level, of pragmatic philosophy.

Pragmatists are especially open to change and to the hope of doing better than before. This should not be taken to imply that pragmatists are not also distinguished by particular and substantive beliefs about one thing or another. Perhaps the most characteristic of doctrines that are shared by pragmatists in general is their theory of knowledge. To know, in the archetypical sense, is to believe that if some specific action is undertaken, then certain anticipated experiences will follow. It is further believed that knowledge confers upon those who know a power to control, in some degree, their relationships with kinds of environments. Thus, to gain in knowledge of the world is to gain in power to assure better, rather than poorer or merely accidental, outcomes of our active relationships with the environment. For purposes of contrast and clarity, this may be compared with a belief, held by many traditionalists and conservatives, that we know simply for the sake of knowing or, if for other reasons, then for passive meditation and acceptance of the way things are. A typical humanist, with that kind of conception, does not look kindly upon pragmatism.

Closely related to the pragmatists' conception of knowledge and power is their belief about values and valuations. In pragmatic philosophy, a judgment of value is thought to be a form of knowledge. This is distinguished from a mere subjective opinion or the expression of a feeling, but different from factual knowledge in that we are lacking a technology by which to assure intersubjective agreement about what is true in such judgments. This means that, in typical pragmatic opinion, to know what is good or aesthetically pleasing is to have increased one's power to secure what is good and to increase the having of aesthetic experience. This does not accord with ordinary opinion. These individuals who say that they may not know much about art but know what they like are not only philistines, they are also not entitled to speak of "knowing" what they like. To know, in a veridical sense, what one likes in art or in serious music is to have achieved a high level of knowledge, a feat that can be accomplished only after prolonged study and observation; in short, it is to have become a part of the cognoscenti, or to have achieved sophistication in the arts.

It is easy to see why pragmatists have been especially interested in contributing to theory of knowledge and logic — as was true of C. S. Peirce, John Dewey, and C. I. Lewis — and to value theory and aesthetics, equally true of the same persons. Superficially considered, a wide gulf would seem to separate logic from aesthetics. But as pragmatists think of these domains, they become closely related by reason of a third domain, that of theory of mind. The mind, or intellect, functions in its most characteristic way whenever we seek to learn about the world in order to gain better control over how it affects us and our welfare, and this in turn requires an awareness of what it is that promotes our welfare or in any way contributes to the realization of the good. Logic is the systematic accounting of rationality, and to be rational is to be self-consistent in building a structure of beliefs and values so that we do not both do and undo, march and retreat, in our passage toward a better realization of the good life.

From this brief mention of a pragmatic concept of "mind," it is only a small step toward consideration of education, or more specifically, of schooling. Schooling is commonly understood to have something to do with the cultivation of mind, and if one is to think about the improvement of schooling (and of music education) it may seem best to know what we are talking about when we speak of the mind and of taking steps deliberately to improve how it does whatever it is that we suppose it does.

One of the best-known aspects of John Dewey's philosophy was his proposal that the mind is an instrument for dealing with emergencies as they arise within the environment. This was pragmatic, at least in part. It had the virtue of recognizing that the mind is *not* to be conceived as engaged in the disinterested search for knowledge as matter for contemplation or in passively reasoning about abstract systems. Instead, the mind is thought to be engaged with the world as a place that offers goods to be won and forces to be dealt with when they stand between us and our purposive actions. But an emergency theory of mind has serious flaws: it requires of us that we conceive of mind as quiescent between emergencies, and also, of mind as stimulated into action not because of its own processes, but as somehow prompted into action by external events. A more genuinely pragmatic conception would avoid these errors.

For these introductory purposes, where theory of mind is instrumental to something else, let us propose that the mind is more or less constantly employed in perceiving an environment and in interpreting what is perceived by means of the mind's ideas and concepts. The purpose to be served by such interpretation is to link up a particular here-now environment with the rest of the world, with a past and a future, and to spot trends that may be used to advantage, or forces that threaten our values and that might be overcome. (Thus, to discover an emergency is the result rather than the instigator of the mind's activity.) This is a greatly simplified and abbreviated conception, but for this context it will have to suffice. Anyone who employs it will notice that when persons find themselves in unfamiliar environments, they must learn enough about those scenes to be able, at the very least, to dismiss them as of no further import. That is to say, a novel environment stimulates at least a minimum of mental activity simply because it is novel and one doesn't know what it might portend for good or for harm. But whether an interpretation yields reason to inquire further than a cursory once-over is a function partly of mental habits, whether they be sloppy or else sharply honed, and partly of the conceptual apparatus that the mind has at its command. A simpleminded individual, when confronted with environmental presences that are of a largely intellectual or artistic nature, may be quick to dismiss them as of no further import. This stuff, he or she may say, is of no interest to me. An intellectual, on the other hand, might sit up straight with anticipation of an occasion to learn or to enjoy. Here, at last, we have reached an educational issue.

Simpletons and intellectuals are not born that way; persons become one or another largely as a result of their educative experiences. It is easy to see that intellectuals become that way through the kinds and qualities of their educational experiences. They discover in themselves a facility for academic learning and a pleasure in the exercise of it, thus forming predispositions to approach further experiences as occasions for learning, especially for the kind of learning that is mediated by abstract language and communication.

The institutions of schooling, including the system of grading and rewards, has a large part in that process. Normal operations include constant and public evaluations of each student's performance, and those who do well — the potential intellectuals — are praised and in other insidious ways rewarded for their academic talents. But this same process means humiliation and discouragement for the many whose grades are, of necessity according to the iron laws of grading, low. These children are ruthlessly damaged in self-esteem. Schooling is, after all, their career at that stage in life, and they are told constantly that, career-wise, they are pretty lousy. They learn to disparage themselves and to find other resources than intelligence. We teach people to become simpletons. This, of course, is not supposed to be our intent, although conservatives and traditionalists are happy with it. We are not aiming to make of everyone either an intellectual or a simpleton, but in a democracy marked by equality of opportunity, we do intend to encourage in everyone a capacity to apply informed intelligence to experience and in general to the conduct of one's life. This topic needs further consideration.

People are born with differing degrees, and perhaps kinds, of intelligence, and the brightest people are very much more intelligent than the average. This fact has been taken to mean that schooling beyond the more elementary levels is mostly for those who are above average in intelligence; it is said by conservatives that an academic high school program requires an IQ of 115 or higher, which would mean that academic high school curricula are suitable for considerably less than half of the population. This elitist conception accords with the historic role of schooling, but not with democracy.

In America, the intent of public schooling is to make formal education available to everyone. But there are two ways to interpret that intent. A conservative says that everyone should be given an opportunity to show whether he or she has the requisite intelligence, and then be provided with an amount and kind of schooling suited to that degree of aptitude. Liberals see it differently. They believe that equal educational opportunity means providing quality education for everyone, and this requires that we improve our technologies of schooling until they become adequate to the task.

On this issue the pragmatic philosophy is aligned with a liberal perspective — not necessarily because of any strong bent toward liberal politics, but for a different reason. It stems from the pragmatic conception of mind, or intelligence. The presence of mind in the regulation of behavior is bound to make a favorable difference in the quality of life, no matter whether the degree of intelligence is small or large. The role of intelligence at its most functional best is to use what we know or can learn about the environment by figuring out how that knowledge may help us to force, from a sometimes reluctant world, the favorable action of its processes and structures. This increases the odds in our favor as we attempt to reach our goals and to satisfy our needs and desires. The presence of an informed mind in control of behavior means that what befalls an active person is less a product of chance or accident and more of a deliberate intent and insight. This is true for anyone, even for a person who is developmentally disabled. Recent experience has shown that if persons of limited intelligence are encouraged to use whatever degree of intelligence they have, they become much more self-supporting and effectual than anyone had ever suspected was possible.

In this little essay, it is now time to begin a consideration of music education. The universal values of music are the various kinds of qualities that they contribute. Some of these qualities are more universally recognized and appreciated than others; a marching band, for example, stimulates militant or patriotic emotions, which are thought to help one's football team to victory. Conversely, the listening to some forms of popular music by adolescents may be used as a sign of revolt against older generations or to shock one's parents. This particular value is often appreciated by high school and college students. But these are among the least central, or the most peripheral and accidental, of musical values. Coming closer to the heart of the matter we could mention music as that to which we dance. However, these values are so widely recognized that schools need have nothing to do with them. If music deserves a special and prominent place in schooling, then it would have to be for teaching about music that which is not already well dispersed within the population and its common culture. What would that be? Well, it could be the skills of musical performance, and this has indeed been accepted widely in our schools. But teaching for skill in performance is a part of public schooling that reaches only a few. What then is there for the public at large?

The only suitable answer is to teach the values that accrue to human life from experiences with serious music. There is much of cognitive content available for school music — not just music notation and solfeggio, but also the history of musical periods and styles and the evolution of forms. However, the most important of educational objectives is the cultivation of a capacity to attend to and to hear with understanding the kinds of music that qualify as serious, and thereby to have experiences of strong aesthetic quality. This is something that is missing from mass culture; it is a part of our cultural heritage that the great majority must learn about from school or else not at all. Indeed, for most persons, it is still not at all. Even jazz, which used to be a part of the popular music of an older generation, is now often too highbrow for most people. It also seems that most of today's youth don't realize that there are musical instruments other than electronic keyboards and amplified guitars.

You might think that this kind of carping is just what one would expect from an older generation. But to a person of a certain age, who sees almost no young people at the concerts he attends, it seems that schools have failed not only to teach the basics, but they have also failed to teach a new generation about the aesthetic qualities to be experienced and perhaps prized in serious music. If this impression is veridical, then there must be reasons for it.

My first suggestion is that music educators have not yet taken to their bosoms an idea I tried to convey in the 1958 edition of *Basic Concepts in Music Education,* namely, that their educational efforts should be directed toward aims that respect the integrity and the unique qualities of music rather than toward generalized aims that are shared with teachers in other fields of learning.

A second observation is that music educators are bent upon persuading everyone that music education, along with all other parts of a sound educational program, is also vitally important. We too are a part of the main endeavor. This is probably natural enough, given their sensitivity to a tendency to look upon music in the curriculum as a frill that can be cut whenever economies must be made. It seems to me that in a publishing enterprise such as this, our first concern ought to be to convince music teachers themselves that they have an important role in schooling, an *essential* role, and that they can be clear in their own minds about what that role is and be *passionately* devoted to it. Their allegiance is to teaching about music, and about music that possesses the strongest aesthetic content. Alas, the clarity of purpose, the conviction, and the passion are not there.

The biggest difficulty, however, is that we are not of a common mind about equality in music education and what equality should be taken to mean. Here we have a tradition to be overturned. Serious music is commonly thought to be, like other forms of art, a special privilege of a social and economic elite. Attendance at the concert hall or the opera is almost entirely middle class — that portion of the middle class that is nearer to the upper than to the lower end of the socioeconomic distribution. There is no pressing economic reason for this. Today's youth spend more for pop concerts and recordings than would be needed for their concertgoing, if ever they were to try it, even in those few cities where the great (and most expensive) symphony orchestras are located. They simply don't know that powerful music with potential for aesthetic and sensuous experience is there to be enjoyed in concerts and recordings. No one has ever succeeded in removing the blinders and opening their senses to this kind of potential. The reason, of course, is that whereas popular music is usually easy to understand and to like, serious music is a cultivated taste and cultivated over a lengthy period of learning. To further complicate the educational task, there are two special forms of opposition to the achievement of success. One of these is contained within the widely distributed levels of commonsense culture, and the other in the more rarefied levels of conservative ideology, the humanities, and philosophy.

It is sometimes suggested that common sense is a repository of wisdom and is a necessary antidote to the foibles of intellectualism and of passing fads. That may be so for carefully selected bits of our common sense. But the most widely distributed levels of mass culture contain beliefs and values that reproduce in new generations the false beliefs and harmful attitudes that perpetuate the worst features of human societies, those that are oppressive and demeaning. Among that kind of cultural material is a belief that the working class is not meant to be well educated, having no use for advanced levels of knowledge or for refined tastes in music and art. A similar attitude is associated with rural people and small-scale farmers. This kind of pervasive cultural influence is the main reason why schooling in our large cities and in rural communities is so difficult. Teachers are challenged to show that school-taught materials have utility in the life of the neighborhood, and the challenge seems to be too great. Many American adolescents of the working class are so deeply imbued with a bad common sense that nothing seems able to get through to them. Middle-class children are somewhat more educable, but usually for the wrong reasons. They are willing to work for good grades because they see themselves as competing with one another for entrance into good colleges and then into the more prestigious corporations with the higher salaries. Neither class is easily persuaded that serious music has a potential for adding something exciting to the quality of their lives.

Teachers vary in their approach to this major problem. A conservative teacher says, in effect, "Give me students who are well motivated and willing to work hard and I will try to help them learn." Progressive teachers, by contrast, feel that a first requirement, before they can teach anything successfully, is to show why schooling is valuable and in what senses it can contribute to a more interesting life. And, perhaps most of all, their obligation is to teach all learners, without exception, that they can indeed learn and grow and win rewards for their accomplishments.

This is not an appropriate place to write at length about the motivation of learning. Nevertheless, the problem cannot be skirted entirely. Let me offer this: A significant change in chances for success in teaching (about serious music as well as about anything else) can come about by changing the way we conceive our educational task. At the present time, in this era of triumphant conservatism, we think of schooling as a matter of teaching various school "subjects," and of some subjects like mathematics as being more important than others. Progressive educators conceive the task in a very different way: they believe that instead of teaching subjects, we ought to think of our educational task as that of teaching our students about the kinds of environment that lie beyond or behind the familiar environment of home, neighborhood, and school, and which are in some significant ways contiguous with the known environments and exert influence upon the welfare of students and their futures. If schooling is ever to be judged successful in its democratic mission, this could happen only when students have become aware of environmental forces and events that are not of immediately pressing concern but that are nonetheless significant. Forces and events in the nonimmediate environment are significant when they push and pull us in this direction and that — without our consent and sometimes without our even knowing of their action upon us, unless by reason of fortuitous intervention and instruction through the formal school. It is from the school that we learn about much of that in the world which must come under our surveillance or control if we are to increase the odds in our favor. The mission of schooling is to teach about environmental forces and processes, those that work against our welfare and those that can be used to gain advantage. The various academic disciplines must be taught only when and as we see how they can be of assistance in that mission.

A pragmatist realizes quite well that as we pursue our destinies, we are only partly in charge. Try as we might we cannot control everything that determines our fate, or even a very large part of it. If nothing else cuts us short, cancer is lurking about. However, if there is any chance that we might direct our lives deliberately toward achieving the good life, it would have to come from learning where to intersect favorable winds, where to push back the forces of darkness, what to cultivate, what to prize, and what to seize from the flux. The more we learn about environmental forces that determine outcomes in our experiences, the more we gain in power to intercede and to force a reluctant world to do our bidding. If there is any chance for happiness and any true meaning for the concepts of responsibility and individual integrity, these must come from our reliance upon informed intelligence and from our active interventions. From a pragmatic point of view, to accept poverty, hopelessness, and misery without putting up a good fight against them and without making full use of our minds and of our power to learn is not only stupid and barbaric, it is also a waste of life and of human potentials.

Now, let's try to deal with the pressing issues of music education. The first of these is a belief typical of most people in most segments of society. It holds that serious music and serious art is especially for those who inhabit the higher ground, those whose income and education are considerably above average, and who have the cultivated taste of an elite. If this belief is taken to include a corollary, namely, that being of an elite is a necessary prerequisite to enjoyment of art and music, then of course a democratic and equalitarian education would be bound to fail.

I am assuming here without further argument that music educators are on the side of democratic and equalitarian education. They believe that the aesthetic qualities of serious music are of potentially great value to anyone and everyone. I am assuming that serious music is not effete and languorous, as may be the case with a small part of chamber music, but rather vigorously stirring, stimulating, sometimes beautiful and usually capable of helping to make one's life more livable with enriched quality and emotional force. This is true for almost anyone, and therefore the cultivation of a taste for serious music is not among the special privileges of an elite. As things now stand, this is a minority point of view that cannot prevail except through successful combat against all the many entrenched opinions and values opposing it.

Among those whose opinions and values are especially negative are the inheritors and bearers of lower middle-class and working-class cultures. Children of the lower classes don't know, for example, that many of their acquired values and attitudes, imposed upon them in their unguarded formative years, are antieducational in effect, working against their own best interests and depriving them of opportunities to use informed intelligence in surveying their options and opening up choices. The only way to deal with this is to direct the attention of children and youth to a critical examination of their immediate sociocultural environment, to reveal the subtle forces that are crippling them and making the use of their minds difficult. A study of what one's culture — the everyday culture of the masses — does to people and to their educability should be a first and continuing concern of the schools. This, of course, requires the use of anthropological and sociological instruments to open eyes toward that which otherwise cannot be seen because it permeates the atmosphere and is so pervasive and so ordinary, so much inhaled daily that it has become a part of one's fiber. It means using the critical and rational parts of the mind against other parts of the same mind.

This prerequisite kind of educational endeavor — prerequisite because it is necessary to promote the educability of students — is necessary not only for the children of the lower classes. It is necessary for *all* classes, but the kinds of transmitted beliefs and attitudes that stand in the way of children becoming truly educated are different for those reared in presumably well-educated families and households. For them, and for a great many music educators, the cultural forces that work against their chances for success are more insidious and more deeply entrenched in the humanities and philosophy. On the most widely distributed front there is mere snobbery: a belief that upper-class people are made of finer stuff than the masses, and that class distinctions are a necessary part of social reality and, like poverty, are always with us. On a somewhat more intellectualized plane, we have the heritage of certain parts of ancient Greek philosophy, particularly that part of it contributed by the enemies of democracy and the open society, among them especially Plato and Socrates.

Primitive Greek philosophy is still being used by humanists to justify an elitist educational system, in which schooling, both in its contents and in its length, is different for each of the supposed three classes of humanity. For academics whose minds are shaped by this primitive perspective, it would be a violation of social order and its virtue to propose that the masses have a right to enjoy the subtleties and divine harmonies of serious music. Since the masses, by almost any accounting, are by far the largest class of people, then it would follow that the cultivation of the mind and soul are appropriate only for a small proportion of our present-day student population. If we were to try to extend our educational mission to everyone, we must fail for having suffered a peculiar kind of hubris that leads us to buck up against the realities of the social order. Even worse: to uphold a pragmatic ideal, offering quality education to everyone, with a romantic expectation that it can be made to work, is to fall victim again to the lure of the sophists.

The distribution of primitive Greek ideology among academics is now so wide and deep that music educators actually turn to classical realism for intellectual guidance! This is the ultimate gaffe. I have no doubt that the gods are laughing uproariously. To witness the irony, it may be helpful if first of all we give attention to the issue of motivation.

Suppose, for the sake of argument, that we had agreed upon a pragmatic and democratic purpose for schooling, and we took seriously the hope of educating everyone alike to make full use of mind and intelligence. For our learners in school, this would be bold and maybe intimidating, especially for students of average ability. They have already learned that they are not the very brightest of people, and they are already adapting to a world in which they are tossed and bossed, told what to do, and threatened with unimaginable badness if they stray from the flock and the right expectations of one's little world. As they see it, "fitting in" is the safe route, and the idea that "the likes of them" could learn to challenge the way things are and the *mos majorum* is to have become haughty, and even worse, to commit a kind of sin for which they have no name. In the world as we inherit it, the majority of people learn to be humble early in life. And now, here come persons like me, wanting to teach them to challenge unkind fates, to redo the distribution of educational goods, and to pursue the good life with insight, sensitivity, and the smarts. For most people, to be asked to take seriously the tasks of intellectual learning about the world and how to turn its powers to our advantage, and to expect that by our intelligence alone we can intervene in the course of events to shape our own destinies, is very bold and scary. It is like keeping our eyes open when we want to duck under the covers and shut out the shadows. So, in the face of self-doubts, humility, and low expectations, what shall we do? Shall we not try to encourage, to open up the discovery of the joys of learning, to stimulate each person — every one — to discover the kind of self-esteem that comes from having tried, struggled, and then succeeded? Shall we not reward each faltering step, trumpet each little triumph, cherish every little gain in learning, and sympathize with every little error? Shall we not make of our schools the arenas in which everybody wins in the long run, everybody grows and flourishes, and the mind is nourished with so much good employment? Shall we make certain that our students succeed more often than they fail, and will they learn from experience that a temporary bit of postponed pleasure in order to accomplish useful work is a way to feel good about one's self and to brighten the day? How else could the humility of mediocrity be overcome and all people be taught to expect of themselves that their informed minds can really make a difference? Well, you see the problem and its delicacy.

So what do the humanists and the Greek realists propose? They propose "education for excellence." We are asked to represent our schools as places wherein we try to get our students to try to excel. It is understood by everyone, of course, that the achievement of excellence is, by definition, rare and approachable by only the few. The talented will rise to the top, and all others must learn to accept their humble place in the lower levels of society, as determined by their relative place in the hierarchical distribution of intellectual or artistic talents. To suggest that everyone can approach excellence if they will just get into the spirit of the race is to do violence to our language. To excel is to get ahead of the others, to win the race. Excellence has no meaning if it extends beyond the few.

"Education for excellence," along with our penchant for grading on a bell-shaped curve, requiring as many low grades as high ones, is ideally suited to an educational system designed to rake over the coals and to mark all students with a sense of where they belong in a class-structured society. The masses learn to accept their humble place. They agree that the higher levels of culture are not for them; the opera, the ballet, the Brillo boxes of Andy Warhol are part of the privileges of the elite. Under the influence of classical realism, the working classes are supported in their indifference or hostility to serious music. The symphony orchestra, with its strange instruments, belongs in another world. The masses want no part of it. A teacher who might try to teach them otherwise would find the weight of lower-class values, when combined with academic tradition and the seekers after excellence, too heavy to overcome.

The difficulty is not only that primitive Greek philosophy and academic traditions together confirm people in their acceptance of the past and its inequities, making it difficult to change anything in the cultural heritage no matter how odious; it is also that the ancient mentality distorts thinking on practically anything. This becomes strikingly evident in the presently popular literature of music education. There we find it said that "the ability to detect form is the heart of musical education."

This emphasis upon form, musical or otherwise, is also the heart of Platonism. And Platonism is a powerful force. The writings of Plato before he became old and crabby are charming, and coming as they did at the very beginning of Western philosophy, they deal with issues of universal concern in a simple way, uncluttered with any prior inheritance of sophisticated philosophic systems. In that early dawn light it seemed to Plato that for every kind of thing for which we have an honored name and a cluster of expectations, there is an essential and unchanging nature. In our sensory experience, where we might find a particular thing belonging to its kind, we expect to find something less than the pure essence of what it is, some little flaws or imperfections that, we have learned, arise from its materiality. A beautiful red rose is blemished on one petal with a spot of white, which surely doesn't belong there. It is, let us say, an accident, not of the essence. The only perfectly pure thing, unblemished in every way and representing the pure nature of its kind, is the Idea or the Form of the kind of thing it is. In the mundane world of our sensory experience, we find that objects encountered are changing and imperfect, and to the degree that they are thus qualified, they are unreal. The most truly real world is a world of pure Ideas, pure Forms, unblemished by the accidental properties that becloud perceptible experience. When we try to know what is real and to embrace reality with our minds, we search within the objects of knowledge for their underlying forms, which constitute their true nature. This way of thinking may be applied, mutatis mutandis, to music and the perception of music.

In listening to an extended piece of music, we are enabled to perceive it as a unified and unique object by means of memory and anticipation, those being the processes by which all of the changes that occur are felt to belong to a single work. The task of remembering is made not too difficult by carefully spaced repetitions, but a simple repetition of the same material too many times would fail to hold our interest. To keep a listener's attention, a composer will introduce variety, often by use of a contrasting theme, or by dramatic tension, achieved perhaps by modulation and a new key. During the career of Haydn, he and other Viennese composers worked out a particularly useful way of doing these things called the sonata form. A composer who masters this form could then carry a listener through many exciting ups and downs, variations and returns, lights and darks, and by means of the sonata form keep it, as it is heard, a single work of art, cohesive and integrated. If we think of form in music as that by means of which a great variety of sounds and rhythms, and changes of these along with all the other musical elements, is made a single entity, then it would indeed seem that form is the heart of the matter. It is similar, let us say, to the parti in an architectural design. This much is true.

But now, Platonic realists will carry their recognition of musical form a bit further. They will say that it is only through its form that a musical composition achieves its reality, and therefore the hearing of any music penetrates to the reality of it only when its form is perceived. Without that perception the experience of music is only of sensuous materials, incoherent and blind, and tending to stimulate the baser feelings and instincts. (Plato was a prude about sensuous experience.) Thus it could be made to seem that the ability to hear and recognize form is the aim of music education. Those who make serious music a significant part of their lives will feel uneasy about this. If they ponder the cause and come to realize what is afoot here, they will discover that this conception of music education in relation to musical forms is an egregious error. Regardless of anything having to do with metaphysics and the nature of reality, it is an error for several reasons.

In the first place, this conception is established upon a confusion of means and ends. Any particular musical form is a means, chosen by a composer along with other means like, for example, the sonorities of differing instrumental groups, to achieve a musical end. The goal in a composer's mind is not the achievement of Form, perfected and shimmering in its pure ideality, but rather a work of art that brings to its audience the possibility of experiencing aesthetic quality; *sensuous* aesthetic quality, enlivened by the immediacy of sounds and rhythms. Obviously, for composers, a knowledge of musical forms is a professional requirement, a tool of their specialty.

Whether an audience is better off for knowing the technical details by means of which a composer achieves his or her magic is debatable. On the one hand, a knowledge of forms might be said to enlighten expectations, helping to perceive the distinguishable parts and to give one a feeling of understanding why this or that happens in the way that it does. But it may be also that this habit of expectation is what brings about the well-known phenomenon of critical rejection for highly creative music, new music that breaks out of the patterns as they have evolved up to any given point in musical history. Take any great work from the symphonic repertoire, and then read what the learned critics had to say about it when it first burst upon the scene. It makes you wonder how they could have failed to hear the glorious music that we hear now. It is a historic fact that a learned audience given to trained expectation of musical forms is likely to reject the music of its contemporary composers, and like humanists in general, to hark back to the greater glories of the past.

A second point is that any composer who gains great facility in using already established forms, and who then uses them precisely as they have become formalized, will surely produce large quantities of second-rate music — pretty, perhaps, and flowing easily in well-worn patterns, but lacking in passion, and mostly superficial, light in weight. Many examples of this could be drawn from the Baroque period. For growth in powers of composition, a first-rate composer breaks the molds of established forms and pioneers in new ways of achieving aesthetic quality. Indeed, the greatest works of art have an extra role to play, beyond that of giving aesthetic pleasure; they are required by the state of the art to *teach*. They teach those who are truly sensitive to see or to hear in a new way or to discover aesthetic merit in a new kind of source. The more of this burden to teach that a given work carries, the more difficulty it has in gaining acceptance, the more rejection it suffers at the hands of critics, conservatives, and academic humanists. But it does teach, and sooner or later it becomes accepted as a work of art, first by the truly sensitive and adventurous, and finally by the scholars, who then explain why it is so powerful. New generations wonder how it could ever have been rejected.

There is one further point to be made concerning the teaching of musical form. In any given piece of music, its form is that part of it shared in common, either actually or implicitly, with other pieces of music. These other pieces include those that are merely mediocre or even poor in aesthetic quality, however much they might exemplify the correct use of established musical form. Form is, so to speak, a naked mannequin waiting to be clothed in ways that make the finished project an original. And surely the most important educational outcome, toward which our teaching ought to strive, is a capacity to respond to what is *unique* in this particular work of art, that which makes it more than a finger exercise, more than a filling out of a known form. To look upon teaching musical form as the heart of music education is to teach people to look for that which makes no contribution to the greatness of a work of art. It is to teach people to prefer the music of Salieri to that of Mozart.

I don't mean to suggest that there is no proper place for instruction in the forms that music employs. But I do mean to propose that we look upon such instruction as, for us too, a means to an end. The end we seek is to teach students to hear, in serious music, the sensuous excitement, the flowing line, the tensions and climaxes, the sometimes passion and always the contents of feeling or emotion that provide an aesthetic experience. Persons who are new to serious music, especially when young or adolescent or sophomoric, approach this music with very strong negative biases. They can't really hear what an experienced audience hears, no matter how loudly it plays and no matter how often they are told to shut up and listen. They treat any promises from teachers that this is great stuff with skepticism or rejection. Their behavior is the result of cultural imprisoning, of socially transmitted attitudes, values, and false beliefs, plus, of course, peer group pressures to conform.

In this section, I have been trying to show that music educators, too, are suffering from a like imprisonment. Their beliefs and attitudes, soaked in illiberal humanities and conservative values, leave their thinking in professional matters tied to the past, and for many, even to the distant past of an ancient culture. No one seems to have been looking when the ideals of democratic education were being conceived. Here a helpless infant has come upon the stage and we aren't noticing that its growth to a vigorous youth requires us to redo the nursery in radical ways. It won't do to fix up an old place with a coat of paint and some flimsy gauze.

We live in an unbalanced society, wherein the lower classes live their lives in ways that are markedly different from the upper classes, and this has been reflected in the kinds of music that people learn to enjoy. Generally speaking, the lower classes enjoy simple melodies and rhythms. For the upper classes, it is elaborate variations and sophisticated forms, and in the best of music, great beauty and aesthetic excitement, with such richness of content that a masterpiece can be experienced over and over for a lifetime without its ever growing stale. Shall we be very stingy with this, keeping it only for a fortunate few? Much of our school ways and even our educational philosophies are geared to perpetuating this tradition of cultural differences. Making of our schools a race for the swift, a proving ground for the competitive and ambitious, a striving to excel, is to perpetuate the social class divisions of the past. It reproduces within the school the divisions of humanity, including for some the gentlemanly values, the polite customs, the supposed sportsmanship of playing to win, and the whole long history of swells and humble folk, boss and worker, fine linen and coarse homespun.

We are giving consideration (I assume) to an idea that challenges a part of our unbalanced cultures. We are thinking that everyone, even those lower in their inheritance of talents and other goods, may be taught to rely upon their minds and to cultivate their intelligence, and to become as discerning, as sensitive, and as devoted to quality in life as their capabilities will allow — will allow, that is, when we have really reshaped our schools to accomplish this new goal and developed new technologies of schooling that are suited to the challenge. This is a very radical ideal, and so different from the values and expectations of our traditions that it requires much creativity and boldness. Among the first requirements is that we become aware of what is there, in the world and its cultures, which is working to defeat us, and above all, what is there in our own educational heritage and educational literature that would perpetuate false values and wrong goals. We must come to know the enemy. The enemy might be that charming, cultivated scholar with more than a little Greek in his or her mind, who glitters and warms us with wry humor and deft touches of elegant humanism. The enemy of quality is a seductive fellow.

A kind of schooling that teaches everyone to use informed intelligence in the control of conduct, that promotes a reliance upon mind and its rightful place in dealing with the environment as we find it, and that thrusts aside the obstacles that a cultural heritage puts in the way of intelligence as a universal reliance rather than a specialty of the elite, has not yet been tried. Even among the founding fathers, in their proposals for schooling in the new nation, it was Jefferson the Platonist and elitist rather than Franklin the pragmatist and champion of the common man who won praise for "wisdom" and for "democratic" values. Imagine that! Today, pragmatists and other possible agents of democratic enlargement are a small minority. But the history of civilization is a history of occasional setbacks in man's spiritual quest, followed nearly always by new gains. The rich and powerful have always lived the good life as they understood it, with the moral equivalent of stretch limos and useful movie actors at their service. With the advance of civilization, it has been the common people whose share of worldly goods has greatly increased, and whose hopes for a better life have materialized. The cultivation of informed intelligence and of attachment to the refined products of artistic genius are the next frontier.

3

A Realistic Philosophy of Music Education

Harry S. Broudy

PRELIMINARY OBSERVATIONS

AIMS AND PROCEDURES OF MUSIC EDUCATION

Whenever experience can be analyzed into patterns of melody, harmony, rhythm, and tonal color, we call it musical.

Not all experience is musical, and music education is only a part of education. If music plays a considerable role in the lives of only a few individuals, or a trivial role in the lives of most individuals, it has no place in *general* education. If, on the contrary, it does or should play a considerable role in the lives of all humans, then how to assure its proper place in general education is a task of the first importance.

By music education, in this discussion, is meant all deliberately instituted procedures designed to shape the musical skill, knowledge, and taste of the learner — and only such procedures. Some of this education will be *formal,* that is, when the primary goal of the procedure is instruction. It will be *informal* if the instruction is incidental to some other goal, e.g., as when a mother in the midst of doing the laundry takes a little time out to teach her child a song.

But musical education, in this discussion, does not mean the multitude of environmental activities that without intent to instruct nevertheless produce or affect musical learnings, e.g., singing commercials and the playing of Christmas carols in department stores.

Originally published in *Basic Concepts in Music Education, I,* Nelson B. Henry, editor, 1958. Reprinted (revised) with permission from the National Society for the Study of Education.

Formal education tries to guide the behavior of learners into specific routes of value realization, and when this guidance is rational, educators select materials and methods according to some principle or theory. Principles may be used by one group or many, for a long or short time, but choosing according to principle is essentially different from acting according to impulse or well-established habit.

Principles of choice become *standards*. If there are no defensible objective standards of musical quality, then music education is an indefensible imposition of the teacher's taste upon the pupil, and such terms as "good," "better," and "best" are deceptions, for they sound as if they were describing the music whereas they are only describing our reactions to the music.

These are some of the topics and issues that belong in a philosophy of music education. Any serious attempt to defend one set of basic concepts in this area against another will lead into general philosophy. This is so because to describe the musical experience is, in part at least, a problem in *aesthetics;* to define the role of musical experience in life as a whole is a problem of *ethics and value theory;* to test the relation of music to cosmic and human nature is a problem of *metaphysics,* and the entire discussion should be respectful of the rules of logic.

SOME REALISTIC EMPHASES

Twenty centuries have developed standard approaches to these problems. These are called idealism, naturalism, pragmatism, realism, and so on. There are numerous variations and combinations of these views. The author of this chapter has been asked to present some basic concepts in music education from the point of view of the philosophic position called realism.

As used in art, realism refers to both a kind of subject matter and a way of presenting it. Realistic art utilizes for its subject matter the objects and actions of ordinary people in ordinary life as opposed to highly idealized or romanticized scenes, characters, and actions. Thus, to paint ash cans in an alley would be more "realistic" than to depict the well-groomed landscapes so beloved of the French court.

Realism also refers to the faithfulness with which an artist imitates an object, e.g., when automobile horns, thunder machines, and steam whistles are used in an orchestra to get "realistic" effects.

Unfortunately, neither of these meanings, nor the one encountered in everyday usage (namely, to face situations without blinking the facts), has more than a remote relationship to the use of the word in philosophy. To understand why this is so, it is necessary to go back to Plato whose doctrines are the ancestors of both philosophical realism and idealism.

Plato was impressed by what seemed to him a fact, namely, that whenever we judge a horse, an automobile, or a sonata as good, we have some ideal (model) in our minds that we use as a yardstick. It is the model that is perfect rather than the horse, auto, or sonata we are judging. Indeed, whatever goodness things around us have comes from their participation in the perfection of the ideal or model. If we now say that the perfect is the most real, that is, the most perfect horse is the most real horse, the most perfect sonata is the most real sonata, then we can understand why ideals (universals in more technical language) are regarded as real and the doctrine that proclaims this is called realism. Platonic realism places these ideals in a realm of their own not visible to the human eye and discernable only to the eye of the mind. Aristotelian realism brings the ideals down to ordinary individual horses, automobiles, and sonatas and calls them the *forms* that give them a design or structure peculiar to themselves and yet common to other members of their class.

Let us go back a few steps. Suppose it occurs to us that the Platonic ideas or ideals, which are most perfect and most real, must come from some cosmic mind or the mind of God or the mind of the absolute. We might argue in this way because every idea or ideal we know about does come from some mind. In that event we would be idealists rather than realists.

Between the current use of the word *realism* on one hand and the original Platonic meaning on the other lie a bewildering variety of philosophical realisms, such as critical realism, classical realism, neo-realism, scholastic realism, and realism combined with this theory of knowledge and that theory of reality. Obviously, no single chapter could do justice to this philosophical variety. As to what each says about education in general and about music education in particular one can only speculate. Some have said a good deal; others have said little; and still others, nothing at all.

For the reader who wishes to become acquainted with the historical development of realism in philosophy there are standard histories of philosophy as well as current expositions.[1] Here we can only indicate a few general theses to which philosophical realism is sympathetic and show what, in the view of the present author, a realistic approach to music education would have to say about certain problems.

1. One of these theses is that, although the world comes to each filtered through his or her own sense organs, nervous system, and a particular pattern of space, time, and history, one does not create the objects that are apprehended; nor are they merely ideas in one's mind. If three of us hear *Yankee Doodle* and disagree on its pitch or rhythm, we do not conclude that *Yankee Doodle* has no single pitch or rhythm. On the contrary, we try to find the peculiarities in each individual that would explain hearing them differently.

The realist does not insist that every quality of music must lie wholly in the object, where they indeed appear to be. The objectivity of pitch, timbre, tempo, and formal design is easier to defend than are certain "expressive" qualities, such as nobility, religiousness, strivingness, dignity, sublimity. Clearly the "humanness" of these latter qualities makes it seem plausible to believe that they are creations or projections of the human consciousness onto the patterns of sound that we call music. Yet, even here realism is reluctant to give up objectivity altogether. Plato, and even the more moderate Aristotle, would try to find some correspondence between the structure of the music and its fitness to express human passions and aspirations. Thus, the Phrygian mode was held to be appropriate to the mood of courage.

2. Why is realism so concerned with whether the qualities of music are in the object or added to it by the listener? For one thing, if there is no sense in which the musical object is independent of the listener, then it makes little sense to talk about standards for music; one can only talk about standards for listeners. If enjoyment, as such, is to be the sole standard of listening, then the child, the symphonic musician, and the music critic might all be listening to *Peter and the Wolf* with equal enjoyment. It would seem that those who are willing to affirm this have to explain why music education is necessary. Those who are reluctant to accept this conclusion are assuming standards of listening other than enjoyment as such, or they are assuming that knowledge or skill can affect the quality of enjoyment.

For another matter, realism holds that, in knowing or hearing anything, we do not alter it.[2] Musically, this means that our previous experience or expectations do not create or change the sound patterns emanating from the voice or instrument, however much or little they affect our interpretation of these patterns. In other words, they would hold that a piece of music, although related in many ways to the culture in which it was composed and the experience of its auditors, nevertheless has musical qualities and structure independent of these and peculiar to itself which can be progressively explored in any culture and at any time by the musically cultivated person.

3. However, we cannot banish relativity altogether. As has been mentioned, it is doubtful whether music would be "expressive" to any but human beings. It seems more in accord with experience to say that if music has a given structure of tonality and rhythm, it *invites* appropriately tuned human beings to apprehend them as being expressive, i.e., as sounding sorrowful, joyful, noble, dignified, or sublime. Music is alleged to have charms even for the subhuman organism, but, although a lullaby may make a tiger gentle, it is doubtful that for a tiger the music expresses gentleness or anything else.

Realism in company with other philosophic systems has the problem of accounting for the fact that what people like and what is judged good music do not always agree. If we are to dispute about taste, then we have to be able to say that there is a standard for the cultivation of the listener as well as for the construction of the music.

Theoretically, realism provides for this by the hypothesis that human nature is a pattern of striving for perfection. Cultivation of the virtues, that is, the excellences of the mind, of the will, of the senses, of the body — all are signs of perfecting and perfection. In other words, although music, structurally and qualitatively, is what it is apart from the listener, it takes a "tuned" human being cultivated in music to discern the goodness in the music. Therefore, the standard of both music and listener is the connoisseur.

4. In both Plato and Aristotle and the long tradition they founded, music, although delightful to the ear and charming on that account alone, derived its significance elsewhere. First, music was made up of tones that bore certain mathematical relations to each other. For Pythagoras and Plato, mathematics was the science of measure and, therefore, of order. The orderliness of the cosmos was attested by the mathematical relations the planets bore to each other. Hence, the audible music of men was somehow the representative of the inaudible but more perfect music of the celestial spheres. Music revealed a reality deeper than itself, and the more reality it disclosed, the better it was.[3]

Second, Plato and Aristotle believed that music could be used in character training because it affected the emotions directly. Thus, Plato was concerned lest certain softening musical modes, e.g., the Lydian and Ionian, would undermine the hardiness of the guardians.[4] Aristotle felt that the emotion induced by music and poetry could knock out of the person the more harmful forms of that emotion (catharsis).[5] Good music, therefore, could mean more metaphysically significant music or music that helped build better character.

This brings us to the problem as to whether art can refuse to be evaluated in other than artistic terms. The ancients recognized the difference between music that was good musically and that which was good morally or intellectually. Plato was adamant on this point: aesthetic experience had to be judged by its *effects* on the whole life of a person or a society as well as by artistic standards alone. The musician may resent this as an infringement on his artistic autonomy, but the educator cannot have a curriculum made up of discrete, unorganized types of experiences. One can argue that the expressive qualities of music, as distinguished from the more specifically musical characteristics, are those that bring music into relation with the other areas of life and that one meaning of "greatness" in music is the way in which it does so.

Harry S. Broudy

PROBLEMS IN THE PHILOSOPHY OF MUSIC EDUCATION

We now turn to a set of topics or problems that face any philosophy of music education, if by philosophy is meant a reasoned justification for a set of beliefs rather than a mere assertion of these beliefs. A philosophy of music education is to be assessed in terms of its answers to certain questions. Although, in what follows, one cannot speak for any or all realists, it is presented as an approach that does differ from both idealistic and pragmatic approaches and which may not be uncongenial to many realists.

1. What are the components of the musical experience?
2. How is musical experience related to other types of experience?
3. Which phases of musical experience can we hope to improve by instruction?
4. What principles can justify setting up standards for musical judgment and music education?
5. What can we meaningfully demand as outcomes of music education in the public school?
6. What does realistic philosophy seem to signify in the way of a program of general music education and the training of teachers of music?

THE NATURE OF MUSICAL EXPERIENCE

It may seem silly for grown people to ask: What is music? What is the nature of the musical experience? Everyone has heard music, and, aside from such borderline cases as the clashing of pots and pans, we have no difficulty in distinguishing musical experience from any other kind.

Nevertheless, the question does arise again and again, and books continue to be written to answer it. Says John Erskine: "Some chords and sequences of chords make upon us an unfinished impression — they ask a question. Other chords and cadences satisfy with an answer. Out of question and answer come the subject matter of music, and also its language, and at last its form."[6] Music, on this view, is a kind of tonal conversation and, like verbal conversation, may be simple or profound, and one question may lead to another.

But if music is a conversation, it is difficult to get even competent students to agree on what it is *about*. Thus, Schopenhauer said that it expresses the will, the driving force of all existence. Mendl holds that the conversation, when not trivial, is about the prayers, joys, and sorrows of life, life in general.[7] Still others are reluctant to say that the conversation is *about* anything: they insist that it is a more or less interesting conversation carried on more or less expertly about nothing in particular.

In this chapter we shall not concern ourselves with all the ways in which one can talk about music. For example, the physicist has many important things to say about the vibrations that cause the musical stimulus, and the mathematician can talk about the number relations of harmonics. The musician is more likely to talk in terms of instruments, musical types, and the technicalities of composition and performance. Historians and critics of music have their own special interests and their own special vocabularies.

Our own interest is a combination of the pedagogical and the aesthetic. We are interested primarily in music as a type of aesthetic experience. In aesthetic experience we perceive objects in order to grasp their sensuous characteristics and not *primarily* to further knowledge or useful enterprises. Aesthetic activity may accompany practical, moral, religious, intellectual, and social activity and enhance our enjoyment of them, but it is not to be confused with them.

Nevertheless, one cannot ignore the relations of musical experience to the other strands in the texture of life. However sharply we distinguish logically between the aesthetic and practical attitudes toward an object, however much we might wish the learner to be satisfied with the artistic values to be derived from the art object, it remains true that, for most people most of the time, experience arrives in chunks in which many values are mingled.

Certainly the learners will approach music with all their goals and purposes and not simply with an artistic intent. The school program likewise is fashioned as a rough compromise among the diverse values of life. Thus, although music and labor are distinguishable types of experience, and although work songs have little to do with labor legislation, the place music may achieve in a specific curriculum often depends more on the relations of music to other areas of value and life than on aesthetic considerations.

AESTHETIC ELEMENTS AND AESTHETIC FORM

The raw materials of musical experience are tones. Each tone has its own qualities of pitch, loudness, and timbre. These qualities constitute the sensuous material of music, just as colors and lines are the sensuous materials of painting.

In addition to hearing and recognizing single tones, we hear combinations of them in chords and sequences. Each of these combinations also has a sensuous quality of its own.

"Each interval . . . has its own unique formal character. . . . The fifth is hollow, flat, and a bit commonplace; the major third, lively, rich, compact; the major seventh, raspy, bitter, disjointed, etc."[8]

Or as Erskine says, "The simplest form of question in music is the dominant seventh chord; the most complete answer is the major triad."[9]

We may call these small patterns of tonal material musical elements, because out of them or with them larger patterns are woven. There is a level of listening on which one simply hears these elements come and go and responds to them with feelings of pleasantness or unpleasantness. It is something like enjoying the changing colors of a kaleidoscope.

This simple mode of enjoyment probably is the basis for all musical enjoyment, for, if listeners cannot enjoy simple sound combinations, they cannot enjoy complexes of them. But to stop at this level of listening is to sadden the hearts of the musical composer, performer, and educator. For the whole purpose of composition is to weave these materials into a pattern that has continuity and dramatic structure. That is to say, the materials are put together in such a way that tensions are created, sustained, and resolved; questions are asked and answered, balances achieved, upset, and restored. Let us call this continuity and structure the form or the design of the composition. And let us call this dramatic or tensional structure of the music its *aesthetic form* to distinguish it from the more specific *musical* forms such as the concerto, rondo, or fugue. The more general aesthetic form is that arrangement of elements that attracts, holds, and directs the interest of the listener. The composer achieves this by using one or more of the standard musical forms.[10]

In music, as in all art, form makes or breaks the work with regard to both the composer and the listener. Unless the listener detects form, he is limited to the most rudimentary level of appreciation, namely, the apprehension of the aesthetic qualities of isolated tones and phrases. Hence, as we shall have many occasions to note, the ability to detect form is the heart of musical education.

THE PROBLEM OF AESTHETIC SIGNIFICANCE

Aesthetic elements combine to form patterns that also have their own individual characteristics. We can distinguish three types of such characteristics.

1. We say that a piece of music is slow, fast, jerky, smooth, graceful, light, heavy, rising and falling. These descriptions are admirably suited to indicate the motions of a physical object in space. Note that they do not carry with them any emotional meanings.

2. We also say that music is gay, martial, serene, peaceful, spirited, gloomy, soothing, irritating or disturbing. These adjectives do have a definite emotional meaning. Whenever we use them we are saying, in effect, that some music sounds the way we sometimes feel.
3. On other occasions we speak of music as being religious, noble, pastoral, warlike, victorious, exalted, tragic, comic. These qualities are not only carriers of emotion but also seem to refer to special kinds of human activity that give rise to the emotion, e.g., war, worship, love, aspiration, struggle, idealism.

We are now ready to take up the problem of expressiveness or significance in music. Does music say anything about anything other than itself? When music expresses something, which of the three kinds of qualities or events listed above does it express? And if music does express something not in itself musical, how does it do so?

A number of theoretical questions now raise their heads:

1. If all or some of the qualities that we hear are *in* the music, how do simple vibrations of the air achieve these emotion-like qualities?
2. If these qualities are not in the music but added to it by the hearer who has learned to associate certain sound qualities with certain emotional experiences, then we can ask why this particular kind of sound was chosen to express this particular kind of feeling.
3. Why is it that listeners can agree pretty well that a piece of music is poignant or melancholic, but disagree on whether it expresses nostalgia, unrequited love, or a lack of iron in the blood?
4. In teaching learners to perform music or to listen to it, what qualities do we wish them to express and to hear?
5. Are there different levels of listening, and in what sense is one level better than another? What procedures seem to be indicated for leading the learner from one level to another?

A REALISTIC INTERPRETATION OF AESTHETIC SIGNIFICANCE

To the foregoing questions and related questions, a philosophy of music education has to give its attention, and how music is related to other types of experience is at the heart of such a philosophy.

On a realistic view and on the views of certain types of idealism, music and aesthetic experience in general enable us to recognize our striving for perfection. Human emotions are regarded as registers of human success and failure in this enterprise.

Just as some human action is light-hearted because it has no serious consequences, and some is serious precisely because it has, so the music appropriate to each will vary in emotional quality. Music appropriate to express the spirit of a flirtation at a gay masquerade would hardly be appropriate to reflect the mood of a tragedy-charged love triangle. Some human activity is genuinely playful, and there can be a musical expression of this mood just as there can be musical expressions of conflict, brutality, and evil. It will follow, on this view, that if human action varies in its quality, the music appropriate to express it will also vary in quality, so that the more action perfects the human being, the more perfect will the music needed to express it become.

TONAL MOTION AND AESTHETIC EMOTION

Why is music called the language of emotion? Why does not "angry" music make us really angry? How can music express anger if it is not itself angry? Why, in the course of history, have certain musical qualities become symbols of certain human acts and feelings?[11]

A clue to one answer to these questions is provided by Pratt.[12] Human action is a pattern of motion with velocity, direction, strength, and tempo. Smooth, powerful, regular motion is a sign of successful functioning. Whenever the human organism does function well, whether it be in mind or body, there arises, as Aristotle pointed out, feelings of pleasure. The beholders of such motion, through association with their own experience, also find it pleasant, and should they concentrate on the *appearance* of the motion itself, that is, see it or hear it aesthetically, they will call it graceful or beautiful.

Violent, spasmodic, fluctuating action, on the other hand, signifies imperfect functioning, imperfect control of action, and is accompanied by feelings of unpleasantness, anger, fear, frustration, and anxiety. There is some ground for suspecting a correspondence between the *motion* of human action and the *emotion* in our apprehension of such action.

As Pratt points out, we perceive movement not only by the eye but also by the organs of touch and motion. And in music we hear motion, but it is a curious sort of motion because there is nothing that moves. There is no "thing" that changes its position in space as does a moving train or arrow: only one sound pattern disappearing and another appearing. It is a *qualitative* change; a pure movement. Because it is not tied to any particular object, it can be appropriate to all sorts of movement: from the flight of an arrow to the flight of the Israelites from Egypt. It leaves out the arrow but captures its swift glide; it leaves out the battle as it captures the victory.[13]

Pure or abstract music is not free from emotional characteristics, because such adjectives as gay, serene, and agitated can be applied to the least programmatic music, e.g., the fugues of Bach or a Bartók concerto. To say that this type of music does not express anything beyond itself simply means that it does not intend to arouse in the listener the recognition of any specific human enterprise of which these emotional adjectives would be descriptive. Thus, the gayness of the music is not intended to make the listener think of a wedding or a case of champagne; it is abstract to the extent that it is appropriate to a wide variety of gay occasions and not because it does not unambiguously point to any particular occasion.

If musical movement is analogous to the movement of human action, it can express the emotion accompanying action. We do not have to learn to associate specific emotions with certain tonal movements. On the contrary, the music already *is* a tonal movement that is perceived as expressive of the movements of certain human actions. Thus, we do not have to feel angry to hear the music as angry, but we do have to know what angry action is to recognize a certain tonal motion as an expression of it.

That is why emotion felt in listening to music has been called aesthetic emotion, intellectual emotion, and even the "emotion recalled in tranquility." It is not the real thing somehow. For one thing, when we are really angry it is because we are being frustrated or attacked in some way. This arouses widespread bodily activity and a readiness to get rid of the danger. In listening to "angry" music, however, we are not threatened, so there is nothing for us to do. We can maintain a certain objectivity or "psychic distance," precisely because we are not involved in the situation. Yet we do feel something, namely, the anger minus the actions that normally accompany it — a kind of disembodied anger.

It is argued that the sincerity of a performance is affected by the performer's ability to feel and project emotions and therefore the performer must develop an acute sensitivity to moods and a capacity to reproduce them at will, but even here the performance must be kept under technical control so that it is really expressive rather than merely explosive.

BEAUTY

Beauty is what we experience in music when the *motion* it embodies is analogous to the *motions* characteristic of successful action. Art works of varying degrees of complexity can be beautiful because pleasure can accompany good functioning at various levels of complexity. Music to be expressive need not be beautiful, for it may express imperfections and failures as well as their opposites. However, in great works of art the conflict between the perfect and the imperfect is dramatically carried to a triumphant resolution, so that we perceive beauty in the work as a whole, even though there may be discord and ugliness in some of the parts taken separately.

CONDITIONS FOR SIGNIFICANCE

To grasp the significance of music as well as to enjoy its discrete elements and their design, one needs to know a good deal about human action. He who has not experienced directly or vicariously striving against great odds, great longings, great victories and defeats, religious exaltations and humility cannot be expected to recognize their analogous motions in music.

Will Beethoven's *Eroica* express heroic striving for a given listener? That depends, first, on whether the listener knows the nature of heroic action, and, second, on whether the composer has captured the characteristic motion of heroic action in the tonal motion of *Eroica*. If both conditions are fulfilled, and if no individual subjective psychological factors intervene, then a careful, cultivated listening may result in the awareness of this specific significance. We say *may*, not *must*, because heroic action is not unrelated to other modes of strenuous action to which this music might also be appropriate.

Educationally, the important point of this analysis is that different levels of appreciation may require different approaches. Thus, it may be that we can teach sensitivity to form directly, but sensitivity to significance may involve a growing and deepening experience that has nothing to do with music at all. This, in turn, may affect what we can reasonably expect in the way of appreciation at various levels of the child's development.

MUSIC AND LIFE

Musical experience, while not identical with any other kind, is alien to none and can be appropriate to all. Accordingly, many life activities seem to call for the underscoring that music provides. Religious rites utilize musical accompaniment better to convey their import. Indeed, so closely are they associated that without music the appropriate religious mood may be difficult to establish. Conversely, the music customarily associated with the rites achieves great power to evoke the appropriate religious response.

The waging of war invokes the aid of music, and without music romance seems as incomplete as without moonlight. We have working songs and dancing songs, drinking songs and playing songs. In opera there are murder songs and conspiracy songs. There is no facet of life that cannot enlist music to reinforce its emotional import and impact.

MUSIC IN GENERAL EDUCATION

Because of this relation between musical values and other modes of value realization, no further argument should be needed to justify music education as a part of general education, that is, the education we are prepared to require of all normal learners in the twelve years of public schooling. This claim to full membership, however, needs more specific examination.

For one thing, the social utility of an activity does not of itself determine whether or not it shall have a part in general formal education. Some socially useful activities are not learned formally, for example, the collection of garbage, washing dishes, milking cows, talking, many trades and crafts. Presumably a considerable volume of music is also learned without benefit of formal tuition.

Formal general education includes only what (a) cannot be learned or learned well through informal means and (b) what is judged to be essential for all members of the community to know. When one tries to fill this prescription with this or that subject or course, one is likely to run into difficulty with one or the other of the requirements. Thus, learning to sing popular music would be disqualified on the first count, and learning to read an orchestral score would have trouble with the second.

It is safer, therefore, to think of general education as the cultivation of *capacities* for realizing value. All human beings have the same sort of capacities; however, they may vary in the degree to which they possess them. The realist would argue that to cultivate these capacities is the human enterprise par excellence, and the notion of perfecting human nature means precisely this kind of cultivation. When this cultivation is undertaken deliberately, and when the capacity for knowledge is used to develop the capacities for all other values, then we have formal general education.

If we believe that childish songs and primitive chants are as good as Bach's chorales and Brahms' symphonies, there is no point in including music in *general* education; it would be a dubious luxury for a peculiar few. If we believe otherwise, it is because we are convinced that the individual in responding to the Bach chorale is exercising his human capacities at a higher level than is the child or savage, and to that extent he is "better" than they are, that is, further along the road of self-perfection.

The notion of education as the development of capacity makes it possible to draw several important conclusions: First, the natural disinclination of pupils to practice in order to perfect skills can be regarded as a temporary obstacle to be overcome, rather than as a justification for avoiding the kind of music that requires practice. In the second place, we can speak of *levels* of musical competence with one level being genuinely higher than another.

Harry S. Broudy

SCOPE OF GENERAL MUSIC EDUCATION

To say that music ought to be part of general education is to say that all of us ought to be musically literate, that is, able to express ourselves in musical terms and to understand these terms when used by someone else. These might be called the skills of expression and impression. These skills would include the skills of listening, reading, composing, etc., as well as of musical performance.

Logically, there seems to be no reason for not insisting that everyone be able to express himself in music as well as in words. However, such a claim would not be taken seriously perhaps because we are so word-bound in our thinking and in our action. Nonetheless, the ease with which children use the musical medium makes it at least conceivable that if pupils could develop technique adequate to their expressional needs, they might not abandon music as an expressive resource just when they need it most.

Why the artistic spontaneity of children often subsides by adolescence is in itself a tantalizing problem. At least one hypothesis would suggest that by adolescence the songs we can compose and the pictures we can paint no longer satisfy either our needs for self-expression or adult standards of artistic merit. At this crucial point either new techniques have to be acquired or the medium of expression is abandoned.

If this hypothesis has any validity, then the notion that technical training destroys artistic spontaneity, if true at all, is true only in special circumstances.[14]

What about the skills of performance? Here we have a fairly wide agreement that everyone ought to have some competence; the difficulty being to specify how much and on what instrument (including voice). The arguments for such competence include the following: First, performance in itself can become a creative artistic act. Then, there is the satisfaction that comes from the successful exercise of a skill. Finally, skill in performance can augment musical literacy, that is, skills of expression may help to perfect skills of impression.

That the skills of listening should be among the outcomes of formal music education is not a matter for debate. The disagreement will come in what good listening is to mean and the theoretical grounds for adhering to one meaning rather than to another.

One camp of music educators regards listening as the total activity from which the hearer derives enjoyment. The important matter is that enjoyment accrue and that the desire to listen be established. The more radical version of this view is more interested in the enjoyment than in what music is being enjoyed, and it is based on the notion that good music is whatever music one happens to enjoy. In the same camp one will also find a less radical view;

84

one that believes that there is a difference between good music and music not so good, but it also believes that somehow sufficient exposure to "good" music will eventually produce in the learner a preference for it.

We may call this the exposure theory of teaching music appreciation. As to method, it is suspicious of emphasis on musical techniques, historical accounts of musical works, interpretations by the teacher, and analysis of musical compositions in general. All such dissection, it is believed, threatens to destroy the spontaneous and unified response of the listener. It is, in brief, suspicious of any attempt to intellectualize the act of appreciation.

Opposed to this camp is another that believes the road to appreciation lies in the study of music. Reading, ability to discriminate in matters of melody, rhythms, tempo, and tonality, and ability to apprehend fairly large patterns of tonal material are regarded as essential to adequate appreciation.

LEVELS OF APPRECIATION

If one wishes to listen on what Copland calls the sensuous plane, little musical training is required to do so.[15] Natively, we all respond to patterns of sound with some kind of feeling. The untutored listener may respond to serious music with enjoyment. This is sometimes advanced as evidence for the belief that "great" music will inevitably appeal to all men, if only they are permitted to hear it. But it is also evidence for an even more probable hypothesis, namely, that the fabric of serious music is of varying degrees of complexity, subtlety, and seriousness. A catchy melody, a stirring rhythm, and impressive tonal effects are to be found here and there in the most complex and the most serious musical compositions, and these will not be lost even on the musical tyro.

Art becomes popular most surely when it is made up of elements that can be grasped without formal instruction. There are popular elements in all complex works of art; sex, conflict, violence have a universal appeal. A sex situation, a murder, or a combination of both is as appealing when encountered in a play by Shakespeare as in a popular movie; a nude in a Rubens can be viewed just as pornographically as a picture in an illustrated weekly; the theme of *Tristan and Isolde* is as erotic as that of a thousand popular lyrics.

This may account for the optimism of the exposure theory in art and music education. The natural aesthetic responsiveness of young children and the responses of untrained adults to some examples of serious art produce an illusion of appreciation, if one is not too fussy about what is being appreciated.

Experiments by Kate Hevner Mueller indicate that ". . . progress in apprehending music . . . is significantly related to formal training, interest, attitude, and to verbal intelligence . . ." and probably to auditory sensitivity as well. She concluded that ". . . learning to listen is (a) learning to perceive the details of rhythm, harmony, and form, (b) giving names to these perceptions, (c) building these percepts into more complex and well-defined wholes (concepts), and (d) using these concepts as the framework for comprehending new musical experience."[16]

What did this experimenter mean by listening and learning to listen? The subjects of the experiment, after hearing a composition played three times, were asked to indicate the degree of the agreement or disagreement with certain true and false statements about the music, e.g., statements such as ". . . main theme has two melodic fragments," ". . . keynote well established . . . ," ". . . piece employs 3/4 time," and ". . . no bridge material." The experimenter noted that subjects who scored unimpressively in these musical matters of fact were not reluctant to make confident judgments about the musical *quality* of what they had heard.

Presumably, this experimenter felt that certain musical facts were essential to proper listening, that is to say, that ability to discern certain qualities of the music was essential to proper listening. In other words, proper listening would seem to entail an ability to discern musical structure as well as to undergo glandular disturbance, and listening on the musical level seems to demand not only enjoyment but also discriminative enjoyment.

It would seem that music education can and should make the listener more discriminating and sophisticated with respect to musical materials and musical forms in both the broad and the narrow sense of this word. It may also be urged that mastery of musical skill in listening frees the hearer or performer to apprehend the expressive aspects of music. Finally, such musical training affords the learner a basis for objective and informed judgments about certain aspects of musical quality.

However, when we come to the expressive level of performance and listening, the relation between musical training and appreciation is less clear. Thirty musicians, when asked to describe the character of a piece of music as gay or solemn, were in impressive agreement; when asked to indicate what the music was about, they were in great disagreement.[17] This emphasizes what has already been noted, namely that while certain types of music can be recognized as appropriate to types of human action, the music of itself cannot point unambiguously to specific human actions or even to kinds of human action. At best, music gives us directly an emotional quality that is expressive of the direction of human action, especially as regards that action's relevance to human success and failure.

If what music expresses by its structure of tonal movement is the drama of human action and the emotions that accompany it, then it is reasonable to believe that the listener needs adequate experience to be *impressed* by the musical expression. Thus, for the young, regardless of chronological age, conflict, victory, and defeat are better expressed by a Western melodrama than by Ibsen, and a jukebox serves better than the concert hall.

In front of each work of art, especially if it is complex, stands a symbolic gate. No one enters Shakespeare without going through the symbolic gate of language; no one goes into the music of the "masters" without negotiating the obstacles of complexity in materials and subtlety in form. If this is so, then the duties of music education become clear. First of all, it has to lead each individual to the gate, open it as wide as musical training can, invite all to pass through it and, finally, hope that life and general education will make a whole-hearted entry probable, if not inevitable.

Once the symbolic gates are opened, the hearing of expressive music may itself contribute to listening readiness. The adolescent who has undergone puppy love and who is *musically* ready to listen to *Tristan* may by that experience become emotionally ready to hear the message of *Tristan*. This reciprocal relation between musical readiness and experiential readiness is made no simpler by the possibility that one art form may increase our readiness for the reception of another art form.

THE PROBLEM OF NORMS AND STANDARDS

Education invariably involves some imposition upon the learner of action and attitudes that he or she might not have achieved or even undertaken. To say that the teacher is a guide softens the word but does not alter the fact; it merely means that the pupil is steered by the carrot instead of the stick to which it is tied.

Where right is clearly differentiated from wrong, imposition on learners can be justified because we have reason to believe that the consequences will be judged *by* them as we now judge them *for* them. Thus, we can be sure that acting as if 6 times 7 were 43 will lead our pupils into trouble that they will not relish. But where there is no generally acceptable criterion for good, bad, better, and worse, how can imposition be anything but arbitrary?

Some of the facts do not encourage a belief in objective standards for the arts. Not only do cultures differ in what they regard as good, but even within a culture individuals differ in taste even more than do the various cultures. Is there any way of asserting that one concerto is better than another? One popular song better than another? A concerto better than a popular song? If not, then on what ground is it better for the learner to spend time on one concerto rather than another? On a concerto rather than on a popular song? On music rather than on anything else?

If the subjective enjoyment of an experience is its own and only justification, there can be no argument about good or bad, better or worse, ought or ought not. Without principle, there can be no argument, and enjoyment is a fact not a principle. On such a philosophy of *de gustibus non disputandum* music education can mean either that we help the learner satisfy whatever tastes he or she may have at a given moment or maneuver them into adopting the teacher's tastes. Since the latter has no justification (when there are no objective standards), only the former meaning remains. But can we seriously argue that we need schools and music curricula to help pupils hear what they already happen to like?

What can be said for the objectivity of standards? Let us examine these variations of taste on which relativism so heavily leans. Where do we find them? How great are they? Are they equally great in all aspects of musical judgment?

We have already referred to Gilman's experiment in which thirty musicians disagreed as to what a given piece of music was about but displayed remarkable agreement when asked to identify the mood or character of the music. Had these musicians been asked to judge the technical quality of the performance, would there have been wide variation or substantial agreement? Had they been asked to judge the quality of the harmony, counterpoint, and orchestration, would there have been agreement or disagreement, and to what extent?

The disagreement among experts is probably overemphasized. Technical standards of performance, standards of composition, ability to achieve certain effects are remarkably objective in every value area as far as the experts are concerned. It is on the expressive level that their disagreement is so evident, and we have seen why this is probably unavoidable. Indeed, if it were not so, much of the imaginative activity involved in appreciation would be superfluous. Even on this level experts are willing to argue the matter, and usually they disagree because their premises differ to begin with rather than because of what they find in the art object. In other words, the subjective individual value patterns of listeners play a greater role in judging on the expressive standard than they do on the technical or formal standards. It is important to keep the distinction among these standards in mind, because it gives us perspective in deciding what we can expect of all learners and in what areas variation will be the rule.

The possibility of highly objective technical and formal standards gives the music educator an intelligible and practicable criterion for measuring progress in the learner. To perform well and to listen well mean to approximate the performance and listening of the expert, even though general music education does not aim to produce experts.

SERIOUS AND POPULAR MUSIC

This much can be said in favor of the expert's standard of judgment: It is based on knowledge, experience, and study. Certain art objects exert a fascination on generation after generation of experts. Either this fascination is due to a cultural conditioning or to the fact that the object somehow expresses a profound and permanent insight into the import of human life. If knowledge and study cannot transcend conditioning, then probably nothing can, and music education can be only one more species of conditioning.

Why is a delightful quatrain not so good as a good epic? Why is a good concerto better than a good ballad? As far as sheer aesthetic impact is concerned, there is no way of comparing them, and each may be perfect in its own *genre*. Functionally, moreover, we may need a quatrain at one time and an epic at another. There are at least two ways in which it would be meaningful to compare them. First, by the technical demands they make on the composer, performer, and recipient. In other words, one work can be better than another artistically, and one *genre* can be at a higher level artistically than another. We may have the case, therefore, that tone poems *as a class* are artistically better than ballads *as a class* but that a particular ballad may be better artistically than a particular tone poem.

Within any *genre* the connoisseur is the only reliable source of standards. For the expert, the better is that which is more subtle, more complicated, less obvious, whether the music is serious or popular. It is significant that even among the devotees of popular art there develop "long-hair" *cognoscenti,* experts, sophisticates, and they have about as much use for the "short-hairs" in their field as "long-hairs" in general have for "short-hairs" in general.

The ultimate justification of the expert is, of course, that in the long run the technically and formally good works of art will also achieve greater expressiveness and have greater import for human life than the inferior sort. There are enough exceptions to this generalization to require some faith for its adoption as a guiding principle, but is there any alternative?

In the second place, we can compare works of art philosophically. Thus, the epic *as a class* is better than the quatrain *as a class* because it presents to us aesthetically a bigger slice of life, of reality, of truth, and of goodness. If it is objected that we should not go outside of music for our standards, then it must be retorted that the educator has no choice because, without a yardstick that measures all the values, he cannot construct a rational curriculum at all; he can merely assemble an aggregate of activities that will offend as few of his constituents as possible.

SHAPING PREFERENCES

Granted that we can be fairly confident and insistent on certain formal and technical standards of musical performance and listening, can we be equally confident or insistent about the evaluation the pupil places on a piece of music? Can we hope to shape the taste of the learner without arbitrary imposition?

We are aware, of course, of the shrewd approach of educators who appeal to the Philistines with tidbits of melody and rhythm taken from "long-hair" music. Once the Philistine admits that he "likes" it, its source is triumphantly revealed, and presumably the Philistine is converted into a lover of serious music. This is not only pedagogically unwise, but clearly immoral. For it seems to promise that all serious art is really as easy and sense-tickling as the sample. This is deception and betokens either ignorance on the part of the teacher or a tendency toward virtuous prostitution — probably the worst kind.

That musical preference or taste is the product of conditioning is beyond debate. The issue is to what degree taste is so formed and whether it can be justified. There is a lollipop-method of getting children to like Bach and Beethoven, namely by giving them something sweet, figuratively or literally, whenever Bach or Beethoven is played to them. Conceivably, children could be so conditioned that the very sound of these compositions would elicit the same delightful sensations as did the sweets.

There is no way of preventing all conditioning of this kind because musical performance is usually accompanied by explicit or implied approval or disapproval. The disc jockey announces a record as being a hit, wonderful and sensational and another piece of music as a classic, noble, and inspiring. Can the school avoid the kind of imposition which binds the victim glandularly to like this and to dislike that?

It can, only if it accepts the authority of the expert as a standard. If the expert is picked on the basis of competence, and competence is not the result of agreeing with what we happen to like in music, then conditioning may be justified until the learner is ready to form taste on the basis of experience and knowledge. Educators in whom this rouses the fear that the classics in music will be foisted upon children as conventionally fine and great should be reminded that in any age, and certainly in ours, experts of equal technical competence and training are partisans of the old *and* the new. Experts approve Bartók and Schoenberg as well as Bach and Beethoven. Indeed, it is the expert, rather than the multitude, who nearly always heralds the new. Why each child should have to discover the standards of music any more than discover anew the standards of sound history, sound sociology, sound morality, and sound health is difficult to understand.

But realism would hardly stop at this point. Surely it would follow from its respect for knowledge and for the expert that the goal for every rational person is a taste shaped by knowledge and discriminative experience. To be sure, one starts with the taste of others, but as knowledge and skill grow, freedom to experiment, to be creative, to judge, and to choose and to reject also grow. The goal of the realist is an informed taste rather than eccentric taste, and the former is as genuine and individual as is the latter.

GENERAL-EDUCATION PROGRAM IN MUSIC

From what has been said, the following points can be made with respect to (a) a program of music education for general education [and] (b) the qualities needed by a teacher in such a program.

1. As regards the program, the key concept we have employed is that of connoisseurship. Growth in taste and appreciation has been held to be correlative with growth in musical skill, knowledge, and the ability to comprehend and discriminate the musical qualities. If this is so, then the program can be formal, systematic, and deliberately instituted and conducted, for both knowledge and skill can be taught systematically. It also makes sense to speak of a method of teaching music if there are skill and knowledge to be taught, and if there are gradations of this knowledge and skill in the learner.

The concept of connoisseurship encourages the use of materials that the experts of successive ages have regarded as good and important. It does not exclude the contemporary and experimental, but it does evaluate them in terms of musical *knowledge* and *cultivated* taste.

Further, this view sees value in having the learner aware of the continuity of the musical tradition. Thus, the study of a twelfth-century chant aids listeners when they hear it used or simulated in a contemporary work; and its presence in the contemporary work expands the understanding of it in its original form.

2. As regards the qualification of the music teacher, the concept of the connoisseur likewise provides a few guiding principles.

If there can be method in the teaching of music, it makes sense to ask that teachers master it. This means that teachers will not be left to blunder through some impromptu pattern of music instruction as best they can. Nor can they rely upon enthusiasm, love of children, or even on love of music itself to make up for deficiencies in method.

Teachers cannot use a tradition of connoisseurship in music of which they are ignorant. There is a selected body of knowledge about music —

91

historical, theoretical, and technical — that ought to be part of the educated person's experience. In the teacher, this ought to be underlined and augmented with respect to the requirements of music-teaching at various levels of instruction.

Finally, if the justification for shaping preferences is the faith of the teacher that the learnings they are "forcing" upon the pupil will enhance the pupil's enjoyment of music and life, then this phenomenon of effort and reward must have *come to pass in their own experience*. Otherwise, standards are secondhand and conventional, and their faith unfounded. To demand that elementary-school teachers achieve this order of musical experience and cultivation is asking a great deal, but is the conclusion escapable — even if it should be objected that the other arts will make similar demands upon them?

On the other hand, the music-teaching specialist will have to be *generally* educated as well as musically cultivated. The problem of maintaining the delicate balance between technique and knowledge performance and appreciation, skill and enjoyment will never be solved by the ignorant layperson or the overspecialized expert.

NOTES

1. For a good general introduction, see John Wild, *An Introduction to Realistic Philosophy* (New York: Harper & Bros., 1948), and for a realistic approach to a philosophy of education, see Harry S. Broudy, *Building a Philosophy of Education* (New York: Prentice-Hall, Inc., 1954). For an advanced treatment of realism, see John Wild, editor, *The Return to Reason* (Chicago: Henry Regnery & Co., 1953).

2. Philosophically, this point gets its emphasis from the insistence of the experimentalists that the situation as given to us is transformed in the process of our inquiry into it, e.g., John Dewey, *The Quest for Certainty* (New York: Minton, Balch & Co., 1929, pp. 85 ff.). In Aristotelian realism it is held that during the act of knowing, the mind and the object become formally, although not numerically or existentially, identical. For this difficult doctrine, see John Wild, *An Introduction to Realistic Philosophy*, chaps. xiii, xviii, and xix.

3. Julius Portnoy, *The Philosopher and Music*, New York: Humanities Press, 1954, pp. 14–30.

4. "Rhythms and music in general are imitations of good and evil characters in men." Plato, *Laws*, Bk. VII, 798.

5. *Politics*, Chap. VII, 1342a.

6. John Erskine, *What Is Music?* New York: J. B. Lippincott Co., 1944, p. 13.

7. R.W.S. Mendl, *The Soul of Music*, London: Rockliff Publishing Co., 1950, p. 2.

8. Carroll C. Pratt, *The Meaning of Music*, New York: McGraw-Hill Book Co., 1931, p. 7.

9. Op. cit., p. 35.

10. Cf. John Dewey, *Art as Experience,* New York: Minton, Balch & Co., 1934, pp. 138 ff. It is in its form that the work of art captures the dynamic structure of the adjustive act so characteristic of the life process.

11. On this point cf. Mendl, op. cit., pp. 46 ff.

12. Op. cit., pp. 184 ff. Also consult Leonard B. Meyer, *Emotion and Meaning in Music.* Chicago: University of Chicago Press, 1957.

13. Pratt, op. cit., pp. 187–88. Just how music delivers its message is discussed by Susanne K. Langer in *Philosophy in a New Key* (Cambridge: Harvard University Press, 1942), chap. viii. See also by the same author *Feeling and Form* (New York: Charles Scribner's Sons, 1953). Aristotle remarked, "Why do rhythms and tunes, which after all are only voice, resemble moral characters, whereas savours do not, nor yet colors and odours? Is it because they are movements, as actions also are?"

14. On this topic and its ramifications for art education, the reader may wish to consult Harry S. Broudy, *Building a Philosophy of Education,* chap. xiii. (New York: Prentice-Hall, Inc., 1954).

15. Aaron Copland, *What To Listen for in Music,* New York: McGraw-Hill Book Co., Inc., 1939, p. 9.

16. Kate Hevner Mueller, "Studies in Musical Appreciation," *Journal of Research in Music Education,* IV (1956), 1, 3–25.

17. B. I. Gilman, "Report on an Experimental Test of Musical Expressiveness," *American Journal of Psychology,* IV (1892), 558–76.

4

A Plea for Pluralism: Variations on a Theme by George McKay

Wayne Bowman

Monoliths are just dandy — in stone. They do not belong in the world of ideas.

— Harry Partch
Source (January 1967), Vol. 1, No. 1:103

My contribution to this reexamination of basic music educational concepts will revisit some concerns raised by G. F. McKay in "The Range of Musical Experience," his chapter in the original *Basic Concepts* volume. I will not pretend that all the positions I take here were his; nor is it likely he would concur with everything I have to say. But it strikes me that at least part of McKay's basic argument, that musical education should reflect and respect the dramatic scope of musical endeavor, is as cogent and relevant today as it was in 1958.

One of McKay's major points was that a genuinely musical education is not the achievement of a passive, uncritical mind. Becoming musically educated involves learning to experience and to think about music in a variety of ways. This is simply because music (and the assumptions that influence its creation, performance, and appreciation) is less an "it" than a "they." Rather than a single thing, music is an open, loosely textured network of practices guided by diverse, complex, ambiguous, and often contradictory values and priorities. Music is as multifarious as the human mind, which has created and enjoyed it for millennia. Music is the name of vast webs of interlocking and overlapping similarities (or, after Ludwig Wittgenstein, "family resemblances"), with no common essential features beyond the sonorous materials from which they are wrought and the fact of their deep embeddedness in human culture.

McKay did not say all this, but it is implicit in many things he did say. He urged that music education become less contented with pat, easy answers and judgments. He urged that music education wrestle with complex musical and philosophical issues like the nature and value of the particular music at hand. He sought the kind of musical education that would liberate society from the kind of "restrictive ignorance" that attends exclusive immersion in what he called musical "localisms" (p. 126). The musically educated individual differs from the musically naive in being conversant in a variety of styles and idioms and in the capacity to engage perceptual habits and expectations appropriate to each. The musically educated individual does not, for instance, approach plainsong anticipating harmonic complexity or a "good beat" or judge it inferior if features like these are absent. Nor does the musically educated individual attempt to engage the same set of "ears" when listening to Duke Ellington as when listening to Mozart. At the same time, within each of these disparate domains or idioms, the musically educated individual can distinguish the musically trite or crass from the genuine article.

If this seems altogether obvious, perhaps it is an indication of the extent to which our profession has successfully confronted and resolved certain aspects of the issues McKay sought to raise. It does seem clear, for instance, that music education is less musically parochial than it was in 1958. When it comes to music education philosophy, however, I am less sanguine. We like our philosophy like we once liked our music: neat and unitary. We have rightly proclaimed philosophy a guiding beacon for music education. But it fulfills that promise only to the extent that it clarifies musical understanding and opens ears. Philosophy is a tool with tremendous illuminative power, but it can also be superfluous and irrelevant to existing problems and practice. More dangerously yet, it can obfuscate and distort what it purports to describe.

I shall argue here that the seemingly innocuous assumption that all worthwhile music is and does essentially one thing is precisely such a distorting notion, one which it is time music education disavowed. There is no one way all music is, no one way it must be experienced. Music has no single common essence or nature or value ("aesthetic" for instance, or "expressive"). There are, rather, myriad ways music may be and a startling number of things it may do. If this is so, McKay's contention that appreciation of the range and diversity of musical experience is basic to any musically educational endeavor deserves careful reconsideration.

"THE MANY"

McKay began his discussion with the ancient but provocative philosophical problem of the one and the many: of universals and particulars, of permanence and change, of unity and diversity. And it seems to me that he was arguing for pluralism as opposed to monism. He was urging a perspective that would emphasize music's dynamism rather than some supposedly static, unchanging "essential nature." He sought a philosophical and pedagogical perspective that would take as its point of departure music's marvelous multiplicity, instead of an ideal abstraction designed to confer unity upon the disparate. He conceived musical education as an endeavor devoted more extensively to the illumination of music's many sides and faces than to the revelation of some unitary, monolithic musical "essence." In short, McKay was more interested in "the many" than "the one"; what he thought basic to music education was an appreciation and understanding of the full range of musical experience.

In pre-Platonic times, Heraclitus observed that one cannot set foot in the same river twice. Rather like Heraclitus, McKay is uncomfortable construing music as a single thing. It is a vast constellation of what he calls "regional dynamisms" (p. 125), of what we might rather call musical styles, genres, and practices. And even within these "regional dynamisms," the individual things we designate "pieces" are more highly valued for their distinctive features than their affinities to one another or their representativeness of a particular genre.

Both musical styles and the pieces "within" them are embedded in assumptions as to music's nature, purpose, and value. But these assumptions are as variable, diverse, and contradictory as the human mind. This being the case, McKay believes that a musical education has two fundamental obligations, each intimately wed to the other: first, to introduce the young to the "philosophical ferment" (p. 124) that permeates all musical endeavor, exploring "the whole gamut of artistic-philosophical conflict" (p. 136); and second, to introduce them to the tremendous diversity of musics generated by this "ferment." Music education for McKay is a process of liberating, of opening both minds and ears, of expanding awareness: an induction into the profound diversity of the human condition. His orientation is diametrically opposed to the presumption that all music is cut from the same cloth. Such a notion emphasizes only "the outer surface of the art" (p. 125). It undermines the "flourishing of each regional sensibility" (p. 126) and obstructs awareness of the "artistic antitheses" (p. 124) that undergird them. These tensions are the sources of music's dynamism, the necessary conditions for its proper perception and understanding.

Because McKay was clearly struck by the tremendously broad range of potential musical experience in the 1950s, one cannot help but wonder how overwhelming he might find the last decade of the twentieth century. The multicultural "global village" is no longer a fanciful utopian vision, but a fact of life. Technology has dramatically transformed the creation, the reproduction, the accessibility, and even the sound of music. Ethnomusicologists have exposed and explored fascinating music from the most remote corners of the earth, and we can listen to it virtually wherever we please, on equipment that emulates with greater fidelity than ever before the quality of the real thing. The status of jazz has been elevated from musical pariah to musical art form in scarcely more than a decade. Digital sound synthesis is no longer the curious preoccupation of eccentric composers with esoteric tastes, but an accessible and pervasive fact of the musical mainstream. The conventional instruments and idioms to which instruction in our schools and universities is geared may not be antiquated, but neither can they claim to constitute the center of the musical universe as they once did. It sometimes seems that the only thing less debatable than the ubiquity of change is its rate of acceleration.

In the 1960s and 1970s the music education profession in North America struggled to broaden its musical purview to reflect the conspicuously changing musical facts. McKay's chapter and many other publications reflect the profession's growing sense that its conceptions of music were rather parochial and ethnocentric. But curiously, the profession's philosophical inquiry drew its inspiration more from the past than from the musical reality of the times. While John Cage and dozens of others struggled to free music from the "tyranny" of nineteenth-century assumptions as to what it "ought to do," and while music educators were beginning to recognize the validity of musics outside the mainstream European aristocratic tradition, music education was busy crafting an advocacy argument for school music based on the assumption that the ultimate value of all music lies in its universally "expressive" nature and its capacity to enhance "aesthetic" sensitivity.

In its thirst for basic concepts, music education was strongly attracted to the belief that beneath the overwhelming diversity of musical practice was one set of universal principles that somehow bind it all together, one set of musical criteria that enable the segregation of the musically significant from the trivial, one way that all music must be, one universally valid justification for the inclusion of music in public school curricula. Would that it were so. Life would be so much easier for the music educator if a particular doctrine would address all musical problems for all times, if we could simply impart to our students the answer (the way to listen, the checklist for distinguishing musical substance from musical fluff). Serene though it might make our existence, there is no such doctrine. Instead, we must listen, we must think,

97

we must explore, we must weigh and compare, we must criticize, we must choose.

One of the "basic" challenges confronting twenty-first–century North American music education is the realization that there is no way the world (or its music) "essentially" is, but a rich, almost staggering diversity of ways it may be; there is no immutable, universally valid prescription for musical value, but there is a fascinating array of ways music may be found and experienced — each valid in terms of its own particular stylistic priorities, assumptions, and imperatives. Plato was right: music does exert profoundly powerful influence upon human and social values. G.W.F. Hegel was right: music is a phenomenon borne of mind and a profound shaper of human ideality. Edward Hanslick and Edmund Gurney were right: music does consist simply of tonally moving forms. Arthur Schopenhauer was right: music does often parallel the patterns of tension and release in our felt life. John Cage was right: there is music to be found in random, goalless sonorous "events." Phenomenology is right: music is a bodily acquisition. Nor, I hasten to add, are musical Formalism and Referentialism silly products of naive minds, but important, if partial, truths.

But how can all these blatantly contradictory and incompatible philosophical perspectives be valid? Is this not tantamount to conceding that none of these are valid? Isn't this unmitigated relativism? I think not, although it is definitely an assertion that the problems of music's nature and value are a good deal more complex than we have traditionally assumed. It is a confession of doubt as to the universal validity of any single account: none, in other words, is applicable to and descriptive of all musics for all times. To put it still more directly, there is no such thing as music, only musics; no single nature, no single value, but a rich and provocative variety of musical natures and musical values, whose revelation is one of the most "basic" tasks of genuinely musical education.

If the nature and value of music are plural, relative to, and often specific to particular styles, and if (as I think we have correctly maintained) the nature of music education should be determined by the nature of music, the implications for music education are a bit unsettling. We have access to a broader range of musics than ever before in history and should be committed to broadening the range of musical understanding — to developing respect and appreciation for multiple musical "realities," different yet equally valid musical values. Both our democratic ideals and the character of our subject matter seem to dictate pluralism. Yet at the same time we must ensure that our students experience music with sufficient depth and engagement to nurture and sustain personal and cultural values.

THE SECURITY OF PHILOSOPHICAL MONISM

In the 1950s and 1960s, music education discovered a particularly promising weapon for its advocacy arsenal: the rather intractable branch of philosophical inquiry known as aesthetics (notable, among other things, for its determined efforts to articulate the ineffable). The special attraction of the aesthetic rationale, as it came to be called, was its seeming invulnerability to criticism, especially compared to the "utilitarian" or "extrinsic" justifications for musical instruction that had been employed to placate and persuade skeptics since earliest recorded history. As an advocacy argument based upon a set of values supposedly unique to music, one that was music's alone, the aesthetic argument was understandably quite alluring. In its wake, outmoded claims to citizenship, cooperation, group participation, and the like were discarded, and the aesthetic rationale rather quickly achieved the status of doctrine. Its values were intrinsic, pertaining to nothing outside the music itself — except, of course, for the "aesthetic sensitivity" it was held to enhance. On the precise nature and value of this aesthetic sensitivity or the distinctive manner in which music nurtured it we were none too clear, but never mind. The conviction that music could teach people things that nothing else could was an important step forward for a music education anxious to authenticate its claim to professional status.

Music education drew much of its inspiration in this effort from the Idealistic philosophical tradition of the nineteenth century, in which music's primary value derives from its capacity to render conceivable the otherwise inconceivable: the patterns of human sentience, the forms of feeling. Music, Susanne Langer convinced us, was a "symbol" of the form of human subjectivity, a vehicle for conception of the innermost essence of humanity that, were it not for musical experience, would utterly elude us.

Several ironies attended this new self-concept, with its extensive (if little-acknowledged) debt to Hegel, Schiller, and Schopenhauer. First, the theory was most clearly applicable to music of the nineteenth-century European aristocratic tradition that spawned it. It could scarcely help distorting (indeed, often denigrating) music that did not share its stylistic assumptions and priorities. Second, the argument to "intrinsic" value was, despite its claims to the contrary, functional or transitive. It was grounded in music's capacity to reveal (or "portray," or "symbolize") something not music: the patterns of sentience, the forms of feeling. Feeling was music's raison d'être, the condition to which all music aspired, the source of musical value. And this feeling was not some purely musical feeling, as Formalists like Hanslick and Gurney had insisted, but everything felt. The claim to "intrinsicality" was erected on an exceptionally precarious foundation.

In a further irony, as we turned for justification of our existence to a philosophical realm concerned primarily to illuminate commonalities among "the arts," we found ourselves thinking less and less about specifically musical education and more and more about "arts education."

Obviously this abbreviated account of the aesthetic rationale is to some extent a caricature: it does great injustice to what we all recognize to be many subtle and valuable insights. It exaggerates (though I do not think it distorts grossly) in order to make vivid several points that cannot be pursued at length here. What strikes me is that the "aesthetic" philosophical stance was embraced not so much for its cogency or internal consistency, or even so much for its capacity to guide and improve educational practice, as for its inspirational value and its promise to fulfill an apparently insatiable need for the ultimate ironclad advocacy position. Never mind that musical education thrived in the early history of North America because it met people's practical, social, and everyday needs. Never mind that music won its way into the school curriculum on the persuasive power of the very "extrinsic" merits now considered passé. Never mind that the ubiquitous presence musical instruction now enjoys in North American schools came about because of the public's love for performance spectacles like festivals and marching bands. We had outgrown such things, and in our maturity promised to turn our full attention to enhancing society's sensitivity to the patterns of human subjectivity.

It is also striking how the ascendancy of this philosophical stance coincided with a veritable explosion in the range of musical activity that could hardly have challenged monocular expressionistic doctrine more directly had it been expressly designed to do so. Serial techniques, aleatory, music that was coolly cerebral, rowdy rock 'n' roll, and that ever-impolite jazz idiom: each offered profound challenges to the aesthetic philosophy's orthodox precepts, above all the canon that holds that all music can be adequately described by one philosophical perspective and evaluated by one universally applicable set of criteria — whether "subtlety and abstractness of expression" (Leonhard and House 1972), "syntactical excellence and profundity of expressive content" (Reimer 1970), or "craftsmanship, sensitivity, imagination, and authenticity" (Reimer 1989).

I wonder if this may not have been something of what McKay had in mind when he wrote, "Because of the overwhelming quantity and the almost bewildering variety of possible musical experience . . . the danger is that our teaching and learning will be satisfied with only a small or isolated part of this total wealth of music that has been offered us by the creative spirit" (p. 123). The basic challenges he conceived for music education were to "encompass [the] full range of musical experience in our teaching" (p. 123) and to nurture democratic educational ideals such as "openness to philosophical ferment," "experimental-mindedness," and "open tolerance of artistic antitheses" (p. 124).

There is a marked contrast between this vision of McKay and music education's rather doctrinaire adherence to a monistic philosophical base during the ensuing decades. Surely careful exploration of the profound diversity that attends both philosophy (musical aesthetics) and musical practice should have taken us in precisely the opposite direction. Instead, "philosophy of music education" came to be dispensed as though it were a kind of pill, neatly bottled and mass distributed, so as to make minimal intellectual or musical demands upon its consumers.

The nature of the philosophical quest is far messier than this. Its roots lie in intellectual discontent and ferment, in cognitive dissonance. The capacity to think philosophically (that is, to reason logically, systematically, and critically) is far more crucial to a music education profession than is the capacity to generate convincing justifications for music's inclusion in public school curricula.

If philosophical enquiry is to have any real value to musical education in the twenty-first century, it will be because it is approached as process rather than dogma; because it is as concerned with framing the right questions as it is with dispensing of answers; because it turns us toward music rather than inward; because it helps us think, listen, and teach more effectively. The music education profession has long asserted that philosophy is foundational, while relegating its study to a superficial unit in a cursory and insular "foundations course" that effectively avoids the kind of intellectual discomfort that is grist for the philosophical mill. Most undergraduates have thought more about brass mouthpieces than about philosophy. Rather than using philosophy as a tool to refine our thinking, our hearing, our teaching, our research, our very professional identity, we have generally settled for slogans designed to keep the wolf (the unsympathetic administrator) from our door.

Moreover, philosophy must retain as its constant focus that which it purports to explain, or else it distorts and reduces it to something it is not. To help curb the speculative excesses of Idealism, Wittgenstein urged philosophers to "think" less and to look and describe more. Now, a philosopher would be the last person in the world to denigrate thinking. The trick is to assure that thought remains grounded by (in this case) musical perception rather than becoming seduced by the mind's fondness for ideal types and abstractions. Modern philosophy has for the most part abandoned the conception of its task as a search for immutable essences that lurk behind predominantly illusory surfaces. It has come to conceive its primary task more as descriptive than speculative. It has become less a quest for ultimate explanations, more an attempt to shed light upon smaller, more manageable

101

issues and problems — to describe as fully as possible what is "given" to experience in terms that are as lucid as possible. Obviously I believe that music education would do well to follow suit.

MUSICAL PLURALISM

At risk of redundancy, let us resume the line of argument with which this essay began. Its main points might be cast in the form of a kind of syllogism:

- *If* most of the fundamental decisions about the conduct of music education (instructional method, repertoire selection, and so on) should follow from a clear understanding of the nature and value of music; and
- *If* an examination of music shows that nature and value to be fundamentally plural, dynamic, and various;
- *Then* our philosophical base must (in order to be faithful to musical art) reflect that plurality, that dynamism, that variousness.

We have long been aware of the first premise's validity. It is the second premise that has been our shortcoming. Endorsing music's nature and value as foundational need not (indeed, should not) commit us to a monolithic conception of music, whether "absolute expressionism" or "absolute" anything.

A twenty-first century philosophy will have to espouse a range of potentially musical experience broader than ever before in history and embrace the fact of multiple natures and multiple values for music. For the moment we enshrine one set of characteristics as constitutive of music's essence and think of one style or set of conditions as exemplifying the highest condition that "musical art" can properly attain; a whole host of musics that do not necessarily subscribe to these value assumptions are automatically demoted to the status of nonartistic music, substandard music, or even non-music. Again, though the 1960s apparently taught us the necessity of opening our ears to a variety of musics, the kind of philosophical inquiry that might well have been expected to dialectically inform that more open attitude has been conspicuously absent. Too often we teach our young charges that "expression" is the exclusive aim of musical art, the only valid determinant of musical worth.

I am not suggesting that we discard nineteenth-century metaphors like "organism," "feeling," or of music as a "language of the heart"; I am only suggesting that we can no longer delude ourselves that these are absolutes, eternal essences, or universals. Not only is the security these assumptions afford false, they also have the capacity to restrict and distort perception. They describe ways that music has been and can be, but not what it must be or always will be. We must respect the complexity and diversity of musical reality and renounce our vain attempts to force all music into one mold, to articulate one set of criteria that presumes to prescribe for everyone and for all times what music must be. As a product of the human mind, we must expect music to assume as many forms and functions as that marvelously complex organ can contrive, and we must recognize that music will continue to evolve along multiple paths, some convergent, some parallel, and still others strongly divergent. Like other cognitive functions, much of musical pleasure derives from making connections — connections that may be intramusical or extramusical; connections that may be the contribution of composer or performer or listener; connections that draw upon the musical past, refer to its future, or speak to nothing but the present moment. They may speak to the head, to the ear, or to one's entire body and its many other senses, as well as to the "heart."

Some music may indeed be taken as a kind of narrative interpretation of the dynamic patterns of human feeling, as a "tonal analogue of emotive life"; but to impose this template upon all music and all musical experience is to distort it in subtle and often not-so-subtle ways, to occlude our perception of what music often is. Philosophy may and often does enlighten and reveal, but so may it obfuscate, distort, and divert — dangers few philosophers have doubted since the intellectual disaster of Hegel's unbridled speculative adventures. The metaphors of nineteenth-century Idealistic aesthetics may vividly describe a certain range of musical experience, but that range is far more restricted than we often assume.

As Lewis Rowell (1983) documents very effectively in a chapter entitled "Clotho and Atropos" (Plato's symbols for the present and future), a great deal of the music composed during this century blatantly rejects the assumptions of goal directedness and temporal linearity, which are so central to the organismic/feeling metaphor. Music has been variously conceived, rather, as object, as pure kinetic process, as an indeterminate state of being, as the architectural juxtaposition of discrete sound events or aural images, as pure space, as ritual, as stasis, as a field of action, as an intensely earnest or an utterly frivolous affair. Music may resemble life processes or even perhaps the "shape" of an entire human life. But its experience may also be predominantly visceral or corporeal, cerebral or contemplative. Music may be found in nothing more than what Hanslick designated "tonally moving forms," whereas a great deal of it entails reference to things like seas or events like the crucifixion. Musical experience may be seamless, integrated, and perceptibly coherent (as nineteenth-century philosophical heritage insists it must be); but it may also be disjunct and atomistic — a mere succession of discrete "nows." Music may support a sense of self-integration and confer "meaning" through contemplation of its harmonious unity; but it may as well be crude, rude, jarring, violently active, alienating. The effort to subsume all musics under one philosophical banner, one set of philosophical doctrines, and a monolithic account of music's "essential, singular, unifying concept" (Reimer 1989, 8) is a fascinating mental exercise. It is not, however, necessary to a philosophy of music education. Nor is it particularly helpful.

The security of monistic doctrines will be sorely missed, but what alternative do we have? What set of criteria for musical "worth" can possibly be identified that will adequately subsume Gregorian chant, a Puccini aria, a Bach fugue, a late Beethoven string quartet, Dixieland jazz, a Fauré song, a requiem mass, an aleatoric John Cage piece, the free improvisation of Coltrane's "Ascension," a highly determined serial composition? And what will subsume music of Australian or Inuit aboriginals, a Tibetan Buddhist ritual, a Balinese gamelan orchestra, an African drumming ensemble? The Rolling Stones or The Beatles? Muddy Waters, Billie Holiday, Thelonious Monk, and Duke Ellington? Surely, to say these all constitute profound manifestations of the human spirit is to speak the truth. But their differences are far more provocative than their similarities. And each is "great" for different reasons. Even our perception of the unitary nature of "common practice" European art music has for more than a decade been yielding to a preference for performance on authentic "period instruments."

There is no single idea that can illuminate such a profoundly disparate range of music and musical experience. There is, rather, a provocative array of alternatives, each with its own distinctive assumptions, priorities, and values. A twenty-first–century philosophy of music education must renounce the quest for air-tight definitions of the musical art. It must overcome the temptation to mistake the particular for the general, the individual for the universal, and to trivialize perspectives that lie outside the range circumscribed by such narrow purviews. It must recognize musical value as an open-ended and ever-changing constellation of what McKay so graphically designated "regional dynamisms" and what Leonard Meyer calls stylistic "universes of discourse." It must dedicate itself to opening minds (our own as well as our students') to the splendidly diverse and dynamic adventure that is musical experience.

Expressionistic doctrine is a noble and inspiring vision of one way music may be. But it is not the only valid one, and it cannot help but create a jaundiced view of musics (and approaches to the teaching of music) that do not conform to its presuppositions. Its Idealistic heritage renders it ill suited to illuminating musics that confer their highest priority upon kinetic drive or vitality; upon social or religious significance; upon "extramusical" meaning or reference; upon the vivid enjoyment of sound as it purely "is"; upon spontaneity rather than careful premeditation; and upon individuality and freedom rather than homogeneity and uniformity.

To opt for a pluralistic value orientation is neither to abdicate philosophical responsibility nor is it to retreat into utter subjectivism. It is only to concede that music, like knowledge, is more a matter of perspective than immutable absolutes, and to commit to exploring the assumptions and practices underlying such perspectives. This stance commits us to recognizing music as a culturally dynamic phenomenon rather than a unitary or monolithic set of practices. It necessitates that each music be approached with a view to its kind, in terms of what it aspires to be and to do rather than from the presupposition that its first obligation is to express, or entertain, or reveal, or any other single thing.

Clearly this implies a shift away from philosophy as traditionally conceived, and toward criticism. But music education could do far worse than to take its cues for educational practice from actual, first-hand experience of music itself, from open-minded deliberation of its merits on the basis of that experience and whatever knowledge can be brought to inform it. We might well, in this way, foster greater respect and appreciation for the rugged as well as the "fine"; for the playful as well as the reverent; for the visceral as well as the cerebral; for the disposable as well as the permanent; for the free and spontaneous as well as the reflective or self-conscious or carefully controlled; and for the earthy as well as the spiritual.

Pluralism does not need to mean that music education deteriorate into anything less than a quest for the best — only that we recognize that just as there are many musics, so are there many "bests." Our endorsement of one need not, and probably should not, occur at the expense of others.

IMPLICATIONS AND PROBLEMS

There is at least one conspicuous educational dilemma that attends the contention that reality is complex, indeterminate, and various: for what does one teach in the absence of absolutes? If the answer is not easy, at least it respects the complexity of reality. We must develop respect for the multiplicity of musical value, and at the same time help our students develop personal musical values deep enough to sustain continued musical involvement. We must, on the one hand, assume a liberal stance toward the diversity of ways music may be, while on the other, fulfill education's conservative obligation to preserve our cultural heritage.

The trouble is that deep personal commitment to even a small portion of the world's musical heritage does not follow automatically from an appreciation of the vastness of the range from which it is drawn. Nor does mere awareness of the cultural value of music dispose one to the sense of personal commitment so essential to the preservation of music that is the best in its kind. We must accept the obligation to provide sufficiently rich experience in at least one musical world that it may take root and grow. There is, in short, a significant tension between the two democratic ideals of openness and tolerance on the one hand and value commitment on the other. But surely this is not so much cause for dismay as it is itself fertile ground for animated and extraordinarily valuable debate with our students.

McKay argued that students must encounter the "whole gamut" of artistic/philosophical conflict, the ferment and struggle that are among the "principal glories of our intellectual life" (p. 136). And yet, at the same time, we owe our students the opportunity to become sufficiently immersed in at least one music, sufficiently familiar with its exemplars (and sufficiently aware of why they are indeed exemplary) that it can assume a meaning deeper and more personal than mere appreciation of its status as a cultural artifact. We must help our students embrace as "their own" the very best of at least one musical domain; but in so doing, we must avoid the false impression that its standards and priorities are universally applicable and that, therefore, the endorsement of one music entails the necessary rejection of others.

"We should," wrote McKay, "teach the importance of the full philosophical range in understanding music," using musical examples to "challenge every value point of view," balancing consideration of every musical point of view with "its opposite, as a means of developing the young mind into full-fledged intellectual citizenship" (p. 138). McKay's vision of musical education was decidedly not indoctrinative. He envisioned a musical education devoted to critical exploration of the variousness and ambiguity of musical value, to the development of profound respect for music's many faces. His fervent wish for music education was that it ensure students' commitment to preserving and honoring not just some narrow range of musical experience, but instead the vast constellation of music's "regional dynamisms."

In addition to challenging our basic conception of the aims and purposes of music educational practice, McKay's perspective appears to bear some equally unsettling implications for the philosophical education of prospective music teachers. We have long argued that philosophy should fulfill a dual role in music education: as an advocacy tool and as a guide for practice. Both functions are more easily met if we conceive philosophy as a product rather than a process, as a unitary set of doctrines rather than an open and complex set of possibilities. As a result, instead of engaging and sustaining the kind of intellectual ferment to which McKay alludes, we have tended to approach philosophy as the dispensation of answers; to this extent, our philosophical endeavors have become matters of training rather than of education. We have not nurtured philosophical skills as much as we have dispensed slogans and prescriptions. We have sought refuge in the relative security of ready answers instead of exploring the strengths and shortcomings of contrasting perspectives. But philosophy is a manner of thinking, not a body of doctrine; and music's dynamic diversity must be the "basic concept" it is dedicated to elucidating.

In short, music education should strive to transform its conception of philosophy to a vital mode of inquiry instead of a perfunctory, dogmatic exercise. Furthermore, the profession must overcome the temptation to dismiss claims to music's social, referential, extramusical, or formal values (to name but a few) as philosophical aberrations. These are ways music has been, can be, and indeed often is. We must derive our philosophical propositions about music and music education more extensively from description and criticism (based on firsthand observation of what music is and does) than from presuppositions as to what it "should" be or do. Instead of insisting that "all art does the same thing and that all art can and should be judged by the same criteria for success" (Reimer 1989, 111), we must surely recognize that not even all music is of one cloth. Only by injudiciously segregating "art" from "nonart" music in a way that begs the question can the monistic position be sustained. If our minds are to open our ears rather than close them, our ideological and value bases must become as pluralistic as the phenomenon of music itself.

CONCLUSIONS

I should close with a few words of consolation or reassurance for those who believe that the position outlined here leaves us without basic concepts, without principles, and without any basis for claiming that a Brahms violin sonata is among the world's great treasures. If I have created this impression neither has it been my purpose nor do I believe it. But I do believe it is essential that we more conscientiously explore questions of musical value with our students, whether in the school or in the university. I do believe that the time is clearly over when we could complacently maintain that there was only one reasonable way to think about music and about musical education. Again, I am not proposing the renunciation of all values, only urging that we explore rival claims more sympathetically, more open-mindedly, more amicably. I am urging that we not allow our minds to rule our ears or to attenuate what they hear in ways that inappropriately restrict the range of valid musical experience.

Because I have used McKay's ideas as a point of departure in my discussion, it is fair to ask whether, among the principles he offered, there are any that are still valid today. Obviously I think there are, although not all are equally germane to the specific lines of argument I have pursued. These points in particular (slightly abridged) strike particularly resonant chords:

1. We must nurture an attitude of humility and gratitude toward the "vastness of human musical achievement."
2. Our teaching must convey to our students the dynamism and vitality of music.
3. We must challenge our students' "natural curiosity" and inquisitiveness, their desire to further explore this marvelously diverse and distinctively human realm. We cannot be content to be museum curators.
4. We must introduce our students to the "full philosophical range" of musical thought, in all its contradictions and complexity.
5. Although it is imperative that we help students make music "their own," we should not expect everyone to value the same music or to value music for the same reasons. Nor should we create the false impression that valuing one kind of music means "choosing sides."
6. Every student is the creator of his or her own musical culture, and at the same time, an essential agent in the preservation of the very best in our collective musical culture.

In addition to these points of McKay's, I suggest we consider the following:

1. We will understand and appreciate music better, and teach it more effectively, if we remember its numerous and divergent faces — teach musics rather than music. We should not allow ideal types to divert us from the unique splendor of individual pieces and performances.
2. The fact of musical pluralism implicates philosophical and pedagogical pluralism as well. There is no more one nature or one value of music than there is one music. We must be cautious of the rationalistic propensity to force everything (all music, all philosophy) into a single, all-inclusive system.
3. We should emphasize multiplicity, but not to the detriment of personal appreciation of what contributes to greatness in each respective domain of "regional sensibility." Pluralism should enhance and nurture musical commitment, not undermine it.

4. Respect for a broad range of philosophical and musical values is not abject relativism. To maintain that there are multiple valid philosophical perspectives, or numerous valid musical values, is not to maintain that they are innumerable. Within each stylistic "universe," musical instruction must strive to kindle a thirst for the best and impatience with anything less. There are many kinds of "best," but this does not relieve us of the obligation to help our students seek them out and judge them in appropriate terms.

5. We should take a more pragmatic approach to explaining, advocating, and justifying musical instruction in the public schools. It deserves to be taught first and foremost because it is among the most distinctively human achievements conceivable, because people love it, and because greater understanding enhances and enriches the quality of its experience.

6. Finally, ironically, we need to remind ourselves that among the many things "basic" to music education, music is the most fundamental. Perhaps rather than deducing our orientations toward musical education from preordained philosophical stances, we should more often proceed inductively — taking our direction from music itself. This is not to suggest that we abandon philosophical reflection, but that we make open-minded music criticism a fuller partner in music education. Our philosophical convictions should never be permitted to obstruct the music's opportunity to be simply what it is or to "say" what it aspires to "say."

There is an important difference between debate over the relative merits of musics in different styles and comparing pieces or performances within a particular musical "universe of discourse" — musics that share the same stylistic assumptions or priorities. Philosophical monism has encouraged us, often against our better musical judgment, to compare the relative merits of musical apples with oranges; to speculate, for instance, about the "expressive" virtues of music not particularly concerned with expression; and to rank musical genres as though they were in competition with one another. Such activity is, I believe, musically and intellectually pointless.

On the other hand, the critical comparison of pieces and performances within stylistic frameworks is positively essential to musical education. The search for clear and defensible reasons to substantiate the claim that "this is better than that," and the careful examination of the assumptions that undergird musical beliefs and values, are crucial to any musical enterprise that claims to be educational. Without some idea of which cognitive and perceptual schemata to employ, and when and how, our students remain complacent in the false conviction that judgments of musical worth are mere matters of personal "taste," a belief that hardly qualifies as musical understanding and seriously strains the concept of musical education.

REFERENCES

Langer, S. (1951) *Philosophy in a New Key*. Cambridge, Mass.: Harvard University Press.

Leonhard, C., and R. W. House (1972) *Foundations and principles of music education*. New York: McGraw-Hill.

McKay, G. F. (1958) The range of musical experience. In *Basic concepts in music education, I*. Chicago: The University of Chicago Press.

McMurray, F. (1958) Pragmatism in music education. In *Basic Concepts, I*. Reprinted as Chapter 2 in this volume.

Reimer, B. (1970 and 1989) *A philosophy of music education*. Englewood Cliffs, New Jersey: Prentice-Hall.

Rowell, L. (1983) *Thinking about music*. Amherst: The University of Massachusetts Press.

5

Growth Processes in Music Education

James L. Mursell

THE MEANING OF GROWTH IN MUSIC EDUCATION

The concept of *growth or development* — and in what follows the two terms will be used as synonyms — has very wide currency in present-day educational thought and practice. Too often, however, either expression is used without precise understanding of its significance for musical experience and consequently without application of its operational implications for music education. Accordingly, the purpose of this chapter will be to set forth the chief pertinent characteristics of the process of growth and their most important bearings upon music education.

Many years ago it was said that education should be considered as guided growth, and the dictum has found wide acceptance. What is the positive, specific meaning of this celebrated statement? What does it indicate in the way of desirable policy and practice with reference to music? These are the questions with which the substance of this chapter will deal.

THE PROBLEM OF CHANGE IN RELATION TO MUSICAL EXPERIENCE

At the outset it will be helpful to point up a contrast, since this tends to bring thinking to a clear focus. The view of education as guided growth implies a great deal. But also it excludes a great deal. What, then, does it

Originally published in *Basic Concepts in Music Education, I,* Nelson B. Henry, editor, 1958. Reprinted with permission from the National Society for the Study of Education.

exclude? What conceptions of mental life and functioning does it rule out? What types of policy and practice does it disallow? It seems well to begin by considering these negative questions.

The basic datum with which we have to deal is the phenomenon of behavior change. The capacity to modify and change behavior is one of the most striking characteristics of higher organisms, and supremely so of man. According to developmental theory, behavior change is brought about by growth or development, and numerous practical consequences follow. The opposing account is the theory known as associationism; and this too yields various practical consequences.

On the associationist view, behavior change is produced by connecting specific stimuli with specific responses. A rat in a problem box comes to connect one doorway with food and another with a mild electric shock, so it soon begins to seek the former and avoid the latter. A child comes to connect the word "times" with the technique of multiplication. Or he comes to connect the symbol "1492" with certain names and events, so that when the date is given the names and events can be produced, or vice versa. Multitudinous considerations of this kind have been generalized into an inclusive theory. It is this account which stands in contradistinction to the belief that all behavior change is produced by a process of growth or development.

There are many variants of associationist psychology, and many differences in emphasis, with which the present brief discussion cannot deal. It stems from remote antiquity, being represented by certain Greek thinkers, by Hume and Locke, and by Pavlov, to mention only a few. Its wide acceptance in this country has been due largely to the earlier work of E. L. Thorndike, whose position was substantially that just indicated, though numerous qualifications have necessarily been omitted. In any case, associationism in this form has deeply influenced, and still does influence, our educational practice in music and in many other fields. It stands in striking contrast, both theoretical and operational, with the development viewpoint. Out of many such contrasts, two will be considered here.

1. The clear purport of associationism is that behavior change (which, of course, is the educative process itself) is brought about by the *accumulation of specific connections*. This immediately translates into a certain type of curriculum planning and organization, to wit, the setting-up of lengthy series of specific learnings. Numerous courses of study in many fields, emphatically including music, are set up in precisely this way. The presumption is that, if these specific learnings are established, they will be retained and permanently available.

The radical objection is that such accumulation is largely a myth. Investigation has shown that many children, when they pass on from addition to subtraction, forget the "fifty addition facts" before they have mastered the "fifty subtraction facts." No comparable research has been done in music, but undoubtedly the situation is the same here. Evidently the accumulation of specific connections cannot be considered the cause of behavior change. Plans for periodical reviewing (i.e., relearning) are not availing, for relearning, in a vast number of cases, leads only to reforgetting. Practical reliance on a largely mythical process of accumulation is certainly a chief reason for the astonishing ineffectiveness of a great deal of teaching, including the teaching of music.

The contrary view would be that behavior change is produced by a gradually clarifying understanding. Such working musical concepts as "six-eight time," "dotted quarter note," or "phrase" are not, and cannot be, acquired once and for all at some given moment and thenceforward retained. They are, at first, very vaguely apprehended; and the process of education relies in part on their progressive clarification and explication. Obviously this points toward something very different from the conventional course of study organization.

2. A central associationist doctrine is that connections are formed usually, though not always, by repetition. The doctrine has a venerable antiquity, but for American educators, it is best known as Thorndike's celebrated "law of use." Here again arise many practical suggestions for teaching, chiefly of quite an obvious kind. An analysis of the role of repetition would be irrelevant here, as we are merely indicating contrasts. But it is notable that Thorndike himself, on the basis of a great body of research, in effect repudiated the law of use and denied that repetition is a cause of learning, i.e., of behavior change.

What, then, is the cause? The answer of developmental psychology, very briefly put, is that behavior is changed not by the repetitive establishment of specific connections, but by the reshaping of total patterns. For instance, when a child becomes able to respond properly to the key signature of E major, it is not because he has connected the sight of four sharps with a given reaction. His understanding of the staff, of clef, or other key signatures, of key itself, is involved. Indeed, conceivably he might come to understand and respond to the key signature of E major by understanding other key signatures, i.e., without repeating it at all! So what superficially seems a specific, definite connection is really a shift in a far-reaching pattern, every constituent element of which affects all others, and is reciprocally affected by them.

This, then, is the psychological doctrine to be translated into instructional practice, if education is to be conducted as guided growth. The undertaking is not simple! The notion of repetition yields an easy, foolproof teaching formula, albeit a futile one. But the developmental doctrine is hard to apply. Still, application is possible. Reliance must rest on the intelligent treatment of significant experience. Repetitive drilling on the key of four sharps is probably not repaying. But an *ad hoc* exposition of what it means when it occurs in music with which the child is dealing, and with which he wishes to deal, will be far more promising. For it will tend to produce that process of clarification and explication which is the essence of growth.

The critical reader will be aware of an unstated apparent assumption that must be faced before passing on. It has seemed so far to be assumed that development depends upon experience alone. Does not maturation also play a part? Certainly it does; but the extent of its effect is a matter of dispute and doubt. Clearly, it is not an independent influence. No one can mature over the years without having experiences. No experience can affect anyone not mature enough to be sensitive to it. That, perhaps, is all that need be said here on this far-reaching and intricate subject. However, since the present purpose is practical, and since we can control experience but cannot control maturation, our chief concern must be with the optimum planning of experience with a view to desirable behavior change.

Numerous additional contrasts between the associationist and developmental viewpoints could readily be drawn. But the two just considered are crucial, theoretically and practically; they serve to define the issues and to set the stage for more positive discussions. What is the nature of the developmental process? Which of its characteristics have the most important bearing upon educational organization and instructional practice in music? What types of planning and teaching do these characteristics imply? To these questions we now turn.

THE IMPORTANCE OF CONTINUITY IN GROWTH PROCESSES

The most striking single characteristic of the process of growth is its continuity. That growth is a continuum is a familiar and often-repeated idea; but often it is left quite vague and ill-defined. Numerous writers have stressed the negative meaning of the proposition and have pointed out that growth does not go through a series of self-contained stages, each separate from and exclusive of the rest. This, no doubt, is true and significant; and it has many important practical implications. But the positive meaning of developmental continuity is far more important, both theoretically and practically.

It is the strong belief of the present writer that the notion of developmental continuity cannot be made fully meaningful without reference to the associated concept of what Gesell and his associates call the "growth gradient," and what this writer has called the "developmental line."[1]

This concept is basically very simple — so simple, indeed, that it is often overlooked. What it means is that, while growth in general has certain universal characteristics, we always deal with some specific type of growth. We speak, quite properly, of the growth of an oak tree or a cabbage plant, of growth in reading ability, or mathematical competence, or social adequacy. These are lines or gradients of growth. Of course they do not go on in isolation from one another, for everything in mental life, and indeed in nature in general, affects and is affected by everything else. But for purposes of clear thinking and intelligent practice, it is very important to recognize them and to work in terms of them. Much of the vagueness and cloudy sentimentality that infect so many discussions of growth and development arise from the ignoring of definable growth lines or growth gradients. No doubt they are, in a sense, abstractions, but since our minds are finite, abstractions are quite essential.

In terms of this concept the continuity of growth means that any given growth gradient or developmental line retains its own distinctive character throughout its entire course. The oak tree remains an oak tree from the first sprouting of the acorn to its final majestic maturity. The cabbage plant is always a cabbage plant. And each must be treated according to its own distinctive nature if its development is to prosper.

The same is true of mental functions. Of this, the work of Gesell affords numerous impressive illustrations. One such example is his account of the development of reading behavior. At fifteen months the child pats an identified picture in a book. At eighteen months he points to an identified picture in a book. At two years he names three pictures in a book. At three years he identifies four printed geometric forms. At five years he recognizes salient capital letters. At six years he recognizes salient printed words. Here we have a schematic account of a segment of the evolution of a well-defined behavior pattern, the behavior pattern of reading. The evolution of the behavior pattern is continuous in the sense that it always retains its distinctive basic character; for reading, always and at all levels, is the response to and comprehension of visual symbols. Reading always has this character, all the way from the rudimentary response of the infant who pats an identified picture to the performance of the expert who can master the content of a technical work at the speed of a thousand words per minute. Moreover, it must always be treated as such, cultivated as such, and taught as such if its evolution is to proceed under optimum conditions.[2]

Such considerations have far-reaching and profound implications for the organization of the curriculum and for teaching. If the claim that education is guided growth is to be more than a form of words, we must stringently ask ourselves exactly what the functions are with which we are dealing, and then set up conditions for their development, remembering that their essential nature remains unchanged at all levels of maturity. If it is agreed that mathematics, in essence, is relational or abstract thinking, then it must always be taught as such, from the beginning on, and never as the routine manipulation of number symbols by rule of thumb. If it is agreed that natural science is essentially objective thinking, then again it must always be taught as such and not as the accumulation of facts and information. So on for the entire curriculum. Here is the meaning, theoretical and practical, of the assertion that the process of growth is a continuum.

How does the idea apply to music and the teaching of it? In precisely the sense just indicated. From the developmental point of view the teaching of music is not the teaching of a subject in the conventional sense, but the promotion and guidance of a growth gradient or developmental line, with a distinctive character of its own — and a character which remains, constant at all levels of maturity.

Psychologically speaking, the whole art of music depends upon the existence in human nature of a mental function to which has been attached the convenient term "musicality." Musicality may be defined as responsiveness to the tonal and rhythmic patterns which are the substance of the art of music. So far as we can tell, it is universal, or very nearly so, among human beings, and it seems to be present also among many subhuman species. Musicality manifests itself very early in human life, in responses to lullabies and croonings, and to the tones of the mother's voice; and a little later on in lalling, or the repetitive humming of tune-like fragments, and so on. The concept must by no means be confused with the concept of musical talent. The relationship is simply that individuals clearly differ in their innate sensitivity to musical stimuli, which, of course, is true of every type of human responsiveness. But, to repeat, musicality itself appears to be universal and to be one of the fundamental ways in which man responds to the dynamics of his environment.

This, then, is the function with which we have to deal in all the teaching of music. From the developmental point of view, the purpose of all music teaching must be to bring about the evolution of musical responsiveness or musicality. The criterion for judging all policies and practices in music education must be their suitability for this purpose. Moreover, the purpose remains the same at all levels of maturity, for the reason that the essential nature of musicality remains the same. In dealing with kindergarten children, or with the members of master classes, and indeed in the delicate and highly individual coaching of concert artists and operatic performers, the determining aim is always the same, namely, the further evolution of responsiveness to music. Here is the meaning for music educators of the concept of developmental continuity.

This general statement can readily be carried down into particulars, and to do so will make its far-reaching significance more evident.

1. The teaching of music reading is one of the chief points of dispute in music education today. If the notational symbols of music are taught simply as an abstract code, as is sometimes done, then clearly there is a departure from the essential and constant emphasis upon musical responsiveness, which no rationalizations can successfully mask. So there will be a breach of developmental continuity and, in all probability, an educational failure. But the symbols stand for concepts which have musical meanings, the progressive grasping of which is quite essential for any considerable development of musicality. Thus the teaching of music reading can and certainly should be conducted in such a way as to lead to a better and more adequate response to music itself.

2. The teaching of music theory has come to occupy an important place in the specialized music curriculum. Here again a striking, obvious, and disastrous breach of continuity often occurs. Music theory is frequently presented as a sort of formal grammar, with various rules of its own which often appear strange and arbitrary to the learner and which are acquired by the use of practice materials without musical interest or value. One may confidently say that, when it is so taught, it has no relationship whatsoever to musical responsiveness, unless indeed that relationship is negative. Here again, however, our developmental psychology clearly indicates the proper path. The content of music theory has to do with those elements in music out of which its appeal and interest arise; and that content can and should be taught in such a way as to evoke a growing understanding and appreciation of and responsiveness to these essential musical elements. In this case the learning of music theory, like the learning of music reading, becomes an essential influence in the development of musicality.

3. The acquisition of manipulative technique is a formidable and ever-present problem in music education. Very often the acquisition of technique is set up as a separate type of learning, more or less completely divorced from the actual making of music, and technique itself is regarded merely as gymnastic skill. Here again occurs a falsification and a breach of continuity.

As a matter of fact, every musical composition, including even the simplest of children's songs, presents certain problems which must be met if the delivery is to be satisfying both to the listener and to the performer. These may be regarded as problems of musical realization, of expressive and aesthetically adequate interpretation and rendition. But, at the same time, they are also technical problems. The acquisition of technique should result from the attack upon such problems, which are both musical and technical, and technique itself should be regarded as the ability to translate musical conceptions adequately and satisfactorily into sound. Thus, the familiar but most injudicious distinction between musical considerations, on the one hand, and technical considerations, on the other, simply disappears in a sequence of continuous musical development and in the evolution of musical responsiveness which is impossible without growing technical adequacy, but which tends to be frustrated when technique is separated out and treated as an independent function.

This brief discussion leaves many points untouched. But it is sufficient to indicate the positive meaning of developmental continuity and to suggest the many highly significant implications of the idea for policy and practice in music education.

THE NATURE OF GROWTH IN MUSICAL EXPERIENCE

Having seen that growth in general and musical growth in particular are a continuum, a further question immediately arises. What actually happens during this process of growth? What is the nature of developmental change? An answer has at least been suggested in the contrast already drawn between the associationist and developmental accounts of mental life. But now the topic must be considered more at length and in its own right.

Briefly put, developmental change consists of the emergence, clarification, and explication of pattern. A relatively formless response is transformed into one that is specifically structured. To paraphrase in part Herbert Spencer's famous definition of evolution, a vague "indefinite homogeneity" of response becomes "definite" and "coherent." The previous illustration of the oak tree may serve to illuminate the conception. As the acorn is transformed into the mature tree, of course, a great increase in size takes place. But, more importantly, there is also a great increase in structural complexity and specificity. In the same way the vague, indeterminate responses of the newborn infant develop into the relatively clear-cut, highly structured behavior patterns of the adult. It is precisely this progressive organization, this emergence of structure, that is the very essence of developmental change. And it occurs in the development of all mental functions, including musicality. This is the process for which we must provide optimum conditions and effective guidance if the teaching of music is to conform to the claim that education, properly understood and conducted, is guided growth.

But if optimum conditions and skilful guidance are to be provided, it is necessary to go beyond the general statement just presented and to understand how this basic process of structuralization actually takes place. From the great wealth of available material, three points will here be made.

1. The emergence and explication of pattern, which, to repeat, is the growth process itself, takes place through differentiation and integration. A musical example will serve to show what is involved. A group of first-grade children learn to sing a song by ear and imitation. As they listen to the teacher's singing, they are aware of the general expressive intention and appeal of the music, and they are able, to some extent, to project and realize these values in their own singing. Here is a genuine and authentic musical response, and as such it is excellent as far as it goes. But it is necessarily vague, relatively formless, and lacking in precision. The children catch something significant. Indeed one may say that they catch what is the most essential thing of all, which is the expressive beauty of the music. But they do not and cannot grasp it very firmly or apprehend it with exactitude. Perhaps a point here and there may be called to their attention — the turn of a phrase, the rise and fall of the tune, a dynamic nuance, or such like. Here is the beginning of differentiation, i.e., the noticing of significant detail in a vaguely apprehended whole. The suggestion is that, if this small point be duly noticed, a more satisfying projection of the song will result. A trial or two readily proves to the children that this is indeed so. What they have now achieved is a superior and more articulated integration.

Of course, such a simple improvement of a first-grade song is a small beginning, but it is a precise prototype and microcosm of the whole process of musical growth and of the interplay of differentiation and integration upon which that process depends. As the years pass, this interplay of differentiation and integration continues, if musical experiences are wisely chosen and wisely guided. Children come to realize that a piece of music is more satisfying, both to hear and to perform, if its rhythmic organization, its key relationships, its phrase structure, and its melodic and harmonic textures are firmly and clearly grasped. It is in and through this progressive awareness of constituent elements that the pattern itself, as a totality, becomes more articulated, more significant, more adequately appreciated. Such is the process of musical growth.

Two comments, both of momentous importance, must be made before passing on. First, musical growth depends altogether upon study of and dealing with music itself and upon differentiating the constituents which determine its significant expressiveness, its appeal, its beauty. Musical growth does not depend upon studying those constituents in isolation. Second, it becomes evident once again that the all-too-common distinction between the musical and the technical is a fallacy. Rhythmic organization, key relationships, phrase structure, and so on, might be thought of as technical considerations, and in a sense they are. But at the same time they are the constituents upon which the whole effort of music and the art of music itself depend. They must be progressively apprehended, or musical growth itself

— which is but another name for progressively deeper and more adequate appreciation — becomes impossible. Without progressive differentiation, better integration cannot take place.

2. The emergence and explication of pattern involves, and to some extent, manifests itself in, gain in precision and control. A four-year-old child will be clumsy in handling a pencil or in throwing and catching a ball. He acquires precision and control, not by drilling on these activities as isolated skills or techniques, but through the acquisition of more highly articulated patterns of over-all behavior.

In music education, in all its phases and at all levels, precision and control are an ever-present problem. There is the child who "cannot carry a tune," the second-grade group who sings a melodic contour very imperfectly, the instrumentalist who plays "wrong notes," the high-school ensemble performers who fail to grasp a rhythmic pattern and to enunciate it with exactitude. As every experienced worker in the field well knows, these are but a scattering of instances, and more could be added endlessly. What to do about such failures and difficulties is a highly practical and urgent question.

Usually the first thought is to deal with "mistakes" directly and, as it were, in isolation. The "uncertain singer" (less politely called the "monotone") is subjected to drills on "matching" separate tones. The wrong notes played by the instrumental soloist are sharply pointed out. The high-school orchestra repeats the clumsily delivered passage again and again. Such procedures are at best uneconomical and dubious and frequently quite ineffective.

In the earlier stages of any developmental sequence, clumsiness, error, imperfections, and uncertain control invariably occur. They are quite unavoidable. But in those processes of behavior change, which we sometimes call learning and sometimes call growth, the most striking feature is the progressive elimination of error. But, characteristically, this elimination of error is brought about, not by a multitude of anxious *ad hoc* corrections and poorly comprehended drills, but by the emergence of more clear-cut, better articulated patterns. Clumsiness, error, and uncertainty are the concomitants of vagueness and can be overcome ultimately only by transforming vagueness into well-structured response.

Putting the matter in less technical terms, it comes to this. To overcome error, it is not sufficient for the learner to know that something is wrong. *He needs to know what is right.* The high-school orchestra "muddies up" a rhythm pattern because the performers do not really sense and feel it. The instrumentalist habitually makes mistakes in a certain passage because he does not clearly apprehend its musical shape. The second-grade children deliver a tune vaguely because they have only a vague apprehension of it.

120

And as to the "uncertain singer," his difficulty is an inadequate comprehension of the singable contour of the melody, not an inability to duplicate separate tones on order.[3]

Clearly, then, the policy and practice of music education at all levels should be directed to the progressive clarification of musical patterns. Too much should never be expected too soon. Error and imperfection are inevitable at early developmental levels, and well-meant efforts to root them out can do little good and may do much harm. This, of course, is not argument at all for being satisfied with low-level achievement or for rationalizing such achievement by loose talk about the "therapeutic" effects of music. But it is an excellent argument for working always toward the better realization and enunciation of structured pattern. The process in and through which such structuralization emerges cannot complete itself in a week or a year. It must go forward for many years. But it is the process to be promoted by any program of music education centering on the development of musicality.

3. The emergence and explication of pattern involve increasing control by generalizations and abstractions. For instance, as the abstract idea of "fair play" becomes meaningful to a child, his social behavior takes on more definite shape. Or again, as such abstractions as "two hours from now" or "next week" are comprehended, all his actions become more planfully arranged. Abstractions and generalizations are absolutely essential; and if there were not a myriad of them available to us, our lives would be a mere muddled fumbling from one immediacy to the next.

This is just as true in music as it is everywhere else. The doctrine, which seems to be at least adumbrated if not boldly asserted in certain quarters, that music has some mystic power which is dissipated by conceptualization will not bear a moment's scrutiny. It is the sheerest nonsense. Music undoubtedly does have great emotion-arousing effectiveness and, indeed, a highly specific emotional impact.[4] But it has such an effect not simply because of its content but because of its organization. Without organization, music would simply cease to be. So, progressively more adequate grasp of musical organization is the very heart and center of progressively more adequate appreciation. And appreciation, properly understood, expresses itself not only in listening but also in performing.

Now pattern and organization, in music as everywhere else, depend on concepts, abstractions, generalizations. High, low, up, down, loud, soft, chord, scale, beat, key, phrase — these are a few of the very many concepts in terms of which we organize our world of sound. Without such concepts we would have an incoherent chaos, not an ordered cosmos, and the art of music would be impossible. We are able to appreciate, respond emotionally to, and through performance enunciate the musical thought of Mozart because his mind used the same musical concepts as those in which our minds operate. And the better we grasp these concepts, the better our appreciation, our emotional response, and our performance is likely to be. Hence any well-considered scheme of music education is bound to treat the exposition of musical concepts as a central concern.

In order to understand, think about, manipulate, and use any concept, it is necessary to have a symbol. We could not even think about such concepts as "twenty" or "Federal Income Tax" without some symbolic handle for our minds, as it were, to grasp. Here is another universal psychological truth, directly applicable to music. So, it follows that, to develop a grasp of musical concepts, it is necessary to utilize and teach the musical symbols.

A few musical concepts can be conveyed in nontechnical language. But in most cases a special system of symbolism is far more convenient, and often it is indispensable. This, of course, is true of every special field — mathematics, for instance. The standard notation, in spite of its many anomalies, is our best and most adequate means of symbolizing musical concepts. The familiar "so-fa syllables," with "movable do," constitute another symbolic device, and a very useful one, for it represents key relationships and tonality trends with unique clarity and directness. These are our working conceptual tools for coping with and grasping the expressive organization of the ordered world of sound.

It is altogether necessary that these symbols be learned. Otherwise, musical development is bound to remain at a low level, and musical apprehension to be vague, crude, relatively incoherent. But how should they be learned? How should they be taught? How should a grasp of them be developed?

The general answer is perfectly clear. They must be taught always in terms of their musical meanings and in application to musical situations and experiences, never merely in terms of verbal definitions and arithmetical designations. Take, as an example, the symbol "quarter note." The symbol stands for an abstraction, a conceptualized item in the organized time-pattern of music. It is this concept, not the mere verbal or arithmetical definition, that must be grasped. And to grasp it involves a developmental sequence. Children find themselves walking to music. They see, on the blackboard or in books, the notational symbol. They find that quarter notes contrast with other notes — half notes, eighth notes — with other musical meanings and other symbolic representations. They come to realize that quarter notes have a relationship to measure-subdivisions and to time-signatures. Thus the set of conceptual relationships, beginning with something simple and vague yet valid so far, becomes more specific, articulated, and generalized, and so, *pari pasu*, does the ability to grasp and respond to essential elements in the musical pattern.[5]

Here, in briefest compass, is sketched a typical developmental sequence. All the learnings involved must arise directly out of immediate musical experience. For instance, the differentiation between quarter notes and eighth notes must come as a discovery of something worth finding out in music with which one is dealing. Moreover, the differentiation will almost certainly not establish itself at once. It comes as an outgrowth of many, varied, and convincing musical experiences, and clarifies itself with the passage of time.

Undoubtedly much of the hostility of the teaching to the notational and syllabic symbols arises from the all-too-frequent tendency to teach them in and through verbalisms and arithmetic. On this ground criticism is amply justified. But the stubborn and undeniable fact remains that without symbolism concepts cannot be grasped. And if concepts are not grasped, progressive organization is impossible, and development cannot take place.

GUIDED GROWTH TOWARD MUSICAL COMPETENCE

The problem of sequence, that is, of the order in which topics and material are presented, necessarily arises in all curriculum construction and organization. Upon this problem developmental concepts throw much light.

Such clarification is certainly needed, for the problem often proves baffling and is undoubtedly much more subtle and elusive than it may appear at first sight. In many subject-matter fields experience and research have shown again and again that some order of presentation, which seems not unreasonable and has been widely accepted, actually creates difficulties rather than removes them. In music education there is a wide variation, not to say a confusion, of doctrine and practice. For instance, some have argued that the introduction of the standard notation should be postponed until the sixth grade. Widespread practice places it anywhere from Grade II to Grade IV. And it has been successfully and effectively presented in the first grade.

Convincing reasons for such choices are usually impossible to find. What commonly happens is that makers of courses in music either follow some rule of thumb, copy practice adopted elsewhere with some arbitrary variations, or accept without much question the plan of some series of textbooks. When an attempt is made to rationalize these decisions, one encounters formulas, such as going "from the simple to the complex" and "from the known to the unknown," which have a certain obvious validity but afford little reliable guidance because they are so vague that they can be used to justify almost anything. To venture a generalization on the great amount of literature devoted to the problem of sequence, one may say that there is probably no predetermined optimum order of topics in any curriculum field.

Nevertheless, if we adhere to the doctrine that education itself is guided growth, some very useful and tolerably specific leading ideas emerge, applicable to many subject areas and, of course, to music.

1. If the purpose is to provide optimum conditions for growth and development, it is quite clear that no plan turning on a lengthy series of specific and self-contained learnings can be satisfactory. Yet attempts to organize music curriculums, at least implicitly if not explicitly, on this principle are quite common. The so-called fundamentals are distributed according to some chronological plan, and the supervisory machinery is designed largely to make sure that each item is in fact presented when the appointed time arrives. The fatal weakness of all such arrangements has already been pointed out. It is that accumulation itself is largely a myth, which explains at once why the hoped-for outcomes are not forthcoming.

Under such arrangements, moreover, the problem of grade placement becomes insoluble. When should we introduce sixteenth notes, the key of E flat, the minor scale? These are cogent and, indeed, unavoidable questions. Yet, so long as there is a commitment to the notion of teaching such items one by one, with the thought that each can be learned at some given time and thereafter retained, there can be no authoritative or useful answer.

2. Many music educators, aware of these difficulties, have turned eagerly to the concept of readiness, hoping that it might offer a solution, one which is certainly easy and perhaps in keeping with current educational fashions. However, the interpretation of readiness which they seem to have in mind is usually very dubious, to say the least. And the actual practices which it has been used to uphold and justify are of highly questionable developmental effectiveness. Limited space forbids an exposition of the concept of readiness as understood by the best experts in the psychology of language reading, who have done far more than any other group to give it a substantial and well-founded content. Suffice it to say that the interpretation adopted, with suspicious facility, by many music educators, is of an entirely different order.

Roughly speaking, the thought is as follows. Children's early musical experiences should consist of singing songs, playing simple instruments by ear and imitation, rhythmics, dramatizations, listening, perhaps the making-up of tunes, and so forth. It is usually insisted that such experiences should be "rich" — one of those popular eulogistic words that should always give one pause. This should go on for two years, perhaps for three. Then a moment will arrive when the children will be "ready" to study the notation.

Since the uncritical acceptance of this doctrine is extremely common, it seems well to set forth the chief objections to it carefully point by point.

(a) The first and most obvious objection is that readiness so understood involves a glaring breach of developmental continuity. The "readiness stage" is regarded as a distinctive "no notation," "no technicalities" stage. Then a "notational" or "technicalities" stage supervenes. If we ask why symbols and their related musical concepts should be withheld for an indefinite period, there is no answer save an empty formula. Must we believe that a child's musical experiences will be impaired if he learns to realize a little of what phrases are from the teacher's gestures, from curves on the blackboard, or even by looking at a book? If he observes and recognizes quarter notes? If he is brought to understand that the 4/4 time signature indicates a march-like rhythmic beat? The very opposite is true, for developing insight means gain, not loss. A progressive grasp of musical concepts is essential to musical growth and to the deepening of appreciation. There is no reason why children should not begin to understand these concepts very early, and there are excellent reasons why they should. Even the vague and incomplete understanding which is all one should contemplate in the early years is impossible if all symbolism is excluded on some ill-judged principle.

(b) How can one tell when the alleged "music reading readiness" has, in fact, been consummated? The answer is simple. One cannot tell! Language reading experts have devised elaborate testing devices to ascertain the developmental level of individuals, and even about these tests certain doubts may well arise. But in music education there is nothing comparable at all. The proper time to terminate the "music reading readiness stage" is sheer guesswork. And what is not a guess but a certainty is that children will not all reach the same developmental level at the same time.

(c) In actual practice, the notion of readiness as employed in music education tends to work out as a defense of triviality. Musical experiences must, at all costs, be pleasant, appealing, enticing. Superficiality is a matter of indifference so long as there is attractiveness. Now there is an important point here, for musical experiences certainly should and can be a pleasure. But music will not yield its richest pleasures if it is treated merely as happy play and if the fact that it is an organized art is ignored as a matter of policy. Musical growth turns upon a progressive and continuously developing realization of what music actually is. Therefore at least a dawning realization should come from the earliest years.

3. What our understanding of growth and development clearly seems to imply is a cyclical sequence or order of topics. This is a type of arrangement which has appeared in connection with a number of subject fields within recent years.

125

In a cyclical sequence, the various items that need to be presented do not occur once for all at some predetermined time. They appear again and again, always in new settings, always with added meanings. Thus, in elementary mathematics, the concept of *average* may appear six or eight times in the course of six years. At first it is a crude, vague, imperfect notion, though correct as far as it goes. At each recurrence there is a new context, a deeper meaning, wider implications and relationships, more precise definition, more extensive applications. And the techniques for dealing with it progressively emerge along with the progressively better and better understanding of the concept itself. The same plan is followed in the treatment of fractions, and indeed of all the concepts of elementary mathematics.

Such an arrangement is peculiarly well adapted to the curriculum in music. Reference has already been made to the treatment of the musical concept of the quarter note, and it may serve as an illustration here once more. At first the concept, associated with some symbol which may or may not be that of the standard notation, points up, identifies, and gives meaning to a certain recognizable rhythm which can be felt and heard, namely, the rhythm of the walking or marching step. At this level, the idea of "one-fourthness" need not be brought out at all. No more is needed than a way of thinking about and identifying a certain musicorhythmic experience and a symbol to use as a tool for such thinking. But the concept is repeatedly reintroduced, always with more clarification, always with more completeness. As quarter notes differentiate from other note lengths, the fractional designation begins to take on meaning. Then, perhaps later, the relationship of the quarter note to the time signature begins to be clarified, and understanding grows still more adequate. Always the concept is treated as it should be treated, namely, as one of the significant controls of organized musical behavior.

Exactly the same general plan is followed in dealing with all other musical concepts — the minor tonality, key and key signature, rests, phrase, and so on. They are first introduced at a very early level, but only with a deliberate indeterminateness and vagueness and lack of specificity. Their full significance emerges over a period of years, as a result of a variety of experiences and an increasing recognition of their interrelatedness. Such, in brief, is a cyclical curricular sequence. It has numerous and striking advantages, of which the following are the most noteworthy.

(a) In introducing significant musical concepts, there is not any need to wait for a supposititious moment when children will be "ready" to deal with them. They can occur in immature form very early indeed. For instance, it has been claimed that the teaching of the minor tonality should come quite late in the sequence. But an authentic feeling for the difference between major and minor can be established almost from the beginning. Then can come the contrast between the major and minor triads, the significance of the lowered third, the structure of the minor scale and its relationship to its variants, the tonic and relative major. Instead of teaching the minor tonality at some one predetermined point, it is, so to speak, spread out through a number of years. So also with all other musical concepts.

(b) A cyclical sequence meets the vexing and frustrating problem of grade placement. As soon as it is seen that any concept will occur many times, with added meaning, the way is open for a solution. Which concepts should be introduced first? When should each be introduced? When should each recur? How deeply and specifically should it be studied? The general answer is: Whenever any such concept has an important and significant function in music with which the children are dealing; whenever a grasp of any such concept will lead directly to a more adequate appreciation of music that is being heard or performed. Thus it is the musical content of the program that determines the presentation of musical concepts. Music is chosen for its own intrinsic worth, not for the sake of illustrating or teaching the so-called fundamentals. And the concepts needed for dealing with it better are developed as occasion suggests.

(c) A cyclical sequence greatly facilitates the teaching of music. This is of great importance now that so much music is being handled by teachers who are not music specialists. A person with slender music training may well hesitate to explain the minor scale or even the six-eight time signature. But with a little help and guidance such a person may feel entirely able to highlight the effect of the minor mode in a simple song or to emphasize and make clear the characteristic lilting effect of the six-eight time.

As a final question it may be asked how much musical competence a cyclical sequence is likely to produce at the end of the elementary-school or junior high school period. To be still more specific, will it yield any genuine independent music-reading ability? The answer is that it will probably not, but that it may be expected to produce a working insight into the musical organization which is quite sufficient to translate into independent and facile reading very readily indeed.

PLANNING THE PROGRAM TO PROMOTE MUSICAL GROWTH

Two final questions will serve to round out this discussion. What is the general character of a program planned and designed to promote musical growth? Why is the promotion of growth in music important?

A good deal has been said about the nature of the operating program, but a comprehensive statement may be illuminating. The program contemplated will consist of a great variety of musical experiences. Many of them will be spontaneous. Many of them will be informal, even casual. Many of them will arise in connection with social occasions or with units of work in other fields. But some of them will certainly be preplanned with great care and deliberately scheduled. An essential requirement will be that such experiences are of prevailingly high musical quality; for musical growth depends upon the use of music which has a strong appeal because of its worth, and which also repays study because of its worth. Through such experiences, when given their full musical and developmental significance, there will be a constant, sequential teaching and study of the conceptual patterns that constitute the basic structure of the musical art.

The broad administrative implications of such a program are fairly clear. It requires wide co-operation throughout the school. A sufficient body of musical experiences is not possible without the active co-operation of classroom teachers and general teachers. But the development of the quite essential conceptualizations, and the sequential program necessarily implied, are not possible without specialist service. Both generalist and specialist are necessary for an effective program centering on musical growth.

Why is such a program desirable? Why is it important to promote musical growth? This is our second question. It is a cogent one today, for there are some who would deny that such a program is desirable, claiming that musical growth is important only for the few. Their view would be that music is a pleasure and should be so treated. It should be used as an attractive interlude, as an occasional illustration of other topics and other subjects, for its socializing potential, for rest and recreation, for stimulation, and so forth. Often they refer to these as the "therapeutic" uses of music, and they consider them enough.

There is a simple and decisive answer. Education has to do not only with the present but also with the future. The time, the effort, the money we spend on education are not only for the purpose of creating a congenial environment for children and young people here and now but also for the purpose of establishing elevating and lasting values in their lives. How children and young people live today is indeed important. But as educators we are also concerned about how they will live twenty years from now. This also must be the concern of music educators. To deny it is nothing less than a wholesale repudiation of the educational significance of music itself.

Unquestionably, music can be a great and constructive influence in life. Our purpose, as music educators, is to realize this possibility, and above all to make music a *lasting*, constructive influence. This is the central meaning of our work; if it is repudiated, then our work has no meaning. It is, perhaps, just possible to say that we wish to bring to bear the therapeutic potential of music. But if so, it must be a life-long therapy, not only an immediate one.

However, the very notion of therapy is unfortunate, for it is negative, suggesting cure. What we contemplate is the establishment of an elevating, strengthening, ennobling, consoling, lifelong influence, which music can certainly exert.

The only way in which we can hope to accomplish this is by inaugurating a process which can move forward strongly during the school years, and which has good prospect of continuing on when school years are past. This is the process of musical growth. It will be frustrated by mechanical formalism. But it will be frustrated just as disastrously by treating music as a mere classroom amenity, an appendage, an entertainment. Immediate musical experiences should certainly be enjoyable. The contrary is unthinkable. But always children and young people should have revealed to them that there are heights and depths of musical enjoyment still to be explored, still to be attained. This, in essence, is what is involved in musical growth. What is contemplated is the present revelation of the beauty, the appeal, the potentialities of music, while at the same time the way is opened to a continuing and indeed never-ending advance, so that these beauties, this appeal, these potentialities become the benefit and consolation of a lifetime.

NOTES

1. James L. Mursell, *Developmental Teaching*. New York: McGraw-Hill Book Co., 1949.

2. See Arnold Gesell and Frances L. Ilg, *The Child from Five to Ten*. New York: Harper & Bros., 1946.

3. No doubt in all such cases, and particularly the last, complex, subtle, and numerous psychological blockages may be present. But the broad statement stands.

4. The present writer has frequently declared that music has an emotional *meaning*, i.e., that it can arouse highly specific ways of feeling.

5. "Note values" — quarter note, half note, etc. — are excellent examples of the symbolic superiority of the notation over language, for the use of the fractional designations is highly confusing.

6

Music Education Philosophy
and Psychology After Mursell

Bennett Reimer

The word *after* in the title of this chapter is meant to have two meanings: following Mursell's death, and as a consequence of his life. James L. Mursell (1893–1963) was, I believe, a giant in the history of music education. He was, no doubt, the most influential thinker of his time in both philosophy and psychology of music education, and his points of view in both areas have exerted continuing influence. Although I was never privileged to meet him, his writings were so influential on my own developing views about the theory and practice of music education, and they have so pervaded the continued growth of those views, as to make me feel that he was, intellectually, both my mentor and companion. It is with a deep sense of respect, and with no small measure of humility, that I approach the assignment to reflect on what has occurred in music education since he wrote his summative chapter for the 1958 *Basic Concepts in Music Education.*

My comments will focus on the two most characteristic viewpoints defining Mursell's thinking: in philosophy, the notion of music's "inner, living essence," and in psychology, the notion of "musical growth." These two ideas, pervasive in all his writings, are intimately connected to each other. To understand the profundity and unity of his conception of music education (underneath his occasional digressions), one must grasp their interrelations in the fullness of their many implications.

In one sense the conception is simple and elegant: all music is characterized by an essence relating to its power to structure feeling intelligently, and musical growth is the gradual process by which musical structure can be more fully experienced. In another sense, each aspect of the concept is so complex as to defy full comprehension, and the interrelation of the two compounds that complexity infinitely. Having spent most of my career in pursuit of some clarity about each idea and their interactions, I am in little need of persuasion about their intractability. So my attempt in this chapter shall be in the nature of "once more into the fray." We are, after all, dealing here with the two essential issues relating to music education: the nature of music and the nature of education. That Mursell dealt so persuasively and clearheadedly with both is testament to his stature. That they remain unresolved is demonstration that they will bedevil every new generation of music educators devoted to making the teaching and learning of music as significant as those endeavors deserve to be.

IS THERE AN "ESSENCE" OF MUSIC?

For Mursell, of course, there certainly is. That essence is the power of tones to capture the structures of emotion. "Of all the sensory media," he says, "tone is most closely connected with emotion. This is a psychological fact. Thus music is the most purely and typically emotional of all the arts. Here we find its essence. This must be our chief clue to its proper educational treatment, for it is the central secret of its human appeal and its power in the lives of men."[1] But "emotional," for Mursell, is not in any sense to be construed as relating to that which one happens to be undergoing subjectively in one's life at the moment one is interacting with music. That would entirely miss the power of what music does. Emotion is not connected to tones in an arbitrary or extrinsic way. The specificity of how tones are creatively formed into meaningful structures specifies that which must be experienced when encountering tonal structures. The elements of music — melody, rhythm, dynamics, harmony, and so on — are ordered in ways that are musically valid and cause feelings that are dependent on the musical conditions that arouse them. The feelings caused by the music are ineffable. Because they come from tones in structures, rather than from situations in ordinary life, the feelings caused by music are not literal. Yet they are "meaningful" in profound ways because no other medium can duplicate the power of tone to mediate feelings organized by human intelligence and creativity.

The capacity to respond to musical meaning is, for Mursell, inborn. He calls it "musicality." In his chapter "Growth Processes in Music Education" (Chapter 5), he says, "Psychologically speaking, the whole art of music depends upon the existence in human nature of a mental function to which has been attached the convenient term 'musicality.' Musicality may be defined as responsiveness to the tonal and rhythmic patterns which are the substance of the art of music. So far as we can tell, it is universal, or very nearly so, among human beings" (p. 116). The ability to garner musical meaning is dependent on the exercise of musicality to probe within the structures presented by a piece of music: "Music undoubtedly does have great emotion-arousing effectiveness and, indeed, a highly specific emotional impact. But it has such an effect not simply because of its content but because of its organization. Without organization, music would simply cease to be. So progressively more adequate grasp of musical organization is the very heart and center of progressively more adequate appreciation" (p. 121).

Why should we be concerned to share with all humans the meanings music uniquely mediates? There are lasting benefits in human life, Mursell believes, from experiencing the depths and breadths of feeling that music makes available. Some of those benefits, for him, are social, in that musical involvements make people better members of society. (At various times in his career Mursell emphasized particular societal benefits of music education.) But the primary benefit is personal: "Unquestionably, music can be a great and constructive influence in life. Our purpose, as music educators, is to realize this possibility, and above all to make music a *lasting*, constructive influence. This is the central meaning of our work; if it is repudiated, then our work has no meaning. . . . What we contemplate is the establishment of an elevating, strengthening, ennobling, consoling, lifelong influence, which music can certainly exert" (p. 128).

Two important issues are raised by Mursell's arguments. First, how, precisely, do tonal structures, attended to as such, cause percipients to experience them not simply as tones in various arrangements but to experience them "emotionally"? Those familiar with the history of aesthetics in general and the history of musical aesthetics in particular will recognize this as the most-asked question in these fields. It has been asked since the time of the ancient Greeks and continues to occupy a major — perhaps the largest — portion of aesthetic thinking to this day, both about all art and specifically about music. Indeed, it can be argued that the history of aesthetics can be read and understood as the history of attempts to answer this question. It can also be persuasively argued that there is little reason to believe that the end of that history will occur during the short time in which we happen to be alive.

Mursell did not attempt to answer the question. He did what most thinkers about music do whose careers are not focused on solving that age-old conundrum, which is to accept as a given that music causes us to feel and to go on from there: "When we listen to and enter into music we are carried away into a world of feeling. The music possesses us, flows through us, and sweeps us along with it."[2] That is not an explanation, of course; it is a description. So be it. What is important for Mursell is not to attempt to explain what no other human before or since has been able to explain, but to clarify that what "possesses us" when we encounter music is not any particular associations with life outside music (although these can be implicated) but the sounds themselves in their intrinsically organized musical context. That, for him, is sufficient to (1) establish the essential nature of music and (2) suggest how education should be conducted in accordance with that essential nature.

The second issue raised by Mursell's views has to do with the nature of musical emotion itself, putting aside the probably unanswerable question of how structured sounds give rise to it. Here we have an issue that, while as ancient as the first, has turned a major historical corner since the 1950s, when Susanne K. Langer, in a series of books culminating in her three-volume *Mind: An Essay on Human Feeling*,[3] pioneered important advances over the previously influential "expression of emotion" theories stemming from nineteenth-century romanticism. Langer's works (heavily influenced by the thinking of Ernst Casirer), beginning with her explanation of "symbolic transformation" as the characteristic quality of human mentality, and ranging over a host of related issues as she struggled to refine her insights, gave rise to a veritable explosion of scholarship relating to human subjectivity as being far broader, far deeper, far more complex, far more implicated in intelligent interactions with the world than the more narrowly focused "emotion" theories she so thoroughly criticized and found so repugnant. Music, Langer argued, is a mode of human thinking and knowing, and its forms mediate a realm of mindful experience unavailable through ordinary language. That realm of experience is the realm of conscious awareness, or sentience, from which all functions of the human mind stem. The emotions, she insisted, were not, as the romantics tended to think, the subject matter of music. Rather, music potentially can represent, in its dynamic forms, all possible ways that the human mind is itself dynamic.

These insights, and the work of so many aestheticians, philosophers, and psychologists who were influenced by them and who built upon them and refined and corrected them, have had profound consequences for music education, beginning during Mursell's last years but achieving practical applications only since his death. The 1960s were a turning point in music education history largely because these ideas began to liberate the field from the philosophical restrictions under which it had previously labored. The new ideas from aesthetics, combined with the dramatic advances in education of the 1960s, allowed music education to take the first, crucial steps toward a redefinition of its nature and its functions, a redefinition soon to be given the name "aesthetic education."

What are new ways of conceiving the "essence" of music as a result of Langer's (and others') pioneering contributions? It is not possible to give a simple answer to such a question because the corner that was turned with her help led to a vista so open with possibilities that many years — if not decades — will be needed to explore them. Part of that exploration included some careful, critical examinations of the gaps and holes in Langer's thinking — a necessary step in consolidating the gains and moving forward. But having demonstrated the imperfections in her ability to explain the old questions — how sounds relate to feeling and the nature of feeling — the work began to turn toward the questions of how aesthetic responsiveness is mindful, and how aesthetic engagement of the self with intrinsically structured sound-events produces meaning. Feeling, in the older sense of emotion or as always emotion-related, is not as such the content of music or the sole determining characteristic of the experience of music. But feeling more broadly defined as subjective involvement is implicated in intelligent interactions with music, whether composing, performing, or listening. Feeling is itself a cognitive component of the act of structuring musical sounds. The experience of structured musical sounds, including subjective engagement as a necessary component, is also an act of cognition — a remaking in the self of structures of meanings as these particular sounds (this particular musical event) mediate them.

One helpful way to conceive the characteristics of aesthetic encounters was suggested by Monroe C. Beardsley, who posited that five features were implicated. The first was necessary and at least three others were required: object directedness, felt freedom, detached affect, active discovery, and wholeness.[4] Another dimension of aesthetic interactions — the cultural embeddedness on which they depend — was emphasized by John Blacking. Music, he argued, is "a sharing of inner feelings in a social context through extensions of body movement, in which certain species-specific capabilities are modified and extended through social and cultural experience."[5]

Nelson Goodman, in his attempts to develop a general theory of symbols, argued that each art manipulates its particular system of symbols. The experience of music, when it is aesthetic rather than not aesthetic, will be marked by five criterial attributes: syntactic density, semantic density, relative repleteness, exemplification, and multiple and complex reference. To experience a work of music aesthetically is a cognitive achievement in which "the emotions function cognitively: in organizing a world, felt contrasts and kinships, both subtle and salient, are no less important than those seen or inferred."[6] Further, the experience of music requires feeling to discern what properties the music possesses: "Emotional numbness disables here as definitely if not as completely as . . . deafness."[7]

Phenomenologists added another set of concepts to emerging understandings of the breadth and depth of musical experience, in their attempts to study the nature of experience itself as the basic datum from which explanations might arise. The "essence" of music is, in fact, the guiding concept for understanding music, according to this orientation to philosophical inquiry: "A phenomenological description concentrates not on facts, but upon essences, and attempts to discover what there is about an object and its experience which is essential (or necessary) if the object and its experience is to be recognized at all."[8] Musical experience, according to Thomas Clifton, includes several essential features: the "essence" of time; the "essence" of space; the element of play; and the element of feeling, which includes acts of belief, freedom, caring, and willing, all contributing to what he calls "possession." Musical expression requires a reciprocal relation, or a "collaboration" between the sounds and the experiencer: "This collaboration cannot be achieved without the necessary constitutive activities of feeling and understanding."[9]

Several useful ideas emerge from contemporary analyses of musical experience such as these. Feeling, it would seem, continues to be a central concept but has now been fully separated from pre-Langerian expression theories. Beardsley's "object directedness" criterion focuses attention on the condition that the musical object itself, with its phenomenally objective properties of qualities and relations, determines what is experienced affectively (a carrying forward of Langer's concept of embodiment). The social context of what is experienced in music cannot be separated from that which is perceived in music, Blacking argues. But what is perceived within the cultural traditions of a particular societal group can nevertheless be compared with and at a certain level be equated with what is perceived by other people in other cultures. Underneath particular societal subjectivities is a "deep structure" common to all humanity, Blacking asserts, accounting for our ability to be moved by music from cultures other than our own and from times other than our own.

All engagements with music, no matter the style or cultural context, are marked by five defining criteria, Goodman proposes, and the functioning of those criteria in musical experience requires "emotion" as a unifying force. And all musical experience, Clifton adds, requires a possession by the self, in which time, space, play, and feeling are essential elements.

A specifically musical-theoretical orientation to such notions of "essences" is added by Fred Lerdahl and Ray Jackendoff, who attempt to describe the workings of musical intuition (the largely unconscious structures of the mind that an experienced listener brings to a musical engagement). Building on ideas from cognitive psychology, these theorists attempt to describe innate structures of musical understanding that will yield universal principles of musical grammar. They posit four components of music that may qualify: grouping structure, metrical structure, time span reduction, and prolongational reduction. Within each there are two types of rules applied by the listener — well-formedness rules and preference rules. Although these components and rules apply largely to pitch and rhythm, other dimensions of music — dynamics, tone color, motivic and thematic processes — also contribute to the hierarchical structuring of pieces. All musical experience, they hypothesize, requires perceivers endowed by nature with structures of cognition on which musical structures depend. Music theory, as the endeavor to explore the mental constructs entailed in creating and experiencing music, "takes a place among traditional areas of cognitive psychology such as theories of vision and language."[10]

Obviously, the ideas presented here, from among scores of others that could be included, represent an agenda "in process." But that has always been the case; there is likely never to be a conclusion to this ongoing process. Music education is obligated to reflect, in its practices, the most cogent ideas extant about how music works and how it is understood to be experienced and therefore how it can be taught in ways relevant to how it is conceived at the time those practicing music education are plying their trade. To some degree the music education profession at present has been influenced by current thinking and has attempted to apply it in its practices. But of course much more needs to be done to bring educational applications into better synchronization with current theory.

Several crucial advances in music education were in fact made in the 1960s and 1970s as a result of the "opening up" of thinking as influenced by Langer and her successors. The most striking advance was the acceptance into schools of the great diversity of musical styles constituting the "supermarket" of American musical culture. There were some strong negative reactions, of course, to the new initiatives to fully represent in school what was actually going on musically outside school. The older view, tied to assumptions relating to "proper" feelings and therefore "proper" styles, was, after all, pervasive, and it led many to be dismayed that "improper" music — jazz, popular musics, ethnic musics — were getting their foot into the schoolhouse door. Among the invading styles were the new (to many music educators, at any rate) avant-garde experiments so prevalent in the 1960s and 1970s, which further compounded the sense of discomfort with the breaking down of the orderly musical world of "school music" the profession had built. How could all this stuff be reconciled with traditional school literature, which tended to be limited to pleasant songs and judicious selections from the "classics" and "near classics"? Was all this so-called music, associated with cultures not necessarily WASP, not necessarily "serious," not necessarily to be heard in concert halls, and not necessarily respectful of the great classical-romantic tradition to be (1) mastered sufficiently by teachers so that they would be able to handle it, and (2) made freely available to all children rather than *protecting* children from it?

In my *A Philosophy of Music Education,* first edition (1970), I urged music educators to do more about opening themselves and their students to the many musics our culture embraced:

> The music used in music education, at all levels and in all activities, should be good music, which means genuinely expressive music. Because of the belief that only certain *kinds* of expressiveness are good, music education has tended to use music which is generally "polite"; which is safe, bland, sweet, well-behaved, these qualities reflecting the values of most educators. But if music education is to widen children's understanding of the possibilities of human responsiveness, a more open, free-wheeling, more adventuresome attitude needs to be taken toward "proper" musical materials. Music of the many ethnic and cultural groups in American society, music of the past and much more music of the present, music of various types — jazz, pop, folk, as well as concert — all should be considered "proper" sources for finding expressive music.[11]

Although progress was made in this regard over the next couple of decades, I was not sufficiently satisfied with it to delete this admonition from the book's second edition (1989). Nevertheless, if emerging ideas of aesthetic education had done nothing else, they at least have helped break down the previous assumptions linking "good music" to the pre–twentieth-century music of the elite. Such assumptions were simply no longer tenable when it was recognized that *all* musics mediate meaning and *each* music adds to the sum total of musical meaning available to be experienced and shared.

One ploy used to combat the emerging acceptance of the musical validity of various nonestablishment musics was to insist that such musics were not, after all, to be regarded as truly musical, or to be assessed as such. Their value, function, and status were not such as to allow them to be regarded as being as inherently musical — as valid as sources for genuinely musical experiences — as were the accepted styles. So they had to be judged on nonmusical bases. Whereas "serious" music has always been assessed on criteria such as those relating to musical craftsmanship, musical sensitivity, musical imagination, and musical genuineness, such criteria could not possibly be applied to the more rowdy, spontaneous, and unpredictable styles suddenly appearing as if out of nowhere (many music educators had become so insulated from the musical realities among which they lived). Was jazz, for example, to be understood as requiring craftsmanship? Well, said the traditionalist, not if craftsmanship is defined as that which is learned by instrumentalists at conservatories preparing them for orchestral positions. Does jazz require musical sensitivity? Well, they said, not to the subtleties of a Mozartian phrase. Does jazz depend on imagination? Well, maybe, but certainly of an unrefined sort. And can jazz be regarded as an authentic style with its own history, conventions, literature, masterworks? Well, was the counterargument, how could that be compared with the history, conventions, literature, and masterworks of the great classical-romantic tradition?

A second contribution of aesthetic education was to reject the idea that such comparisons are valid. This is not easy to accomplish, because elitist assumptions, whether overt or covert or unconscious, are pervasive among music educators — even among those who think they are antielitist. It is difficult to convince such people that a particular music can be essentially musical and be assessed as such, despite differences from the one style of music assumed to be the "ideal." It is hard for such people to recognize that there is no single, prototypal music that is ideal or exemplary and that solely deserves to be judged or understood as therefore musical. Instead, within each musical stylistic-cultural domain, the very same musical standards are in operation. But that domain itself defines the parameters of goodness as it applies those standards. It is condescending in the extreme — it is, in fact, elitist — to deny to any style the right to be regarded as essentially musical and to not allow particular works in that style to be judged as being more or less successful according to basic musical standards as they are applied in ways that are relevant to that particular style. Musical styles can be compared in many useful ways — useful because they heighten awareness of the similarities and differences among them and therefore make each more accessible for experience. What is to be avoided, I would argue, are comparisons of which style is "better" or "really musical." Those comparisons, I think, are irrelevant and useless.

But what about those musics outside of the broad Western tradition, which itself includes a multitude of styles such as those I have been discussing? This question, also, was raised by the burgeoning movement toward comprehensiveness caused by the new ideas of aesthetic education in the two decades following the publication of *Basic Concepts, I.* The profession recognized that it had neglected musics from outside the West. Because of the shrinking of the world, and because of the increasing presence within the United States of many enclaves from countries outside the West, whose children were altering the cultural landscape of schools, we had better, in addition to everything else, pay attention to the musics of traditions other than our own.

At the practical level, we could get away with activities giving a nod to different cultures — "folk songs from many lands" (with guitar or piano or Orff accompaniments, of course), a few recordings to demonstrate how quaint such music is, a drum activity to teach African rhythms (in 4/4), and so forth. We must be sympathetic to the plight of music teachers in those years (especially general music teachers) who, in a very short span of time, had a load of expectations heaped on them with which their education and musical background had ill prepared them to cope. MENC (Music Educators National Conference) responded with convention sessions, and universities began to offer workshops. It was not unusual to see music teachers, carrying sacks full of strange ethnic instruments, staggering from session to session, bewildered and increasingly insecure, trying their best to become "multi-cultural."

The issues here, of course, are complex. At one extreme, differences among world musics can be so neglected in favor of universals that the distinctiveness of particular musical beliefs and practices gets washed out, leaving a bland stew with no contrasting flavors. At the other extreme, differences can be so exaggerated that qualities characterizing music as being recognizably music no matter the cultural setting are no longer perceived, leaving no room for the recognition that musical intelligence is both ubiquitous and manifold in application. We will have to resolve those thorny issues somewhere in between the extremes, no doubt, balancing our recognition that music is an identifiable art practiced by peoples at all times and in all places, with the equally urgent recognition that differing belief systems and practices make facile correspondences untenable. We will have to accomplish this balancing act within a basic commitment to our own Western culture as foundational for us (as other cultures will have to do with theirs). At the same time we will have to keep our world perspective honest by using an understanding of transcultural aspects of music as a way to better appreciate the intracultural aspects of selected musics from around the world.

The fact is that music is inherently paradoxical. Every piece of music is, in some important respects, like every other piece of music in sharing the essential nature of sounds as humanly meaningful. Yet every piece of music is, in some other important respects, meaningful within a set of culturally determined parameters. Further, every piece of music is, in still other significant respects, unlike any other piece of music in that it is a particular, incomparable event with a unified, unique being. To represent music honestly, educators must highlight all three aspects, for neglecting any of them neglects an essential dimension of the nature of music. This may seem a daunting task, but to ignore the issue would be to hide our heads in the sand. Our treatment of music in schools will have to reflect its complexity as it really exists, and our teachers will have to be helped to understand this complexity in order to embody it in their instruction. That task remains to be accomplished more successfully.

The same principles apply to another issue that the decade following 1958 attempted to address — the proper role in schools of the broad field of the arts, and the obligation to recognize that music was part of this broader field. Here, as we might have expected, efforts to ameliorate the longstanding

139

isolation of music from its larger family by including occasional arts lessons in general music materials, and projecting possibilities for cooperative efforts among the various professional art-in-education fields, caused some people to swing wildly to the extreme of equating one art with another, as if each had no identity requiring it to be treated as autonomous as well as related. As with musics of different cultures, the key to treating the arts authentically, I think, is to use the transaesthetic characteristics of the arts as a means to probe for deeper appreciation of the particularities of *each* art. It would seem strange to argue that learning about various musics from around the world, as each manifests both shared and unique musical qualities, would weaken any particular music or the ability to understand and enjoy any particular music. It would seem just as strange to argue that doing the same with the arts (both from the West and from the rest of the world) would injure the integrity of any art or impede people's ability to enjoy each for what it is.

I suspect that the fears of comprehensive approaches to curriculum development in the arts are similar if not identical to those about including in music education many styles beyond the "established," whether from within the Western tradition or outside it. It is the fear associated with being conservative, self-protective, elitist (usually sub rosa). Yes, there are dangers in opening one's field to new learnings and new challenges. But our future would seem bleak if we did not have the courage to do so and the intelligence to do so properly.

An important guideline in this continuing endeavor, I would argue, is to honor the essence of music as it is understood in each period of ongoing history, as Mursell tried to do in his period and as we try to do with new insights occurring since he contributed his seminal thinking. That "essence" does not limit music or our experience of music; it guides us to appreciate both the staggering diversity of music as music and the remarkable ability we have to share the cognitions mediated by each particular musical style and each particular musical culture. Music education, I think, needs to be far more comprehensive among various musics and the various arts than we were able to be previously, sharing with our students that which is musical as it exists in the real world of their own culture, in other cultures, and in the larger aesthetic domain of which it is an essential part.

HOW CAN WE BEST PROMOTE "MUSICAL GROWTH"?

More consistently than in any other aspect of his thinking, James Mursell embraced an organismic, wholistic psychology of education, the roots of which reach back to the early insights of Gestalt psychology. Just as each individual has the capacity for musicality, intrinsic to being human, each also has the inborn capacity to grow in musicality. For Mursell that means that all planned interactions with music must honor and preserve the essentially musical character of such interactions. Therefore, engagements of students with music should always be centered on the inner, feelingful experience of the music, and should not be centered on the outer, technical, contributory aspects of music as is so often done in the name of music education. Mursell felt strongly that not only is it mistaken educationally to separate and teach in isolation the technical dimensions of music such as notation, key signatures, interval relations, rhythm configurations, instrument skills, and so on, but it is also antimusical at best and inhumane at worst.

His nemesis, in this regard, for which he had a distaste bordering on revulsion, was associationistic psychology, or what we would call behaviorism. Both the premises and tactics of associationism are misguided, he argued passionately. The human mind does not operate by accumulating specific connections (as later computer models of mentality were to posit), and attempts to teach according to a regimen of reinforced connections of particular stimuli with particular responses arranged in step-by-step fashion are doomed to failure. That is because such regimens are inherently foreign to human mental functioning and are also inherently inimical to the nature of music. It is a myth, he argues, that specific associations will accumulate or that behavior change will result, and attempts to shore up the myth by including planned reviews of past associations are not availing, for what was learned this way, and then forgotten, will only be forgotten again after review. Repetition is also fruitless as a basic device to cement associations, and its excessive use makes education a sterile and uncreative task. Mechanistic or atomistic psychologies, for Mursell, are simply wrongheaded, have no positive place in education, are hostile to genuine musical learning and musical experience, and should be expunged from music education.

All of these objections, of course, were based on his general understanding of how the human mind works and how it processes music rather than on a research literature that clarified how this or that learning could best be promoted. Mursell was steeped in the organismic psychologies of his time and rejected the Thorndikian views also current, but music education research was not yet available to more carefully define and explore the issues of musical learning he raised. This is not to say that if he were writing today he would be able to base his ideas on a secure foundation of music education research informing him of which learnings are best produced by which teachings. Such a foundation does not yet exist, and given the history of education research as a whole, is not likely to exist in the foreseeable future.

Yet it might have been possible for him to retain his fundamental value system about music and about people while taking a more balanced view as to the levels and dimensions of musical learning amenable to various teaching strategies. That is, he might have found it possible to be more accepting of behavioristic interventions within his general developmental posture, rather than seeing any incursion of such techniques as being a threat to the total music education endeavor.

That endeavor, according to Mursell, must be marked by several essential characteristics. It must always work from "inside" (the experience of music's affective power) to "outside" (the means by which control over musical tasks in performing, listening, composing, and so on is achieved). There is a continuity in musical growth determined by and governed according to the particular nature of music, which is therefore always, at every point in the learning process, characterized by the development of sensitivity to meaningfully structured sounds. Each subject has its internal veracity as a subject and that veracity must be the key to how each subject is treated educationally. Because musicality (defined above) is the core of music, "the purpose of all music teaching must be to bring about the evolution of musical responses or musicality. . . . Moreover, the purpose remains the same at all levels of maturity, for the reason that the essential nature of musicality remains the same" (p. 116).

In detailed applications of this principle Mursell discusses music reading, music theory, and "manipulative technique" and asserts his conviction that although all are necessary as part of musical learning, each can be learned as an outgrowth of musical experience rather than as skills separated from their meaning within musical experience. The noticing of significant details in music, the interplay of musical differentiations and integrations, the use of musical concepts (high, low, loud, soft, scale, key, phrase, and so on) to help organize our understanding of and therefore our ability to appreciate the inner workings of music, and the self-discovery of how music achieves its nature are all essential aspects of developmental learning. And the curriculum must preserve the constancy of musical experience in its sequence. Music itself must provide the sequence of learnings, including conceptual learnings about the music. The basic principle for curriculum sequence, according to Mursell, is to choose good and appropriate music and to teach all one can about that music, including technical mastery of its performance, its notation, its theory, and its structure. These are among the highlights of his dense and detailed explanation of musical growth; this chapter summarizes a lifetime of his writings on these matters.

What would Mursell think of developments in the teaching of music and in the larger realm of education psychology since the early 1960s? My remarks will focus briefly on two aspects of this development — conceptual approaches to curriculum organization and the rise and fall of behaviorism in music education — and somewhat more fully on the present reorientation of education as a result of advances in cognitive psychology. Each of these, of course, is worthy of several books (many of which have already been written), so my comments will necessarily have to be taken as merely suggestive.

The curriculum organization principle Mursell proposed — choosing music first and then learning whatever could be learned from the chosen pieces, turned out to be insufficient for building a coherent teaching-learning structure in the general music segment of the program (about which he primarily was writing). This was brought home by the major ideas of the curriculum reform movement of the 1960s, which were that for general education in any subject to be successful, the learnings in that subject had to focus on the intrinsic structure of meanings and operations as they defined the nature of that subject. Further, the sequences of learnings in a subject should be determined by its inherent structural characteristics and should reappear constantly in a growing, widening spiral of complexity and sophistication.

The latter of these two principles was entirely in consonance with what Mursell had argued for decades — that musical learnings should be cyclical in nature, always revolving around and further illuminating the "essence" of what makes music musical. Indeed, his prescience in this matter (and, as we shall see, in the matter of emphasizing higher-order rather than lower-order mental operations) was striking.

It was the first principle, having to do with organizational choices, that had to be altered. Choosing pieces (songs, listenings) and then learning about them gave little or no control over developmental processes of understanding, perceiving, appreciating, or performing. What had to occur was a shift in the mechanism of content selection in which the concept to be addressed — some significant aspect of music whether its elements, its organizational principles, its style characteristics, its nature as an art, how people interact with it, and so forth — became the focal point for a teaching-learning episode of shorter or longer duration, and in which the music employed was illustrative of the conceptual organizer. In addition, of course, the music chosen had to be of a complexity appropriate to the capacities of the children to perform it if that was desired, of a subtlety able to be perceived and enjoyed if listening was the focus, and of a broad-ranging stylistic representation so that the essential musical characteristics would be seen to operate diversely in a great variety of different musics. Further, the choice of music should represent good examples of each style and type. This required, of course, some stable, universal criteria of goodness, as explained in the first section of this chapter. These criteria must be applied within the stylistic parameters of each different musical setting and be exemplified successfully by each individual piece, making it a musically convincing example of its type.

These represent formidable criteria for curriculum building, but impressive advances were made, I believe, in applying them. Comprehensive approaches to general music, such as represented by the MENC publication *The Study of Music in the Elementary School — A Conceptual Approach* (1967),[12] and by the textbook series appearing in the late 1960s and 1970s, went a long way toward fulfilling many if not most of these ideas, bringing music education into synchronization with the major advances in general educational theory forged during those years.

But a flaw in the system developed, based on a misunderstanding of what "a conceptual approach" implied. Because instructional units focused on particular concepts (various aspects of melody, rhythm, tone color, form, style, societal roles, creative processes, and so on), the assumption was sometimes made that conceptual learning in and of itself was the goal of music instruction. Conceptualization, understood in its traditional, well-established, widely agreed-upon sense as explained and outlined in the "Cognitive Domain" phase of the Bloom *Taxonomy of Educational Objectives*,[13] seemed to some to be the *end product*, rather than a *means*, of musical learning. This turned the intention on its head, of course, because the desired end was not the learning of definitions and principles for their own sake, but to use them as ways to get closer to the inherently musical perceptions and reactions constituting musical experience as such.

Such experience is essentially and profoundly different from conceptualization as that term is generally understood. Mursell knew that, of course, as did those who used concepts as curriculum organizers in ways he did not himself propose. Yet the confusion developed. I attempted to do some straightening out in an article in the *Journal of Aesthetic Education*[14] and in my revised *Philosophy*,[15] where I contrasted conceptualization in its most widely recognized meaning (as employed by the influential Bloom *Taxonomy*) with the "perceptual structuring" process inherent to musical interactions. In perceptually structuring music — in experiencing music — concepts used to call attention to various musical phenomena are not "thought about" but instead are "thought with."

Despite whether or not this attempt is entirely sufficient or effective, it does call attention to the potential misuse of a powerful idea. The idea itself remains valid, I suggest, and is now beginning to find its way into thinking about how the performance program might be organized to be something more than the rehearsal of pieces chosen solely on the basis of their role in building effective concert programs. Conceptual organizations of curricula also have enormous potential for unifying comprehensive arts programs as well as music programs. If such attempts are made, they will have to take into account the possible flaw of confusing means with ends, and they will have to guard against this reversal by making it eminently clear that in art, verbal conceptual learnings can contribute to aesthetic knowing but do not constitute such knowing.

During the period from the middle 1960s to the middle 1970s, when curriculum reform principles from education in general began to be applied to music education in systematic ways, a second, largely contradictory influence arose both in education as a whole and in music education in particular — a resurgence of reliance on behavioristic techniques and ideas as a basis for curriculum. This manifested itself in a variety of thrusts, including competency-based teacher education and performance-based teacher education, accountability conceived as improvement in measurable learnings, behavioral objectives as a major if not the major device for structuring learning, standardized testing, programmed learning, and so forth. Just as a great many music educators were drawn to the comprehensiveness of curriculum building as suggested by Brunerian approaches, others were persuaded by the specificity and seeming objectivity of Skinnerian approaches. A breach of significant proportions developed, reflecting in microcosm the larger dichotomy in education psychology between those for whom wholes must dominate and those for whom parts are the essence of learning.

There is no question about where Mursell would have taken his stand in this controversy, or how strongly he would have taken it. For him the rise of behavioristic thinking in music education would have been the realization of his worst fears, and no doubt he would have contributed eloquently to the debate, painful as it would have been for him to have had to. He would have, I think, added significantly to the many criticisms of behavioral conceptions of education, culminating most notably in the book *Regaining Educational Leadership: Critical Essays on PBTE/CBTE, Behavioral Objectives and Accountability*.[16] Here, in nineteen essays by writers including J. Myron Atkin, Harry Broudy, Michael W. Apple, Ernest R. House, Maxine Greene, and Elliot W. Eisner, the damages inflicted on education by the technological, teaching-by-training model advanced by proponents of behaviorism were assessed. In particular, Eisner's chapter titled "Do Behavioral Objectives and Accountability Have a Place in Art?" raised serious issues relating to the deleterious effects on aesthetic learnings produced by the behavioral theories of Robert Mager, Ralph W. Taylor, and Robert Gagne (among others). Such theories, Eisner argued, being entirely focused on convergent learnings, misrepresent and deter the expressive and creative learnings the arts exist to foster. And that which is learned about art is chosen on the basis of not what art itself suggests is most important about it, but of what a particular technology of teaching allows to be taught. As Robert Gagne put it, "Once objectives have been defined, there is no step in curriculum design that can legitimately be entitled 'selecting content.'"[17] When education becomes driven by a mechanical model such as this, Eisner asserts, artistic values go out the window.

Protesting voices such as heard in this book began to be raised more frequently, but the fall of behaviorism and of the "learning theory" it spawned was far more advanced in the field of psychology, where it had lost credibility as early as the 1950s,[18] than in the field of education. That it had become a dead issue theoretically was signaled by the psychologists who were invited to participate in the Ann Arbor symposia of 1978 and 1979, who rejected the original title that used the term "Learning Theory" and insisted that it be called "The Applications of Psychology to the Teaching and Learning of Music" instead. The theoretical demise of behaviorism is well described in Howard Gardner's *The Mind's New Science: A History of the Cognitive Revolution,*[19] and its practical waning has become more evident in the largely disappearing instances of programs in the schools based on behavioral objectives and all the other paraphernalia of "learning theory."

At this point the major remnant of behaviorism in education is the continued use of short-answer standardized tests as a basic way to assess the success of programs, teachers, and learners. Significant change in this situation seems likely, as evidenced by, for but one example, the recent conference on "The Uses of Standardized Tests in American Education" (in New York, October 28, 1989), at which speakers were so unrelentingly critical of present standardized testing practices and the assumptions on which they are built that they portrayed them as among the major obstacles to meaningful reform of American education. This conference was sponsored by, of all groups, the Educational Testing Service, which is the most successful purveyor of standardized tests, but which is also astute enough to know on which side its future bread is likely to be buttered.[20]

The major and perhaps sole visible remnant related to behaviorism in the K–12 music education curriculum (behavioristic thinking continues to exert influence in music education research but is waning there as a reflection of its significantly lessened status in education research) is in the work of Edwin E. Gordon, who is the most articulate remaining spokesperson for "learning theory," and whose attempts to apply it in practice are exemplified by his materials for grades 1 through middle school called *Jump Right In.*[21] Few materials in music education history are so precisely based on a specific theory of learning as are these, so those interested in the implications of applying this particular psychological theory of learning to classroom music practices will be well repaid by studying them.

One important reason for the fading of behaviorism was the resistance to it by many practicing educators, who may have been unacquainted with the theoretical issues that led to its being rejected but were nevertheless reluctant to apply it in any consequential way in their teaching because it seemed to diminish the meaningfulness of their subjects and of their work. But the major cause of its decline in psychology (save for its continued uses in clinical and experimental psychology) was the rise of cognitive conceptions of mentality. These are now so dominant in psychology, and have become so with such dramatic speed, as to deserve Gardner's characterization of a "revolution." The literature of cognitive science has become immense, its applications to education are occurring on broad fronts including major shifts in concepts about educational research, and its principles are being adapted to new understandings about how the art of music is processed by the mind.[22]

Of primary interest to music educators are the principles of learning now emerging from the work being carried on in the broader cognitive science domain. In what follows I will attempt to sketch what seem to be the most salient characteristics of a cognitivist approach to learning, each of them mentioning the contrasting behavioristic position.[23] Though I will not apply the characteristics directly to music education, the implications will be abundantly clear.

First, it should be mentioned that the criteria for what constitutes learning are generally agreed upon by both cognitivists and behaviorists, although each sees them somewhat differently. Both positions would define learning as requiring a change that occurs in an individual that is (1) the result of some sort of experience or occurrence in which the learner has been engaged, and (2) relatively long lasting. Cognitivists are primarily interested in changes that are inward, whereas behaviorists focus on changes that are outward. Items (1) and (2) rule out changes caused by maturation, drugs, coercion, and so on. Given this general set of criteria, the following are ways each position explains what is entailed in learning.

1. Most basic, with the most profound consequences for both the theory and practice of education, is that in cognitivist thinking the human mind is a central, necessary concept. What, exactly, the mind is remains the mystery it has always been, of course, but it is not necessary to have forged a conclusive definition in order to both investigate how it functions and assume that it does function as the source and nexus of all human cognitions and actions.

The consequences of this foundational belief that mind is not only a viable concept but a necessary one are that (1) research can focus on how the mind seems to manifest itself in all human endeavors, (2) education can be understood to be the principal societal means to fulfill each person's potentials to be "mindful," and (3) education must be carried out in ways that engage the human mind in enhancing experiences at the level at which human thinking most naturally occurs. That level, as the precursor Gestaltist psychology suggested, is one in which the organization of thinking into patterns, configurations, representations, dispositions, frameworks, and so on is crucial to the processes of knowing and acting.

In behaviorism, the notion of mind was rejected as being either a myth or as being useless for changing and controlling how people act. "Mentalism" was taboo, with all attention focused on explicit activities caused by specific stimuli. Education then consists of arranging the content and sequence of stimuli and responses, any "internal" mechanism being conceived as merely a connection system.

2. In that mind is the central organizer for cognitivist psychologies, and mind is understood to be a distinctly human endowment brought to fruition by and within social-cultural contexts including education as one aspect of such contexts, little credence is given to animal research as being important for insights into human learning. If we are to understand human learning as essentially a function of the human mind we must study learning and provide it in ways indigenous to the characteristically human modes of mindful functioning. Animal "learning" is, therefore, of little consequence.

In behaviorism animal models played an important role, because we can observe, in the ways we stimulate animals and how they respond to our stimuli, the basic principles operating in all learning, whether animal or human. Those principles, being mechanical and universal, can be discovered very effectively in controlled situations with various animals and then applied in controlled ways in school settings.

3. To fully achieve that which the human mind is capable of achieving, suggest the cognitivists, education must focus on the attainment of knowledge as that term applies peculiarly to organisms endowed with mind — human beings. Knowledge cannot be construed as something separate from that which is meaningful to humans. In a certain sense, the mind is that which endows meaning — that which determines what has significance. Significance is a human construct. It pervades all human experience, giving it continuity, selfhood, purpose, import. Education is a process of attaining significant knowledge, and its major signpost is understanding. To understand is to grasp significance — to see implications, ramifications, applications. Behavior is a *result* of attaining significant knowledge and applying that knowledge procedurally. To produce effective behavior the mindful conditions leading to such behavior must be fostered.

In behavioral thinking, terms such as understanding, significance and meaning are deemed unacceptable. They cannot be employed in constructing behavioral objectives because they are mentalistic in essence. Later attempts to adapt behaviorism to cognitivist ideas, such as stating a behavioral objective in terms of "The student will understand how music is used in various cultures (under x conditions and at x level of attainment)" are demonstrations not of the viability or flexibility of behaviorism but of the rigidity of its techniques. One cannot have it both ways: mental constructs cannot be imported and still construe the enterprise as being "behavioral."

4. To understand, or comprehend, as is essential for knowledge to be attained, a wholeness larger than the sum of its parts must be achieved. What is comprehended, if it is significant, is a system of interrelationships in which parts take on meaning *because they are in relation*. Learning is largely a process of building larger and larger systems of relations among more complex parts. This requires high-order mental processes to be constantly employed. One does not work *toward* using processes such as perceiving, assessing, applying, synthesizing, and hypothesizing. Education uses these processes as the basic ways to achieve learning. The "thinking curriculum" (one term used to characterize cognitivist schooling) demands high-order thinking *throughout,* the quality, complexity, and subtlety of such thinking growing as knowledge grows. Skills, facts, procedures, and information are all attained within the overall context of meaningful (high-order) engagements, rather than as ends in themselves.

In contrast, behaviorism, ruling out higher-order processes as being mythical or irrelevant, focuses on lower-order functions in which the key factor is memorization, construed as regular, predictable responses to particular stimuli. Wholes, when considered at all, are conceived to be the accumulative sum of many small parts, which, therefore, must be carefully and exactingly built up step by step. Skills, facts, procedures, and information are the necessary foci, and each, broken down further into as many small parts as are necessary to be controlled, requires shaping into predetermined end states. Reaching such end states is achieving learning.

5. The movement from point to point in learning episodes, according to cognitivist principles, should begin with the largest possible whole (1) that can be managed by the particular students being taught (limited by characteristics such as age, previous experience, and abilities) and (2) that makes meaningful sense out of the subject matter being dealt with. Then details within that whole, including relationships among the details, can be addressed as both important in and of themselves and as significant because they are related to the larger whole. A reintegration of the details into the whole should occur, the whole then serving as part of a still larger whole. So the general sequence is one of top-down-top, more inclusive top-down-top, and so forth. At the level of teaching methodology, strategies should be taken not as rigid prescriptions but as general principles capable of being adapted in a great variety of ways depending on the specifics of what is occurring with particular students and particular subject matters. But the overall progression of learning should preserve the focus on wholes and on parts as related to one another and to wholes.

The sequence of learning in behaviorism is from small part to small part in linear fashion, with as few missteps between parts as it is possible to arrange. Any sense of "whole" is one of longer chains of linked parts. So it is not as much a concept of parts leading to larger wholes as parts linked to larger systems of parts.

6. Within the context of a focus on wholes, learnings should be centered on problem finding and problem solving. Problems, as cognitivists understand them, are by nature wholistic, involving multiple factors and multiple relations among factors. To locate meaningful problems is to demonstrate a sense that there are larger issues than those presently being dealt with: an "upward" thrust is ensured by doing so. Solving problems requires discovery, in that explorations of possible alternatives, applications of various skills or items of information, and hypotheses about what might be done next are necessary strategies and therefore present students with genuinely mindful challenges.

These challenges are based on the *active construction* of the learning process by the learner — a key to effective education in cognitivist views. The learner must be put in the position, by his or her own choices of next moves in the learning process or by the teacher's posing of new problems, to have to call upon what is already known. This ensures that previous learning will be seen as useful for further learning, which both validates the previous learning and invests it with generative power for further learning. Teachers need to assist with strategies for applying previously learned material, skills, and ideas to new problems and encourage students to invent such strategies. The goal orientation is provided by a sense of increasing control over what has been learned, increasing belief in the utility of learning in solving meaningful problems of greater import, and growing awareness of one's own powers to generate solutions and gain significant meanings through doing so.

The contrasting views of behaviorism on these matters are dramatic. Little or no sense of problem solving in the larger sense exists beyond the cementing of particular responses to particular stimuli in longer chains. As with attempts that were made to adapt mentalistic constructs such as "understanding" to a behavioral model (see previous discussion), attempts to construe a complex problem as a "stimulus," and a generative search for solutions as a "response," so as to retain a behavioristic mind-set but with cognitivist contents substituted were to stretch this theory of learning so far beyond the bounds of what it was intended to provide as to abandon its most central tenets. Behaviorism does, in fact, require reinforcement of specific associations arranged in sequential order, overt responses not being conceived as generative but as mechanisms for cementing "Rs" with "Ss." So despite some recent attempts to portray behaviorism as operating at high-order thinking levels, there is a striking and genuine difference in viewpoints between these two theories of mind and education. The goal, it seems to me, is not to subsume one theory within the other — that would only vitiate both — but to allow behaviorism to do what it was intended to do and to use it within education accordingly.

7. A major shift in educational theorizing has taken place in recent years as a consequence of attempting to address the issue of how assessment should take place within a cognitive approach to education. It is impossible to do justice to this complex issue here; it will have to suffice to say that many present practices in evaluation continue to be based on behavioral assumptions, as mentioned previously. In a revised curriculum reflecting a different psychological underpinning, assessment will have to focus on the success of the processes used to generate both problems and solutions to problems. Rather than depending on item recall and task performance as the two pillars of assessment, each of those focusing on end states, feedback about the steps students take to construct problems and move toward solutions will be needed. When are important decisions made about how to move forward? Are such decisions informed by previously learned material or made ad hoc? What resources does a student call upon to help him or her make decisions? (It should be mentioned that given the social nature of mind and learning, some shifts are taking place to add the dimension of communal strategies of learning to the previously exclusive focus on individual learning.) How does a student understand the consequences of having made certain decisions, and how does that understanding help or hinder further useful decisions? To what extent does a particular performance of some task reflect a culmination of learnings rather than a rote activity?

Answers to such questions can be demonstrated by process records (portfolios or process folios) in which students gather a variety of documents evidencing learnings achieved and the processes connecting learnings. These folios themselves are a significant factor in encouraging active ownership of the educational process by those engaged in it. Other means of gathering evidence about learning are being developed, most focusing on demonstration of procedural aptness, use of previous learning in effective applications, quality of self-reflection about what is occurring in project-problem episodes, ability to use both self-generated and communal sources of assistance, and so forth. As these ideas and applications of evaluation theory become more refined and more visible, their use will likely spread to the various aspects of educational assessment now dominated by tests based on responses to separate items, such as are appropriate under behavioristic assumptions about learning.

8. An essential aspect of learning when it is conceived as mindful, self-generated, and project and problem oriented, and when processes employed to

create meaningful higher-order constructs are considered key factors, is the understanding learners have of how they are or are not applying useful strategies within learning episodes. The term *metacognition* refers to this self-awareness of what learning consists of and how one is faring in engaging oneself in learning. Students better achieve success in learning when they are aware that effective learning requires planning, predicting, setting goals and subgoals, sometimes guessing or following informed hunches, calling upon what one already knows and what others know, gathering needed information and honing skills as necessary for progress, organizing parts into configurations, and so forth. It is also important for people to understand their strengths and weaknesses and proclivities so that they can take them into account as part of their exercise of control over their own learning.

The point is that learners need to be and can be intelligent about learning as an activity so that they can engage in learning activity with the intelligence it requires. This is the ultimate meaning of "active learning," because it requires not just activity, which can be and often is unaware, but consciousness about how one is acting and thinking in light of what it means to act and think effectively. Education has often been carried out under the presumption that only one person needs to understand what is going on within the learning process — the teacher. It is now being suggested that it is just as crucial for this understanding to be the property of the learner.

In behaviorism, teachers as technicians, with the help of mega-technicians who write learning programs, apply correct procedures and arrange reinforcing conditions for learning. Learners undergo this arrangement, with no theoretical support for a need to have it otherwise, because theorizing about "active learning" would have to recognize and elevate to prominence what are essentially mentalistic notions.

9. Another key to effective cognitivist learning, in addition to metacognitive awareness, is the use of "schemata" as essential sources for expanding knowledge. Schemata are organized, structured bodies of information previously learned. They are not just collections of facts or actions; they are meaningful units of knowledge that include the inner dynamics of relationships among their parts. They are called upon to make sense of new, related, extended schemata. That is why problem finding is a key factor in learning — it links what is known with a larger issue yet to be known. Learners are not likely to find problems unconnected with already known material. Rather than a teacher always imposing new problems, students need to be expected to generate such problems based on existing schemata but calling for extensions of them. Teachers can encourage this process by setting up learning situations in which hypotheses for needed improvements

can be generated and by helping students be aware (metacognize) that this process is in itself an important dimension of learning.

Behaviorism depends on previously established connections as building blocks for further connections. There is no support in the literature for the idea of problems as wholes larger than the sum of their parts, or of the need for learners to generate new problems as extensions to previous ones, or of the need for learners to be aware of how problem-clusters interconnect.

10. Emerging concepts of transfer of learning from cognitivist literature tend to conceive transfer, not surprisingly, in wholistic terms rather than as the piecemeal transporting of single items from one domain to another. What seemingly happens in transfer of learning is a shift of boundaries in that which is known. This shift occurs because as new knowledge is being gained, previous knowledge being employed as a means to generate new understanding itself shifts in its structure as a result of its amplification and extension to cover new issues. So there is a transfer — or transformation in quality and extensitivity — of what had existed previously. The previous material, in its interactions with new material, both influences the boundaries and relations of the new ideas and is influenced by them, so new configurations of understanding emerge as old and new intermingle. Indeed, education as a process may be conceived as the constant, ongoing reconfiguration of the known as previous and occurrent knowledge interact to form more complex, sophisticated wholes.

Such ideas are foreign to behavioristic principles, which depend on a "similar situation" transfer of previously learned associations into the related context.

11. A good deal of thinking in cognitivist literature has emphasized the domain-specific nature of knowledge and of learning. It seems more apparent that various modes of thought exist, employing a diversity of means of representation, requiring particular sensitivities of mind, or ways to be intelligent, or forms of cognition. And within cognitive domains novices and experts seem to solve problems in different ways, increasing expertise gradually leading to transformations in the way previously learned material within that domain can be applied. It seems to be less likely now that there is a general factor, or a few such factors, to which all learnings may be attributed. Controversy continues over this issue of domain-specific versus general factors as crucial for learning, and it may well be that both will be found to play important roles, the more general aspects being applied as each particular domain transforms them. The important point at this stage of development of cognitive conceptions of learning is that there is growing agreement that more than a "g" factor is needed to explain how learnings take place in differing spheres of knowledge.

153

In the behavioristic tradition learning is conceived as unitary. Its principles should apply no matter the subject. Indeed, that is a central concept in this point of view. Behavioral research focused on identifying the key general principles governing all learning, and behavioral education then attempted to apply those principles systematically in all fields of learning.

12. Cognitive approaches to research focus on the processes involved in performing high-order tasks, including deduction, induction, analogical reasoning, and hypothesis forming. There is also interest in the workings of the mind as it is engaged in being tested, both in traditional and nontraditional settings. Because learning is conceived to require the building of meaningful systems of relations into structures that are themselves adaptable to change within larger, more inclusive structures, research is needed on a broad front, covering all the items in the previous list and a good many more not mentioned. Clearly, research methodologies will have to expand from the limited repertoire employed when learning is conceived more simply and more mechanically.

Behavioral research, as mentioned, aimed to clarify the key principles of learning and to refine delivery systems for them in a variety of educational settings. This agenda allowed a fairly uniform set of research practices to be developed and to be applied with increasing sophistication. The agenda for research in the developing cognitive sciences will have to take very different directions than this. It is likely to aim at diversity in every aspect — methodology, levels from the very specific to the very broad, intrasubject matter and intersubject matter foci as well as relations between the two, studies of individuals, individuals as part of groups, intragroup dynamics as implicated in learning, measurements from the very precise to the very impressionistic, and on and on. We can expect to see a greatly expanded concept of what educational research can and needs to be.

James Mursell, I think, would have found all this fascinating, challenging, and, above all, valid. He would have felt, and deserved to feel, vindicated in his beliefs that learning is the supreme human endeavor and therefore must be understood to operate most effectively at the highest levels of human functioning. Perhaps he would have been sufficiently heartened by these developments to have entertained the idea that important contributory learnings can be fostered effectively by behavioral methodologies, so that they can be considered as positive, even necessary components within a larger concept of educational practice. After all, a good deal of research and experience over the past three decades have led us to recognize that higher-order thinking often relies on the ready availability of information, procedures, and skills, which themselves can be gained efficiently by learning strategies appropriate to nature. Behavioral methodologies seem to be particularly useful for such dimensions of learning and are likely to be so for all learners. In addition, some learners may, in fact, respond particularly well to behavioristic organizations of various other aspects of the curriculum, including some complex learnings that might be amenable, to some degree, to such organizations. A major error would be to assume that certain populations of learners (classified by culture, race, economic and social class, and so on) are likely to respond more favorably to one or the other orientation — a deplorable tendency reflecting social prejudice rather than evidence. Schooling as a whole, and particular programs of study, can include the broadest possible range of learning strategies while retaining a broadly conceived orientation to cognitive development as foundational for all learners. The two orientations, contradictory though they may be in many if not most theoretical aspects, nevertheless need not be construed as antagonistic at the level of practice, I would suggest. If the "thinking curriculum" is solidly established, an appropriate place and function within it for behavioral interventions is likely to be found.

I think James Mursell would have seen clearly the enormous potential for cognitivist concepts of learning to be applied to the field of music education and the need for the entire profession to take as much advantage as it possibly can of these potentials. Doing so would position us as music educators in the mainstream of emerging thinking and acting in education. It would also allow us to provide important leadership for that emergence because music, like all the arts, can be understood as the epitome of all that the cognitive sciences are discovering about the human mind. Music education could be a model of "the thinking curriculum," demonstrating the model's viability as it applies to *musical* thinking, *musical* cognition, and *musical* meaning. We will need to better define what all this means and what it portends for music education and to adapt our curricula as we better understand the implications. It would be difficult to imagine a more hopeful opportunity for music education, at every level from theory to practice, than we are being provided by the current emergence of cognitivist ideas. That James Mursell's thinking anticipated so much of what is now occurring can be regarded as nothing less than remarkable.

NOTES

1. James L. Mursell, *Human Values in Education*. New York: Silver Burdett Company, 1934, p. 35.

2. James L. Mursell, *Principles of Music Education*. New York: Macmillan, 1927, p. 85.

3. Susanne K. Langer, *Mind: An Essay on Human Feeling*. Vols. I, II, III. Baltimore, Md.: Johns Hopkins University Press, 1967, 1972, 1982.

4. Monroe C. Beardsley, *The Aesthetic Point of View: Selected Essays,* ed. Michael J. Wreen and Donald M. Callen. Ithaca, N.Y.: Cornell University Press, 1982, p. 339.

5. John Blacking, "The Study of Man as Music Maker," in John Blacking and Joann Kealiinohomoku, eds., *The Performing Arts,* The Hague: Mouton, 1979, p. 6.

6. Nelson Goodman, *Of Mind and Other Matters.* Cambridge, Mass.: Harvard University Press, 1984, p. 147.

7. Nelson Goodman, *Languages of Art,* 2nd ed. Indianapolis, Ind.: Hackett, 1976, p. 248.

8. Thomas Clifton, *Music as Heard: A Study in Applied Phenomenology.* New Haven, Conn.: Yale University Press, 1983, p. 9.

9. Ibid., p. 74.

10. Fred Lerdahl and Ray Jackendoff, *A Generative Theory of Tonal Music.* Cambridge, Mass.: MIT Press, 1983, p. 2.

11. Bennett Reimer, *A Philosophy of Music Education.* Englewood Cliffs, N.J.: Prentice Hall, 1970, p. 40; 1989, pp. 53, 54.

12. Charles L. Gary, ed., *The Study of Music in the Elementary School — A Conceptual Approach.* Washington, D.C.: Music Educators National Conference, 1967.

13. Benjamin S. Bloom, David R. Krathwohl, and Bertram B. Masia, eds., *Taxonomy of Educational Objectives, Handbook I: Cognitive Domain.* New York: David McKay, 1956.

14. Bennett Reimer, "The Nonconceptual Nature of Aesthetic Cognition," *Journal of Aesthetic Education,* 20:4, Winter, 1986.

15. Reimer, *A Philosophy,* Chapter 5 and pp. 108–110.

16. Ralph A. Smith, ed., *Regaining Educational Leadership: Critical Essays on PBTE/CBTE, Behavioral Objectives and Accountability.* New York: John Wiley and Sons, Inc., 1975.

17. Quoted in Smith, op. cit., p. 241.

18. See, for example, Sigmund Koch, "Psychology and Emerging Conceptions of Knowledge as Unitary," in T. W. Wann, ed., *Behaviorism and Phenomenology: Contrasting Bases for Modern Psychology.* Chicago: University of Chicago Press, 1964.

19. Howard Gardner, *The Mind's New Science: A History of the Cognitive Revolution.* New York: Basic Books, 1985.

20. The proceedings of this conference were published in early 1990 by the Educational Testing Service, Princeton, N.J.

21. Edwin E. Gordon and David G. Woods, *Jump Right In.* Chicago: G.I.A. Publications, 1988.

22. Some recent books on music influenced by cognitive psychology include Jay Dowling and D. Harwood, *Music Cognition* (New York: Academic Press, 1984); P. Howell, I. Cross, and R. West, *Musical Structure and Cognition* (New York: Academic Press, 1984); John Sloboda, *The Musical Mind* (Oxford: Oxford University Press, 1984); John Sloboda, *Generative Processes in Music* (Oxford, Oxford University Press, 1988); Mary L. Serafine, *Music as Cognition* (New York: Columbia University Press, 1988).

23. For this explanation I have drawn on Thomas J. Shuell, "Cognitive Conceptions of Learning," *Review of Educational Research,* 56:4, Winter, 1986. However, I have added a good deal of material for which Shuell should not be held responsible.

7

Psychological Theory and Music Learning

Marilyn P. Zimmerman

In *Basic Concepts in Music Education, I,* the title of the chapter corresponding to this one is "Learning Theory and Music Teaching," by Louis P. Thorpe. The current title, "Psychological Theory and Music Learning," reflects a change in emphasis from learning theory to psychological theory and from the teacher to the learner. This change is more than semantic: the past three decades have shown enormous interest and activity in psychology and music as evidenced by conferences, research studies, and the publication of several major books in psychology of music and developmental music psychology. The major purposes of this chapter are as follows: (1) to summarize the learning theories reviewed by Thorpe, (2) to consider contemporary psychological theories that have had an impact on music psychology and learning, (3) to review the applications of psychology to musical learning, and (4) to suggest psychological principles that can aid the music learning process.

BACKGROUND

Influences from the two learning theories that formed the basis for the earlier chapter, Gestalt and associationist, permeate contemporary psychological theories. Gestalt psychology has had particular appeal for the musician because of its reliance on the role of perception in thinking. James Mursell was a proponent of Gestalt principles, which he viewed as an antidote to the mechanistic approach to learning of the associationists. His synthesis-analysis-synthesis method of musical problem solving derived

157

from a Gestalt insistence on the primacy of the whole over the parts. Other Gestalt principles such as pattern perception, organization, insightful learning, syntactic relationships of figure-ground, contextual learning, and level of aspiration have been incorporated into cognitive psychology and cognitive developmental psychology.

The British associationists, represented by J. Mill, 1869, advocated learning by the association of ideas. American connectionism grew out of this British tradition. E. L. Thorndike was the major proponent of learning as the acquisition of desired stimulus response connections. His laws of learning included (1) the law of effect, (2) the law of exercise, (3) the law of readiness, and (4) the law of disuse. These laws can be stated as two simple rules: (1) put together what should go together and keep apart what should not go together, and (2) reward desirable connections and make undesirable connections produce discomfort. Thorndike's law of effect later became Skinner's theory of reinforcement. Because of its emphasis on stimulus response connections, the theory is considered atomistic, mechanistic, and molecular. Yet the theory's pertinence for the development of performance skills is evident.

Contiguous conditioning is an offshoot of connectionism. One of its famous laws formulated by E. R. Guthrie stated that "a combination of stimuli which has accompanied a movement will on its recurrence tend to be followed by that movement" (Thorpe 1958, 183). This can be paraphrased as what is being noticed becomes a signal for what is being done or what an individual learns depends on what he or she does. Again, the application of this law to skill development can readily be seen. (See Zimmerman 1987, 77).

These short summaries indicate the tenets of Gestalt and associationism that have served as theoretical bases for teaching music. Thorpe elaborated these theories for music educators by applying them to memory and forgetting, effective practice and motivation. He concluded his chapter by delineating relationships between learning theory and problems in teaching music. Nevertheless, Thorpe predicted a future that "no doubt will see an increasing trend toward a needed integration of these theories with method" (Thorpe 1958, 168).

An application of Gestalt principles is found in *Emotion and Meaning in Music* by Leonard B. Meyer (1956). In this influential book published two years before *Basic Concepts in Music Education, I*, Meyer based much of his theory of expectation in music on the Gestalt laws of psychological organization as they function within our cultural context. Chief among the axioms of Gestalt theory cited by Meyer is that of the law of *Prägnanz*, which avers that "psychological organization will always be as good as the prevailing conditions allow" (Koffka 1935, 303) and will tend to continue (the law of good continuation). Continuation of mental activity governed by the law of *Prägnanz* seeks stability and closure. Meyer applies this Gestalt explanation of cognitive activity to music listening. Melodic and rhythmic continuities govern our expectations in listening to music. Musical meaning is embodied in the expectation that one musical event will lead to a subsequent event. These expectations are rooted in specific stylistic and cultural contexts. When expectations are inhibited or thwarted, affect or emotion results. Traces of these ideas can be found in Reimer's aesthetic philosophy (1970, 1989) and Serafine's theory of music as cognition (1988).

COGNITIVE PSYCHOLOGY

Cognitive psychology, a diverse school that covers experimental research in perception, concept formation, memory, language acquisition, and thinking, has particular relevance for music learning and teaching. In 1967 Ulrich Neisser defined the field in *Cognitive Psychology,* a book that also gave the discipline its name. Essentially, cognitive psychology is the study of human cognition as it occurs in natural purposeful activity within the ordinary environment. The emphasis of cognitive psychology is "internal rules, strategies and operations that people employ in intelligent behavior, as well as upon the external outcomes of these processes" (Hargreaves 1986a, 87).

For Neisser cognition is the activity of knowing, which includes the acquisition, organization, and use of knowledge. Within this context perception and cognition are viewed not only as "operations in the head, but [as] transactions with the world" (Neisser 1976, 11). A structural approach to mental processes is also evident in cognitive psychology. Neisser uses the term *schemata* to define "cognitive structures that prepared the perceiver to accept certain kinds of information rather than others (1976, 20)." Hence, perception is selective, and because this is so, an individual determines his or her own cognition. Learning in this context results from a change in perception.

Another early stimulus to cognitive psychology was the founding of the Center for Cognitive Studies at Harvard University in 1960 by Jerome Bruner and George Miller. Prior to this, *A Study of Thinking* by Bruner, Goodnow, and Austin (1956) examined how individuals classify and categorize information in the acquisition and formation of concepts. These early attempts to analyze mental strategies foreshadowed the work of today's cognitive psychologists. Howard Gardner in *The Mind's New Science* (1985) presents an excellent summary of the history and evolution of cognitive psychology, and Jerome Bruner's *In Search of Mind* (1983) also reviews its development.

There are several areas of research within cognitive psychology. One that is particularly germane for music educators is memory. According to the cognitivist, memory is an organized store of acquired information and/or abilities that an individual can retrieve at will (acquisition-organization-storage-retrieval). Everything an individual does is within a context of remembered experience. Present participation in music, for example, depends upon what is already known and remembered and will, in turn, circumscribe future experiences with music.

Development of memory skills involves a composite of many factors and occurs over a wide age span. Active participation of the individual is required. Selective attention, verbal skills, and mnemonic strategies play key roles in the process. Changes over time in the memory system are dependent on differences in the way information is processed, or, in cognitivist terminology, "levels of processing." These include the use of deliberate memory strategies and an individual's understanding of the way his or her memory system functions — the concept of metamemory (Flavel 1971).

In 1972 Craik and Lockhart focused attention on depth of processing information in memory research. They proposed that information embedded with rich associations is more firmly encoded in the memory system and easier to recall. This is an example of the molar, top-down approach favored by cognitive psychologists.

Some of the memory strategies stem from the two memory stages that have been identified: short-term, or immediate, memory and long-term memory, which has more permanence. Miller (1956) suggested that the limit for retention in short-term memory is seven items, plus or minus two. This rule of seven has been confirmed by other researchers. Items in short-term memory can be "chunked" into larger units to aid memory storage for the long term. First and last tones within a pitch sequence tend to be remembered more easily than the middle pitches, a finding that corresponds to the traditional rules of primacy and recency (Williams 1975).

The research evidence points to a developmental pattern in the growth of the memory system. During middle childhood the shift is from an aural centering on the specific pitches to a more global comprehension of the attributes of a melodic phrase.

COGNITIVE MUSIC PSYCHOLOGY

The potential of cognitive psychology for explaining musical learning has not been overlooked by psychologists and those music researchers interested in a psychology of music. Several important books have been published within the past decade, including *The Psychology of Music* edited by Diana Deutsch (1982); *The Musical Mind: The Cognitive Psychology of Music* by John Sloboda (1985); *Music Cognition* by W. Jay Dowling and D. L. Harwood (1987); and *Music as Cognition: The Development of Thought in Sound* by Mary Louise Serafine (1988). A new journal, *Psychomusicology*, reflects the research interests and methodology of a cognitive approach, and an entire issue of the British journal *Psychology of Music* (Vol. 15, No. 1, 1987) was devoted to cognitive psychology and music.

We will consider briefly the theories of Sloboda and Serafine. Sloboda views music as a cognitive skill. He cites two reasons for this viewpoint: (1) most of our responses to music are learned and (2) there is a cognitive component to our affective responses that cannot be explained in terms of conditioning. Sloboda draws a number of parallels between language learning and musical learning. He then considers the cognitive activity involved in musical performance, composition, and listening: "The way in which people represent music to themselves determines how well they can remember and perform it. Composition and improvisation require the generation of such representations, and perception involves the listener constructing them" (1985, 3). These internal representations are central to a cognitive psychology of music.

In his discussion of expert performance, Sloboda suggests that "effective musical memory depends upon the ability to represent music in terms of groupings of notes which can be related to familiar stylistic patterns and structures, and also to other sequences within the same piece" (1985, 95). Fingering patterns and a grasp of the architecture of a composition contribute to the memory process.

Serafine believes that music is best described as a cognitive activity that employs sounds and temporal events within a community context of style. This cognitive definition of music locates music in the activity of cognitive processes under the influence of a community that shares a particular musical style. Serafine proposes a set of pan-stylistic cognitive processes that are indicative of how music is understood. Three categories of processes are defined: field definition, temporal organization, and nontemporal operations. Each category has several components.

Serafine tested her theory through a series of studies in which sixteen musical tasks were designed and administered to approximately fifteen subjects ages five, six, eight, ten, eleven, and adulthood. The tasks covered two of the categories of cognitive processes: temporal processes (succession and simultaneity) and nontemporal processes (closure, transformation, abstraction, and hierarchic levels). Her main findings indicated that (1) the processes are generally well in place by age ten or eleven but are not evident earlier, (2) formal music study does not influence the development of the processes in question, (3) developmental trends for most of the tasks indicated a rapid growth in musical understanding between the ages of eight and ten or eleven, and (4) nontemporal processes appeared to develop before temporal processes.

In Serafine's theory, perception and tonal-rhythmic memory are not sufficient conditions for imagining and predicting in sound, that is, for musical cognition. Her theory of music as cognition goes beyond perceptual theories of development in that the cognitive processes she proposes determine how an individual perceives music.

DEVELOPMENTAL PSYCHOLOGY

The systematic study of human development with an emphasis on child development has been a burgeoning field in the past four decades. Developmental psychologists study patterns of behavior and thought at different points in the developmental process as individuals interact with their environments. Since the mid-1950s there has been a shift from normative descriptions of children's cognitive, affective, and psychomotor behaviors to an emphasis on psychological explanations of these behaviors.

The study of child development encompasses a variety of disciplines, theories, and methods, with each viewpoint recognizing the importance of interactions of intellectual, emotional, physical, and social growth. Most of the theories seem to agree that child development is a process that entails sequential levels, phases, shifts, steps, or stages through which a child's multifaceted growth passes from infancy to youth. Although most developmental theories end with adolescence or young adulthood, development cannot be divorced from the total life process. This section will consider those developmental theories that have particular significance for musical learning.

The cognitive developmental psychology of Jean Piaget "is the best worked-out trajectory of growth in all developmental psychology. While many parts of it are susceptible to criticism, it remains the account of development against which all other formulations continue to be judged" (Gardner 1983, 133). Because Piagetian theory has provided a perspective for research in many areas of learning, including musical learning, key concepts of the theory will be reviewed.

Piagetian theory is a biological theory based on the adaptive interaction of an individual with his or her environment. The twin processes of assimilation and accommodation define and refine this interaction. Interaction occurs as individuals assimilate what can be easily comprehended and/or accommodate their thinking to the new and unfamiliar. Both heredity and environment are essential to the process, but neither is wholly controlling.

Piagetian theory is a structural theory based on the formation of cognitive structures through assimilation and accommodation. Mental schema or schemata that begin as action patterns during infancy are the basic raw materials and building blocks for these cognitive structures. Although the young child's intelligence never stops developing, certain structures at certain levels and at certain times reach a relative stability. Each new assimilation and each new accommodation lead to a higher level and a more stable point of equilibrium. Incomplete systems of thought that conflict with each other are enlarged or integrated through these twin regulatory mechanisms. New knowledge results in and leads to a recombination of existing capacities in order to reestablish the destroyed equilibrium. Development is always solidly rooted in that which already exists and is continuous with past experience.

Piagetian theory is a stage theory of cognitive development that views human intelligence as moving through successively higher stages of thinking from the sensorimotor stage of infancy, to the preoperational stage of the toddler, to concrete operations of the elementary school child, and culminating in the formal operational thinking of adolescents and adults. These stages cut across more than one modality of thought and bring to light important, albeit subtle, commonalities. In Piagetian theory the sequence of stages is both organismic and experiential — organismic because the stages unfold systematically, and experiential because they are dependent upon environment and experience. The age levels at which the stages occur can and do vary according to particularities of physical, social, and cultural environments.

An important concept in Piagetian theory is that of conservation, which marks the transition from preoperational to operational thinking and is the result of reversibility of thought. Conservation refers to a child's ability to maintain the constancy or invariance of a dimension of an empirical object as its other dimensions are subjected to controlled transformations.

In the 1960s a series of music conservation studies (Pflederer 1963, 1964; Zimmerman and Sechrest 1968) focused attention on children's underlying thought processes as they engaged in music tasks and activities. These studies were among the first to view musical development within the context of a cognitive developmental framework, in this case Piagetian. Pflederer (1967) proposed conservation laws in musical development analogous to Piaget's five conservation laws that lead to stability of operational thinking. Since that time there have been numerous research studies, articles, and dissertations in this area. Most of the research has been concerned with conservation and the age at which musical concepts develop. Although the results of these Piagetian studies are mixed, they do seem to indicate that at about the age of nine, qualitative changes in the child's thinking begin to occur. In 1980 Serafine published a summary and critique of Piagetian research in music, an indication of the interest in and importance of this body of research.

Webster and Zimmerman (1983) extended and replicated an experiment from the Zimmerman and Sechrest (1968) research. Rhythm and tonal conservation tests based on listening were presented to 317 children from second through sixth grades. Results indicated that differences in test scores existed between grade levels, with centers of greatest difference at grades two, four, and six; grades three and five seemed to be transitory periods.

Somewhat similar to Piaget's assimilation and accommodation is Heinz Werner's (1961) view of cognitive development through gradual increases in the twin processes of differentiation and integration. In the classification of objects, a young child moves from a global, diffuse, and undifferentiated consideration of the objects to a differentiation into subgroups and finally toward an integration into a conceptual hierarchy. Werner referred to this process as development according to the "orthogenetic principle." Werner applied the orthogenetic principle to musical development by examining the spontaneous melodies of children ages two to five. He determined stages in the direction of melodic movement, the overall form of the melody, and the ending. Melodies of the younger children had tones strung together in a global and diffuse manner, whereas those of the older children were more differentiated and integrated into phraselike structures.

Werner finesses the question of stage versus nonstage theory by insisting that development is both continuous (proceeds without discernible stages) and discontinuous (proceeds in stages). Since development is both continuous and discontinuous, optimal periods of growth alternate with plateaus wherein seemingly little new learning occurs.

Two theories of perceptual development that have potential for melodic processing and memory are the differentiation theory of Eleanor Gibson (1969) and the specificity model of J. Wohlwill (1970). These theories are based on the assumption that the perceptual features of the environment are given rather than formed by mental schema and that development occurs through increases in the ability to extract and organize information from the environment.

For Gibson perceptual development involves an active process of exploration and search that proceeds through abstracting, filtering, and selectively attending to environmental stimuli. Development is marked by an increased differentiation of stimulus features and by the search for invariants in the stimulus field. For Wohlwill perceptual development moves from a decreasing reliance on redundancy to selectivity in isolating relevant from irrelevant cues to continuity of stimulus information over time and place.

Using antecedents of Piaget's cognitive theory and Freud's psychoanalytic theory with its emphasis on affect, Howard Gardner (1973) has developed an elegant theory of artistic development. His prodigious writings in this area, based on years of research with young children in Project Zero at Harvard University, have opened our understanding to more specific ways of viewing musical development and planning for its nurturance. In an attempt to integrate affect and cognition, Gardner posits three systems — making, perceiving, and feeling. These systems are present at birth and combine sensorimotor actions and perceptions with affective reactions. In musical learning these systems translate into psychomotor or skill development, perceptual or listening skills, and affective responses to music.

With Dennis Wolf, Gardner has proposed four major stages of artistic development (Wolf and Gardner 1980). These stages are as follows: (1) child as direct communicator, birth to age two; (2) child as symbol user, age two to seven; (3) youth as craftsman, age seven to eleven or thirteen; and (4) youth as critic and full participant in the artistic process, age thirteen and on.

During the first stage, child as direct communicator, the child gains practical knowledge of the world through the three systems of perceiving, making, and feeling. The child as symbol user corresponds roughly with Piaget's preoperational stage in which the child learns symbols through enactment and imitative play. The third stage, youth as craftsman, covers the years of middle childhood. Spontaneous music making gives way to more deliberate and rehearsed musical expression as children shape and measure their own musical performance against that of their peers. Peer influence thus replaces egocentrism. This is the stage of sustained practice, for the child has an increased interest in perfecting and enhancing his or her performing skills.

In the final stage, youths can deal with the full range of artistic activity. Their capacity for formal thinking allows them to make conscious decisions about style and to consider thoughtfully the full potential of the materials of music. It is at this time that young performers' self-criticism can exceed their competence in technical and expressive execution. They confront their musical futures as they question whether they want to devote time to serious music study or pursue other possibilities among their many wide-ranging interests.

Gardner (1983) proposed a theory of multiple intelligences that includes musical intelligence as one of six autonomous intelligences. His work with brain-damaged individuals and his reading of accounts in the literature of idiots savants led him to theorize that musical intelligence met the criteria for a specific intelligence.

Associates of Gardner at Project Zero have also contributed to the developmental literature. *Invented Worlds: The Psychology of the Arts* by Ellen Winner (1982) outlines artistic development, including musical development. Drawing upon research from Project Zero and others, Winner traces aural ability and song acquisition from infancy through childhood. Davidson, McKernon, and Gardner (1981) studied spontaneous and learned songs in young children. Four phases in song acquisition were determined: overall topology, rhythmic surface, pitch contour, and key stability.

Dowling (1982, 1984) has detailed the underlying cognitive processes that children use in learning songs. He too found a sequence from an apprehension of the overall melodic contour to a precision in tonality and interval size. This sequence parallels his account of the development of melodic information processing in children.

Bamberger (1982) attempted to determine the cognitive processes by which young children, ages four to ten, internalize music. The children drew pictures of the rhythm of a familiar nursery rhyme in a way that they could remember it or another child could clap it. The four- and five-year-olds tried to duplicate the motion of their clapping with swirling scribbles. The six- and seven-year-olds drew a figural representation of each discrete clap. The older children tended to group the claps metrically. Obviously, the role of learning, whether formal or incidental, cannot be casually dismissed. However, a general developmental progression is evident from a figural to a more formal representation.

That developmental psychology of music is a rapidly expanding field is evident in recent publications such as *The Developmental Psychology of Music* by David Hargreaves (1986b). From an initial chapter that outlines psychological approaches to music development, Hargreaves considers thinking and music development beginning with the preschooler and progressing throughout the life span. Also included in the book are cogent discussions of creativity and personality, the influences of social psychology on music development, and curricular applications of developmental psychology. One of the book's strengths is the critical and enlightening analysis of the research literature that undergirds developmental music psychology.

Other publications have contributed to the field, including Hargreaves's "Developmental Psychology and Music Education" (1986a); Funk and Whiteside's "Developmental Theory and the Psychology of Music" (1981); and Zimmerman's "Developmental Processes in Music Learning" (1982).

THEORIES OF INSTRUCTION

This section will focus on theories of instruction that apply ideas about how we learn to the curriculum. One such theory of instruction is that of Jerome Bruner, the widely recognized authority on development, perception, and discovery learning. Bruner does not adhere to a strict stage theory of development. Instead he views development as moving from enactive to iconic to symbolic representations of experience. These modes of representation do not function as discrete stages; they remain intact throughout adulthood. The modes interact with each other and guide and support further actions, images, and symbols.

Three important themes that are recurrent in Bruner's theories have special relevance for musical learning. The first is that a curriculum must be organized to emphasize the structure of knowledge. This is the essence of Bruner's theory. Bruner's concept of structure is an inclusive one: it proposes that knowing involves a grasp of the structural elements of a discipline. These structural elements include principles, concepts, and the modes of thinking peculiar to a particular discipline. Not only does a student learn about the end product of a discipline; he or she also learns something about the process through which that product is shaped.

The teaching of structure also involves the selection of those unifying principles that are basic to understanding. To grasp the structure of a subject is to understand it in a way that permits the mind to see relationships. When viewed in the light of structural principles, details become more comprehensible. The teaching and learning of structure are central to the classic problem of transfer. Learning the structural principles of a discipline prepares a student to solve new problems in that discipline.

A second theme in Brunerian theory is that intellectual activity, whether in the composer's studio or in a preschool setting, is the same; the difference is of degree rather than of kind. To emphasize this point, Bruner claims that "any subject can be taught effectively in some intellectually honest form to any child at any stage of development" (Bruner 1960, 33). The problem is one of communicating with the student, of translating for him or her the structure of a given subject into terms that he or she can understand. This should be the main thrust of our teaching — to open the structure of music to the understanding of our students. To fulfill this dictum, Bruner advocates the spiral curriculum, a curriculum that turns back upon itself at each higher level in order to present structural concepts with expanded meanings.

The third theme reiterates the importance of learning by discovery. At all levels, discovery learning represents a problem-solving attitude toward learning that includes the possibility of solving problems by following one's hunches. This is the heart of intuitive thinking and is manifested in the music classroom through improvisation and composition.

Some well-known applications of Bruner's theory to the music curriculum include a dissertation by Boswell (1969) in which the theory is applied to teaching concepts in beginning instrumental music; the spiral curriculum of the Manhattanville Music Curriculum Project (Thomas 1971); and the generative approach to music learning in *Music* (Boardman, Andress, and Willman 1988), the Holt, Rinehart & Winston elementary series. This approach uses Bruner's three modes of representation (conceptual modes).

Edwin Gordon (1984) has proposed a sequential learning theory that is based an aural/oral method of learning prescribed tonal and rhythmic sequences. Perceptual tasks are apprehended through a process of "audiation," a term that Gordon coined to refer to inner hearing of a musical score without its realization in sound. The hierarchy of Gordon's learning sequence is highly reminiscent of Gagné's (1970) eight types of learning. With David Woods, Gordon has applied his theory to elementary music instruction in *Jump Right In: The Music Curriculum* (1984).

In his studies of musical aptitude Gordon determined that until the child is about the age of nine, his or her musical aptitude is developmental and is dependent on environmental influences. The very young child reacts to immediate impressions with intuitive responses to aural perceptions. According to Gordon, "music aptitude is stabilized potential for achievement in music, and . . . does not stabilize until approximately age nine" (1979, 43).

BEHAVIORISM

Behaviorism is basically a stimulus-response learning theory that stems from connectionism with reinforcement. According to the behaviorist, learning occurs when there is a change or modification in the behavior of an individual. B. F. Skinner has exerted a great influence upon educational practice during the past three decades with his emphasis on behavior modification through the programming of desired responses. Skinner insists on the learner's need for immediate and continual reinforcement, whether this is furnished by the teacher or a programmed sequence of instructional materials. Learners receive reinforcement in terms of feedback, so they know exactly how well they are learning. The importance of feedback cannot be too strongly emphasized. It is both motivational because it creates a desire for further learning and informational because it corrects errors.

Behavior modification techniques have been applied in musical settings by Madsen and his associates at Florida State University and Greer and his associates at Teachers College, Columbia University. Behavior shaping through successive approximation has been used in studies to improve pitch discrimination and intonation. In other applications of behavior modification techniques, music is used either as a reinforcer for nonmusical behavior change or as a reward for behavior change or accomplishment of a prescribed nonmusical task. *Research in Music Behavior: Modifying Music Behavior in the Classroom* (Madsen, Greer, and Madsen 1975) contains excellent summaries of early research findings in behavior modification techniques applied to music learning. Madsen and Yarbrough (1985) present applications of behavioral self-assessment and successive approximation techniques to developing musical competencies such as conducting skills.

MOTIVATION

Several theories of motivation have been proposed in recent years. The theory of personal investment (Maehr 1983) grew out of Maehr's earlier theory of achievement motivation (Maehr 1974) and is basically a cognitive theory. An individual makes choices, demonstrates persistence, and maintains a level of activity based on his or her perceptions, thoughts, and beliefs. For example, level of aspiration and perceived competence in music are powerful motivators, often determining whether or not an adolescent will continue music study.

As mentioned previously, reinforcement theorists approach motivation in one of two ways. Either an activity (music, for example) serves as reinforcement, or reinforcement contingencies such as teacher approval and successive approximation of task mastery are used in a learning situation. Greer (1981) provides an extensive summary of this approach to motivation and affect during the 1970s.

Raynor views motivation in terms of early, middle, and late stages of career striving along a series of steps toward a goal. The young person is motivated by what he or she hopes to achieve, whereas the older individual is defined by and tries to maintain past achievements. Intrinsic motivation, according to Raynor, has two components, "one stemming from the particular kind of activity or task and one stemming from the perceived difficulty of task accomplishment when standards of good performance are inherent in the activity. Intrinsic motivation seems particularly potent in the field of music, because of both the apparently inherent interest aroused by musical sound, and the fact that reproduction of a musical manuscript involves the standard of playing the notes correctly" (1983, 18). Extrinsic motivation enhances task involvement when extrinsic incentives (world-class competitions, for example) are associated with the task and anticipated as an outcome prior to involvement.

CONFERENCES

In this chapter I have attempted to review psychological theories that have influenced music learning and teaching. Thorpe's effort of over thirty years ago to indicate how music educators and psychologists "can co-operate in formulating some common principles and procedures for the direction of effective and enjoyable teaching" (1958, 163) has been expanded by joint research activity (some of which has been reported in this chapter) and conferences and symposia of music educators and psychologists. In 1978 and 1979, two symposia concerned with the applications of psychology to the teaching and learning of music were held at Ann Arbor, Michigan. At the 1978 meeting, twelve music educators presented papers, replete with questions, to which twelve psychologists responded. This procedure was reversed at the 1979 symposium with essentially the same participants. Topics considered at each symposium included auditory perception, motor learning, child development, cognitive skills, memory and information processing, and affect and motivation (Davidson et al. 1981; Greer 1981; Zimmerman 1981). In 1982 a third symposium of different psychologists and music educators, again held at Ann Arbor, considered the topics of motivation and creativity (Maehr 1983; Raynor 1983).

In 1984 a conference of music educators and child developmentalists was held at Brigham Young University to establish a dialogue of common interests based on current theory and research findings (Boswell 1985). Papers from a 1988 symposium on music development and cognition at the Eastman School of Music are also available (*Psychomusicology*, 1989). This list is by no means exhaustive, but the conferences cited here reflect the intersecting interests of both professions.

CONCLUSION

In 1958 Thorpe concluded his chapter "Learning Theory and Music Teaching" by singling out "five fundamental procedures in the field of music teaching which to a considerable extent harmonize with the principal tenets or points of view of the theories of learning" (p. 190) that had been discussed. This present chapter will also conclude with five principles of learning that harmonize with the psychological theories reviewed in the chapter.

1. Learning music proceeds most effectively and efficiently when the skills and materials to be learned match the student's developmental level. Stages of cognitive and affective growth and research into children's thinking can and should inform curricular structure and pedagogy. Modes of representing music differ according to developmental level and should be considered in teaching.

2. Learning music proceeds most effectively and efficiently when the skills and materials to be learned are sequenced according to level of difficulty. This principle is a correlate of the previous one. Learning sequences should at all times complement and reinforce the developmental sequence. Technical study should be sequentially organized to take advantage of and build upon prior learnings and skills. To avoid confusion, the sequence should clarify and define the tasks and problems presented to the student.

3. Learning music proceeds most effectively and efficiently when learning strategies are drawn from the individual's style of learning. Learning is facilitated and enhanced when children are aware of the strategies they use to learn new information. What one learns must fit with what one already knows. The concept of "headfitting" is very useful in determining when and how to teach new skills and materials.

4. Memorizing music proceeds most effectively and efficiently when deliberate memory strategies are used. Students should be aware of how they memorize and what strategies work best for them. Analysis of the musical structure aids the memory process.

5. Learning music proceeds most effectively and efficiently when the student is motivated to learn. Motivation can also be viewed as stage related. An elementary school child is motivated by his or her interest in the task as well as by extrinsic rewards. The adolescent is motivated by level of aspiration and perceived competence. Reinforcement is an important factor in motivation. Musical understanding and technical facility are developed gradually and continuously through successful performance. Reinforcement is most effective when it is an intrinsic part of the learning situation; that is, the music or skill to be learned provides its own reward. In addition, students should be provided with well-defined long- and short-term goals and objectives. Understanding the results of one's practice is an important aspect in attaining goals.

Teachers are not psychologists, but an understanding of psychological principles can add credibility to teachings. For as teachers we are required to confront our students at the level they have reached and do what we can to move them toward new and expanding horizons. As Maxine Greene has so eloquently stated, "He [the teacher] can only be present to his students as a

171

human being engaged in searching and choosing, as someone who is willing to take the risk of new perspectives, as someone who cares" (1973, 297).

REFERENCES

Bamberger, J. (1982). Revisiting children's drawings of simple rhythms: A function for reflection-in-action. In S. Strauss, ed., *U-shaped behavioral growth*. New York: Academic Press.

Boardman, E., B. Andress, and F. Willman. (1988). *Music*. New York: Holt, Rinehart & Winston.

Boswell, J. (1969). An application of Bruner's theory of mental growth to the teaching of musical concepts in beginning instrumental music. University of Illinois, Ed.D. dissertation.

———. (ed.). (1985). The young child and music: Contemporary principles in child development and music education. Reston, VA: MENC.

Bruner, J. (1960). *The process of education*. New York: Vintage Books.

———. (1983). *In search of mind*. New York: Harper & Row.

Bruner, J., J. Goodnow, and G. Austin. (1956). *A study of thinking*. New York: Wiley.

Craik, F.I.M., and R. S. Lockhart. (1972). Levels of processing: A framework for memory research. *Journal of Verbal Learning and Verbal Behavior* 11, 671–684.

———. (1966). *Toward a theory of instruction*. Cambridge, MA: Belknap Press.

Davidson, L., P. McKernon, and H. Gardner. (1981). The acquisition of song: A developmental approach. In *Documentary report of the Ann Arbor symposium: Applications of psychology to the teaching and learning of music*. Reston, VA: MENC.

Deutsch, D. (ed.). (1982). *The psychology of music*. New York: Academic Press.

Dowling, W. J. (1982). Melodic information processing and its development. In D. Deutsch, ed., *The psychology of music*. New York: Academic Press.

———. (1984). Development of music schemata in children's spontaneous singing. In W. R. Crozier and A. J. Chapman, eds., *Cognitive processes in the perception of art*. Amsterdam: Elsevier.

Dowling, W. J., and D. L. Harwood. (1987). *Music cognition*. New York: Academic Press.

Flavell, J. H. (1971). First discussant's comments: What is memory development the development of? *Human Development* 14, 272–278.

Funk, J., and J. Whiteside. (1981). Developmental theory and the psychology of music. *Psychology of Music* 9 (2), 44–53.

Gagné, R. (1970). *The conditions of learning* (2nd ed.). New York: Holt, Rinehart & Winston.

Gardner, H. (1973). *The arts and human development*. New York: John Wiley.

———. (1983). *Frames of mind: The theory of multiple intelligence*. New York: Basic Books.

———. (1985). *The mind's new science*. New York: Basic Books.

Gibson, E. (1969). *Principles of perceptual learning and development*. New York: Appleton-Century-Crofts.

Gordon, E. (1979). Developmental music aptitude as measured by the primary measures of music audiation. *Psychology of Music* 7 (1), 42–49.

———. (1984). *Learning sequences in music: Skill content, and patterns*. Chicago: G.I.A.

Gordon, E., and D. Woods. (1984). *Jump right in: The music curriculum.* Chicago: G.I.A.

Greene, M. (1973). *Teacher as stranger.* Belmont, CA: Wadsworth.

Greer, R. D. (1981). An operant approach to motivation and affect: Ten years of research in music learning. In *Documentary report of the Ann Arbor symposium: Applications of psychology to the teaching and learning of music.* Reston, VA: MENC.

Hargreaves, D. (1986a). Developmental psychology and music education. *Psychology of Music* 14 (2), 83–96.

———. (1986b). *The developmental psychology of music.* Cambridge: Cambridge University Press.

Koffka, K. (1935). *Principles of Gestalt psychology.* New York: Harcourt, Brace.

Madsen, C. K., R. D. Greer, and C. H. Madsen (eds.). (1975). *Research in music behavior: Modifying music behavior in the classroom.* New York: Teachers College Press.

Madsen, C. K,. and C. Yarbrough. (1985). *Competency-based music education.* Raleigh, NC: Contemporary.

Maehr, M. (1974). Culture and achievement motivation. *American Psychologist* 9, 887–896.

———. (1983). The development of continuing interests in music. The Ann Arbor symposium, Session III, *Motivation and creativity.* Reston, VA: MENC.

Meyer, L. (1956). *Emotion and meaning in music.* Chicago: The University of Chicago Press.

Mill, J. (1873). *A system of logic, book 3.* New York: Harper and Brothers.

Miller, G. A. (1956). The magical number seven plus or minus two: Some limits on our capacity for processing information. *Psychological Review* 63, 81–97.

Neisser, U. (1967). *Cognitive psychology.* New York: Appleton Century-Crofts.

———. (1976). *Cognition and reality.* New York: W. H. Freeman and Company Press.

Pflederer, M. (1963). *The responses of children to musical tasks embodying Piaget's principle of conservation.* University of Illinois, unpublished doctoral dissertation.

———. (1964). The responses of children to musical tasks embodying Piaget's principle of conservation. *Journal of Research in Music Education* 12, 251–268.

———. (1967). Conservation laws applied to the development of musical intelligence. *Journal of Research in Music Education* 15, 215–223.

Psychology of music 15 (1), 1987.

Psychomusicology 7 (2), 1989.

Raynor, J. (1983). Step-path theory and the motivation for achievement. The Ann Arbor symposium, Session III, *Motivation and creativity.* Reston, VA: MENC.

Reimer, B. (1970, 1989). *A Philosophy of music education.* Englewood Cliffs, NJ: Prentice-Hall.

Serafine, M. L. (1980). Piagetian research in music. *CRME Bulletin* 62, 1–21.

———. (1983). Cognition in music. *Cognition* 14, 119–183.

———. (1988). *Music as cognition: The development of thought in sound.* New York: Columbia University Press.

Skinner, B. F. (1953). *Science and human behavior.* New York: MacMillan Publishing.

Sloboda, J. (1985). *The musical mind: The cognitive psychology of music.* Oxford: Clarendon Press.

Thomas, R. B. (1971). *Manhattanville Music Curriculum Project, interaction and synthesis.* Elnora, NY: Media.

Thorndike, E. L. (1913). The psychology of learning. *Educational Psychology* 2.

Thorpe, L. P. (1958). Learning theory and music teaching. NSSE Yearbook, *Basic concepts in music education.* Chicago: University of Chicago Press.

Tunks, T. (1980). Applications of psychological positions on learning and development to musical behavior. In D. A. Hodges, ed., *Handbook of music psychology.* Lawrence, KS: National Association for Music Therapy.

Webster, P., and M. Zimmerman. (1983). Conservation of rhythmic and tonal patterns of second through sixth grade children. *CRME Bulletin* 73, 28–49.

Werner, H. (1961). *Comparative psychology of mental development.* New York: Science Editions.

Williams, D. B. (1975). Short-term retention of pitch sequence. *Journal of Research in Music Education* 23, 53–66.

Winner, E. (1982). *Invented worlds: The psychology of the arts.* Cambridge, MA: Harvard University Press.

Wohlwill, J. (1970). From perception to inference: A dimension of cognitive development. *Cognitive Development in Children:* Five Monographs of the Society for Research in Child Development. Chicago: University of Chicago Press. Pp. 73–93.

Wolf, D., and H. Gardner. (1980). Beyond playing or polishing: A developmental view of artistry. In J. Hausman, ed., *Arts and the schools.* New York: McGraw-Hill.

Zimmerman, M. P. (1981). Child development and music education. In *Documentary report of the Ann Arbor symposium: Applications of psychology to the teaching and learning of music.* Reston, VA: MENC.

———. (1982). Developmental processes in music learning. In R. Colwell, ed., *Symposium in music education.* Champaign, IL: Crouse Printing.

———. (1987). The application of psychological principles to the teaching of piano. In J. Lyke and Y. Enoch, eds., *Creative piano teaching.* Champaign, IL: Stipes Publishing Co.

Zimmerman, M. P., and L. Sechrest. (1968). *How children conceptually organize musical sounds.* Evanston, IL: Northwestern University.

8

American Music Education:
Is It Better Than We Think? A Discussion of the
Roles of Performance and Repertory, Together With
Brief Mention of Certain Other Problems

Allen P. Britton

American music education is better than we tend to think it is. In the literal sense of the words, we live in the best of all possible worlds. It is certainly the very best that all of our striving has been able to produce. All of those concerned have thought their best thoughts and tried their hardest tries, and what we have is the result. Ought we despair because some of our dreams have never been realized? Or, taking into account the general cussedness of things, should we not be fairly content with what we have actually been able to accomplish?

I begin with quasi-cosmic considerations of this sort in order to prepare you for the thought I wish to develop in this chapter, specifically, that music education in the United States, on the whole and speaking generally, is truly something splendid, something to be encouraged and preserved largely in its present aspects. This opinion is not widely held among us, nor amongst our critics, both internal and external.

In short, I am going to argue that our heavy emphasis on musical performance is basically correct but that critics of this policy are right in some respects. We certainly ought to try to do a better job of teaching repertory, theory, and history.

Before going on, I want to call your especial attention to a brilliant article by Eunice Boardman that was published in the spring 1990 issue of the *Bulletin of the Council for Research in Music Education* entitled

"Needed Research in Music Education." Boardman's views contrast significantly with the ones to be developed in this chapter. However, she provides an analysis of accepted goals that should be noticed here. As penetrating as she is thorough, Boardman presents the "desired outcomes" of music education as these are typically to be found in our literature and as recently summarized in a publication of the National Endowment for the Arts, entitled *Toward Civilization*. The desired outcomes include giving "young persons a sense of civilization, of their heritage, as reflected in the arts," fostering "creativity by working on . . . reasoning and problem-solving skills . . . as well as the particular understandings of the art form necessary for creative production," developing "students' ability to communicate and to understand the communication of others, using symbolic systems and vocabularies other than verbal," and helping "young persons acquire tools needed for critical assessment and the making of choices based on models and standards of excellence."[1]

She also provides us with an outline of the reasons usually given for our failure to accomplish the "desired outcomes." The "failure explanations," according to Boardman, involve time and money limitations as reflected in staffing, scheduling, and instructional materials, problems of defining content and sequence and of coming to agreement on assessment, problems of teaching technique, and problems stemming from "ensconced teacher education programs unable/unwilling to change." She recommends that research should seek to resolve such problems, and she seems sanguine about the possibilities, even while admitting, with what I detect to be a sigh, that "the list of questions and implications for research seems staggering. It would be easy," she continues, "to feel so overwhelmed that one might decide simply to continue to make public statements of concern while quietly maintaining the status quo and complaining about the forces beyond one's control which make it impossible to create change."[2]

I admire her courage and honesty, but I think she is whistling in the dark with regard to the possibility that further research can solve the problems described. The research proposed can help alleviate our problems, but many of the problems themselves would go away were we to modify our goals. It seems to me that we ought to reassess our whole situation, to abandon goals that may be mistaken as well as impossible of attainment, and to devote ourselves to the improvement of what we have. In so doing I think that we can come to feel better about ourselves.

The general condition of music education has continued, despite occasional setbacks, to improve gradually during all the course of my lifetime. Many of the things that used to bother me can no longer do so simply because they have disappeared from the scene. For example, the musical content of elementary school songbooks no longer features the specially composed songs and the artificial folk songs that used to fill the books from which I sang in school. Our heightened awareness and appreciation of ethnic and cultural differences have permitted us to fill our books with real songs from real countries including our own, songs intended to be performed with faithfulness to their origins.

The very aims of elementary school music have been transformed. Children are no longer subjected to hours of drill on the sol-fa syllables. We seem to have learned the lesson that musicality is the important thing, that music reading is easy to teach to children who are enthusiastic about the music they are asked to perform. We seem to have learned the lesson taught by the Irishman Patrick Keenan over one hundred years ago when he complained about the songs in a singing manual prepared in England for Irish schools. "The tunes," he wrote, "do not pretend to any national character . . . are foreign to all sympathy . . . belong to no country . . . are sung in no home."[3] Tunes like that are no longer to be found in Irish textbooks, nor in our own.

The quality of college music education has also improved, particularly, I think, as regards research. A definite trend is noticeable away from the exclusive use of scientific (that is, mathematical) research techniques that have dominated us for so long.[4] I have treated this subject in detail elsewhere, but at this time and place, it seems appropriate to review briefly some of the principal considerations pertinent to it. In an intellectual world stunned by the achievements of physical science — what with atomic bombs, moon flights, computers, heart transplants, micro- and nanotechnology — small wonder that those of us engaged in other than scientific pursuits took to trading on the name, to pretending for self-protection that we were being scientific too. Some of you will remember the time when historians first took to calling themselves social "scientists." The world of professional education also adopted the external trappings of the physical scientist, even though we possessed no truly scientific theories as bases for research — no theories like the quantitative theories of relativity, quantum mechanics, and atomic weights; in short, nothing that would permit educational researchers to make precise measurements so as to add two to two and get four.

The results of such naiveté have been frustration, bewilderment, and disillusionment, and never has the world of professional education stood in lower general esteem, as Allan Bloom has reminded us. (I will not be discussing Allan Bloom here, but if you haven't done so already, please read his chapter on music — wrongheaded and uninformed as he may be at times, he hits a lot of nails squarely on the head.[5])

But now we have begun to remember that earlier historians and scientists — the Gibbons and the Prescotts, the Galileos and the Franklins —

177

were in fact upper-class amateurs, conducting their investigations for the fun of the intellectual quest rather than for any perceived practical gain. We seem now to be awakening from our pragmatic dreams and coming to realize that research, whether scientific or scholarly, should be pursued not in the hope of practical gain but for the joy of it, for the satisfaction of ascertaining and telling the truth about something.

Another consideration that accounts in part for the intellectual changes we are experiencing is the realization that the mere adoption of scientific method does not produce automatically the objectivity demanded by true science. Quasi-religious wars do take place among scientists as well as scholars. *The Journal of Research in Music Education* abandoned the Modern Language Association style sheet twenty years ago in favor of that of the American Psychological Association. It is only within the most recent past that *JRME* has adopted a more tolerant position, returning to its original practice of using whatever style sheet was appropriate to an individual article. Now one of our new problems is that of relearning the use of straightforward language, of learning how to speak and write in plain English rather than in Educationese.

However all of this may be, it seems indeed that studies in the history of music education have gained increasing respectability. The younger members of the profession are developing a more tolerant view of what is proper for dissertation topics (at least it seems so to me). I am not as sure, however, that the present generally felicitous situation has been as widely recognized among us as it ought to be.

The nicest thing to be said about our own form and style of music education is that it is virtually free of outside controls. No arm of the federal government exerts any jurisdiction over it, and very few states do anything more than make helpful suggestions. Certainly no one outside the profession itself says anything binding upon us with regard to what music we study or how we study it. Because our methods and materials are completely of our own invention, some might think that we can be saved from ourselves only by outside control. But who would be able to exercise this control? One can hear and read lots of criticism of the profession both from insiders and outsiders, but no one yet has offered any suggestions at all for establishing either an inside or outside system of control. The best we have been able to accomplish is to publish lists of aims and ideals and contest pieces, sample curriculums for educating teachers, and the like. And so, as the comic strip character Pogo discovered years ago, if there is an enemy, it is us. Any improvements to be made in music education can be made only by individual teachers, their organizations, and individual school systems; in other words, by ourselves, not collectively, but more or less individually.

We face a number of peculiar difficulties. Americans in general, music educators among them, tend to believe, on the basis of misleading or no evidence at all, that things musical are done better in Europe than here. But such is not really the case. Music education in German elementary schools consists of learning to sing by ear the folk songs of Germany together with a few songs from other countries — that's why all Germans can sing "Oh! Susanna." All other musical education in Germany comes after school and must be paid for by extra fees. Neither Germany nor any other European country possesses anything like our own commercial textbook series. There is little comparable in all of Europe to our high school bands, choirs, and orchestras, or our musicals. European visitors who discover the existence of these performing groups are always amazed that thousands of American secondary schools can afford to maintain fully instrumented ensembles and that so many American schools maintain fully equipped theaters. German schools cannot afford to issue oboes, bassoons, and the like to elementary school students, nor can the schools of other countries. Of course, competent musical instruction is provided everywhere in Europe for a small percentage of students, but, and this is what must be emphasized, nowhere does the percentage reach what we call the "select" 20 percent that we should be happy with but constantly blame ourselves for. European children simply do not have readily available the wealth of musical instruction taken for granted here.

Observations such as these are not intended to lead to complacency about the present status of music education in the United States, but they should provide a better basis than is often used on which to criticize and suggest improvement.

Now let us turn directly to the consideration of some difficult problems that continue to plague us. The greatest of these, in my opinion, is that we still tend to consider musical repertory as the means rather than the content of instruction. I do not speak here of the old pseudo-problem of whether we teach the child or teach the subject, but of whether we teach an actual individual piece of music or, rather, teach the theoretical category to which it belongs — whether we teach songs or song form, sonatas or sonata form. (Have you heard of the teacher who, after completing his lecture on sonata form, went on to remark, "And now I shall play you an almost perfect example of sonata form by Mozart.") We do not learn a Mozart sonata in order to learn sonata form; we learn sonata form in order to more readily understand Mozart.

If we thought our task was to teach certain musical compositions instead of certain theoretical ideas, then we could engage in more rational debates with ourselves as well as with outsiders concerning the actual music taught in schools. We could get right to the point of Plato's ancient educational question: "What knowledge is of the greatest worth?" What music, indeed, is of the most worth? Ought not this to be the most discussed question among teachers? Let us be even more specific. On my desk as I type these lines there lies a page from one of our marvelous state journals, *North Carolina Music Educators,* and it is headed "The 100 Most Popular Marches."[6] Obviously the editor's intent in reprinting this item from a 1976 issue of *The Instrumentalist* was to encourage the performance of the works listed or, in other words, to encourage putting them into the curriculum.

I applaud the effort and simultaneously point out how unusual it is. How many similar lists of the most popular, that is, the worthiest, items of any of dozens of musical categories have you seen? Where is the list of music everyone should know, or of the types of music with which all should be familiar — the standard choral pieces, piano pieces, and so on? Should not our music curriculum consist, first of all, of the world's most beautiful music? Should a child be able to sing in a high school choir or play in a high school band or orchestra for several years and still not have come to know at least a fair sample of the best there is of our musical heritage? For that matter, should not members of high school jazz bands have opportunities to play some of the masterpieces of big band music of the 1920s, 1930s, and 1940s? To construct curriculums with music of lasting beauty would by no means exclude the use of new music or even of the teaching pieces now so widely available. It would, however, ensure that music of the greatest worth would be presented to our students in larger quantities than is now the case, and that they would know some of it when they get out of school.

The obverse of this consideration is our professional preoccupation with method rather than content. Remember the expression "methods and materials"? The materials, of course, consisted of the music. Even if we were to alter our conception of content from musical theory to music itself, we probably would still continue to give content a secondary place to method. To do so is one of the natural pitfalls of teaching. The hardest problem is always to get method and content into appropriate balance. The expression "music itself" has two connotations. It can refer to actual compositions and improvisations, or it can refer to musical performance. Generally speaking, when we say that we are studying music, we actually mean the performance of music: producing tone, reading notation, counting time, caring for the instrument, and so on — rather than a repertory of individual musical masterpieces.

Although each connotation is perfectly legitimate, my observation has been that we tend to downplay repertory and forget that we learn to play in order to learn repertory. Playing is fun, but playing remains only fun unless we play something worth playing. Furthermore, technical ability comes and goes. Almost all musicians ultimately allow their technique to deteriorate a little, especially as the burdens of conducting, administration, classroom teaching, and scholarship settle gradually upon us. But a worthy piece of music once learned, once under the fingers, so to speak, can never be forgotten; we can enjoy every hearing of it for the rest of our lives.

And this brings us to a consideration of our sometimes peculiar attitude toward perfomance. This word also has two connotations. It can refer to public perfomance in recital, concert, or on parade, and it can refer simply to the business of singing and playing music as distinguished from reading and talking about it. Although the typical musician as well as the typical member of the general public never doubts that "making music," that is, performance, is the chief aim of musical endeavor, many critics of music education, including a significant percentage of musical scholars, display real regret that so much attention is given to musical performance in our schools. Let me quote a particularly clear and succinct statement of the critical position taken by many scholars, taken from an unpublished paper by an anonymous scholar. I wish to make use of it here so that I am sure not to falsify that position in any way. As you know, the NEA's *Toward Civilization* concluded that "basic arts education does not exist in the United States today,"[7] and our scholar comments:

> In the light of their penchant to concentrate on performance programs for the talented, music educators would find it difficult to take issue with this assessment. This bias for performance probably contributed to the perception that music education is more devoted to entertainment than to serious learning. Where skill has become an end in itself, knowledge of music is given little attention. . . . In music, particularly in the high schools, all that concentration on skill development for select students in band and chorus has been recognized for what it so often is — not an education in the musical heritage but a perfecting of performance. Our educational practices in the arts have betrayed us. In music the goal has not been education through performance so much as performance as an end in itself. The goal has not been to teach all students their musical heritage but rather to teach production to the talented.[8]

These particularly well-chosen words epitomize the nature of the charges continually brought against us during the past many years, and especially since the publication of the report of the Yale Seminar.[9] The charges have considerable truth in them, but they also display, in my opinion, an unconscious social disdain, a considerable bias, and a serious misunderstanding of the actual state of our affairs. The disdain is that of the liberal arts scholar for the professional musician. The bias is that which values talking about music above performing it. The serious misunderstanding lies in the implication that the general public (which includes about 20,000 boards of education) could somehow be brought to support, in the place of performing groups, senior high school courses in musicology and/or musical sociology (whether designated "music literature," "general music," or "music appreciation").

I wonder if those who suggest that we abandon bands and other performing groups in order to serve the 80 percent or so of nonperforming students have ever tried to imagine how the change could be effected. To require one semester of classroom music of every student not enrolled in a performing organization would mean, and here I guess that I have got to get categorical, (1) providing new teachers, (2) providing new rooms and equipment, (3) solving new scheduling problems, (4) obtaining new budgetary resources, and, perhaps most difficult of all, (5) securing new community and administrative support. These are entirely practical problems, of course, and, so far as I can see, each is insurmountable. Let us consider only the problem of finding the new teachers. Even if every college in the country were to begin right now offering a curriculum for the preparation of senior high school general music teachers, how many students do you think would enroll? All of our past experience teaches us how difficult it is to interest students in existing general music curriculums designed to prepare for teaching in elementary and junior high schools. How much harder would it be to find students who would enroll for a curriculum preparing for a field of teaching for which there is little if any actual demand?

A historical fact that is seldom, if ever, appreciated by educational historians is that no subject has ever secured a place in the American school system until long after there was a genuine public demand for instruction in it, usually demonstrated by the existence of numerous entrepreneurial schools. Privately operated singing schools antedated the introduction of music instruction in the Boston schools by more than 100 years. Many other subjects were never taught in public schools until long after there was obvious public demand, including mathematics, foreign languages, chemistry, driver training, dancing, cooking, and sewing. At the present time, there still exists a genuine demand for instruction in musical performance. Remember that the elementary school general music program is in fact largely based on singing, dancing, and playing simple instruments. Believe me, if there existed a genuine public demand for musicological instruction in our senior high schools, such instruction would have already found its place there.

I believe that the basic wisdom of the public is revealed in this situation. Music is not music until you can hear it, and you can't hear it until someone performs it. You can't enjoy it unless you hear it, and the greatest enjoyment comes in the playing of it. However this may be, it is through performance that one develops the mental discrimination necessary to the fullest under-standing of music. The best way to learn is still to do. I have lived for many years in a university town happily full of music lovers, many of whom have never played an instrument or otherwise involved themselves in practical music making. Some of these, however, can and do engage in what they believe are serious and competent critiques of the quality of the conductors, soloists, orchestras, and composers who perform for us, of their concerts as well as of their recordings. I remember well how surprised I was when one of my longtime acquaintances got me aside one day to ask, rather apologet-ically, about something that had "always puzzled him." I was prepared to hear one of those complicated questions that no one can answer. "Some-times," he began, "a piece will be listed on the program as a symphony in C minor. At other times the program will say symphony in C major. Could you tell me what the difference is?"

This man would on occasion speak with seeming authority on the relative merits of Gustav Mahler and Richard Strauss, and still neither his good musical ear nor his extensive reading had enabled him to understand a musical concept that any beginning instrumentalist acquires immediately. We have here one of those if-you-have-to-ask-you-ain't-never-going-to-know situations. What one knows, one knows, and what one doesn't know, one doesn't know one doesn't know. And on this account it is difficult to convince some people that the purpose of learning to perform is to learn better how to understand music; further, that it is quite difficult to under-stand the finer points of music if one has never subjected himself or herself to the discipline of learning to perform it.

Musicians themselves are usually blind to this circumstance. They as-sume that what they hear and understand is what all their listeners hear and understand. They tend not to realize as they play or hear someone else play a long sequence of musical phrases that the amateur by their side may be hearing only a succession of unrelated pitches, not even realizing that they are organized as phrases. The amateur may not be hearing any of the melodies, really, or the harmonies, or detecting the end of one section and the beginning of another. It is difficult to convince conductors of this psy-chological fact. The conductor may study a score for months before bringing it to an orchestra. He or she will then rehearse it as many times as possible, all the while insisting upon the most delicate nuances of expression. At the concert the audience hears only a series of general effects, not many of them pleasant to the ear. The conductor in his or her heart may then blame the audience for not responding enthusiastically and intelligently to a composi-tion they simply do not know and, in fact, have not, except in the grossest sense, really heard at all.

Such a comedy of errors continues in debates within the profession as well as between the profession and its patrons. When some of us use the word *form* in saying, for example, that for full enjoyment one must understand the form of a composition, we refer to unique form, the specific shape of an individual piece of music. Others — most others it would seem — understand the term to mean generalized form, the Platonic ideal form, perhaps, as in sonata-allegro form, what I have referred to above as theoretical form. No one has ever heard sonata form in the general sense, but for pedagogical reasons we keep on speaking of it and, as a result, we have almost come to believe it really exists. It is truly impossible to recognize any individual piece of music without recognizing its specific shape or form, and it is also impossible to recognize whatever beauty exists in a specific piece of music without recognizing its individuality of shape or form. But to say this is by no means to say that one can't enjoy a piece of music without knowing to what general category of musical form it belongs. Mozart himself never used the term *sonata form* (*sonata,* yes; *sonata form,* no).

Large misunderstanding exists concerning how music becomes music, psychologically speaking. Groups of tones assume form and become music only to the extent that they are repeated. Repetition is the key to making a succession of tones magically become a melody in the mind. Any melody upon very first hearing consists in fact of a series of unrelated tones. Only by hearing the sounds again do we begin to relate them, to hear them as an organic whole. Simple compositions provide for many repetitions of phrase within each performance. It is only by such repetition that the composition becomes intelligible and that the listener can be said to begin to understand the work. It is the performer, of course, in the very act of practicing, who repeats any given set of tones a sufficient number of times to ensure that the psychological miracle takes place.

It has always seemed strange to me that we as music educators seem to be the only branch of education to deprecate performing in favor of observing and philosophizing. Who ever heard of a course in history appreciation? chemistry appreciation? or football appreciation? Has athletics suffered because it has put a heavy emphasis on performance or because so much attention has been given to the select few who make the teams? Of course, athletic programs have their critics too, who deplore competititive sports and recommend that more attention be given to exercise and hygiene. But who can believe that the public will give up the Super Bowl for calisthenics, or that it should?

Critics should keep in mind that music in the schools exists only to the extent that boards of education insist upon it. Boards of education are comprised of ordinary citizens seeking, according to their own lights, the best for their children. Unlike education in other countries, which is controlled directly by central governments along with armies and postal services, education in our country is controlled directly by our citizen boards of education — an exercise in democracy unparalleled elsewhere. We have as much chance of changing the emphasis on musical performance as we do of changing that on athletic performance, mathematics performance, foreign language performance, or actual performance in any subject worthy of being taught in schools.

Educational problems are usually presented as polarities of desirable and undesirable procedures. We get on one side or another of an issue, erect straw men to knock down, and in general act as if one side is all wrong and another all right. With regard to all the polarities of music education, we should almost always avoid choosing one or the other exclusively but rather see to it that both are attended to. We must teach performance, because it is the only sure basis for understanding, but we must also teach history and theory. It's not enough just to learn the dates of historical events; you must also learn the significance of the events. It's not enough just to learn to play beautifully, you must learn to play something that is worth playing. Do you remember when piano teachers would forbid playing by ear? I remember when my old and good trumpet teacher assured me in the late 1920s that, were I ever to learn to play jazz, my career in music would be finished. Surely you have read Herbert L. Clarke's famous letter of January 13, 1921, to Elden E. Benge, which advised him not to change over from the cornet to trumpet, "as the latter instrument is only a foreign fad for the time present. . . . It has sprung up in the last few years like 'jaz' music, which is the nearest Hell, or the Devil, in music. It pollutes the art of Music."[10] (What would he have thought of Mick Jagger?)

Nowadays, I think, our understanding has improved, and there is general agreement that everyone should be taught to play by ear as well as by note. In like manner, we seem to agree that all should learn something about the proper performance of popular music as well as art music, that we should learn our scales perfectly as well as how to play any music expressively. I can remember when the principal aim of public school music was to teach "good music" in order to wean our students away from our own popular music so they might learn to enjoy exclusively the high art music of the European aristocracy. I can remember when all the conductors of and many of the performers in our major symphony orchestras were foreign-born and couldn't have played a jazz phrase correctly if their lives depended upon it. Should the fact that such is no longer the case be counted against music education? And how well, anyway, did we succeed in our efforts to stamp out ragtime, jazz, rock, country, and gospel? Despite all of our sermonizing against them, these musics have remained viable and indeed have captured the attention and admiration of the world. The existence of polarities, at least in music education, has usually meant that the scope of the subject was much greater than the profession thought at the time. Experience has often shown that both poles were good ones to aim for and that the middle ground was not to be neglected either.

The continued emphasis on performance in the schools, despite all criticism from outsiders, has resulted in the production of a host of marvelous singers and instrumentalists together with an enormous number of symphony orchestras, opera companies, and other civic performing groups. For this happy result we have to thank the elementary and secondary school teachers on the front lines rather than their presumed mentors in colleges and universities — the former did not pay much attention to the latter. So, our major orchestras and opera companies no longer need to import performers from Europe. Rather, we now do the exporting.

We have learned at last that folk music is good, that popular music is good, that jazz is good, that rock is good, and that Mozart is good. The upper classes, as spoken of by sociologists, now listen to and understand lower-class music, and vice versa. The world has changed, as it always does, not usually according to our hopes or expectations, and all of us now must be able to converse in a number of languages, musical as well as social and political.

Claude V. Palisca, the director of the 1963 Yale Seminar on Music Education, was asked in 1978, fifteen years after the event, to prepare some reflections upon it. What he said constitutes a remarkable vindication of what music education has accomplished, a vindication to which not enough of us have paid proper attention, in my opinion. I can't say it better than he does, so here is a paragraph quoted directly:

> The clamor for returning to the 3 R's has distracted educators from the fundamental place the arts should have in partnership with those basic skills and cognitive learning. Amidst the consternation about SAT scores, the public has not been told the encouraging news that students are arriving in college today so much more sophisticated and accomplished in the arts that if there were a score to express it, it might be a multiple of that of 1963. Music in particular has attained a status among young people that the most optimistic among us in 1963 could not have predicted. The Woodstock phenomenon is only the most visible and least attractive side of this music boom. Those who read applications for admission to colleges and meet the freshmen who arrive are struck by the large number of musicians whose level of performance is nearly professional; these are products of high schools, private schools, private teachers and neighborhood music schools concerning which my colleagues spoke so despairingly in 1963. They were obviously doing some things right.[11]

If the chairman of music at Yale University, who is also one of the nation's most distinguished musicologists, does not in any way deprecate performance, why should we? If our music education profession has failed in attempting the impossible but succeeded in accomplishing the possible, that's pretty good. Let's not complain. Rather let us study the means by which success has been achieved and seek to utilize such means in carrying out our long-term aims, which can only be to bring more music to more of the American people. Remember that we have been most successful when we have been truest to music itself. Music, as the poet suggests, is its own excuse for being. Austin A. Harding, Joseph E. Maddy, Marguerite V. Hood, William D. Revelli, and thousands of others have demonstrated over many years that the way to win children to music is to give them as much of the best of it as the day allows. There is no way in which music can serve other social ends unless it is first of all music.

NOTES

1. National Endowment for the Arts, *Toward Civilization: a Report On Arts Education* (Washington, DC: U.S. Government Printing Office, 1988).

2. Eunice Boardman, "Needed Research in Music Education," *Bulletin of the Council for Research in Music Education,* no. 104 (Spring 1990), pp. 6–7, 9.

3. From the Appendix to the *Twenty-second Report of the Commissioners of National Education in Ireland, 1855,* in Marie McCarthy, *Music Education and the Quest for Cultural Identity in Ireland, 1831–1989* (Ph.D. diss., University of Michigan, 1989), p. 74.

4. See Richard Colwell, "The Organist's and Scholar's Contribution to Music Education Research," pp. 13–22 in Anthony Kemp, ed., *Research in Music Education: a Festschrift for Arnold Bentley* (n.p., International Society for Music Education, Edition No. Two, 1988). See also, as soon as you can, the as-yet unpublished paper by Robert G. Petzold, "Music Education Research: A Historical Perspective and Implications for the Future," which he read at the Indianapolis meeting of the Music Educators National Conference on April 21, 1988. See also my own paper, "Research in Music Education, With Particular Reference to the Historic and the Scientific," originally delivered on August 28, 1988, in connection with the Symposium, Music in American Schools, 1838–1988, A Sesquicentennial Celebration, held August 26–28, 1988, at the University of Maryland, College Park, in cooperation with the Music Educators National Conference. Michael L. Mark was the chairman, and the papers are being edited for publication by Bruce D. Wilson.

5. Allan Bloom, *The Closing of the American Mind: How Higher Education Has Failed Democracy and Impoverished the Souls of Today's Students* (New York: Simon and Schuster, 1987), pp. 68–81.

6. See the issue for September 1988, p. 33.

7. National Endowment for the Arts, *Toward Civilization,* p. 13.

8. This is from an unpublished paper sent to me privately.

187

9. Claude V. Palisca, *Music in our Schools, a Search For Improvement. Report of the Yale Seminar on Music Education.* U.S. Department of Health, Education, and Welfare, Office of Education (Washington, D.C.: U.S. Government Printing Office, 1964).

10. For a facsimile, see Clifford Lillya, "About That Famous Letter," *ITG* [International Trumpet Guild] *Journal,* 12 (December 1987), pp. 12ff.

11. Claude V. Palisca, "Prefatory Remarks," *Bulletin of the Council for Research in Music Education,* no. 60 (Fall 1979), p. 3.

Part II

Music in the Schools

9

The Role of Music in General Education

Clifton A. Burmeister

> The problem is that basic arts education does not exist in the United States today. . . . The single greatest drawback . . . is . . . emphasis on skill development at the expense of the art form as a whole.
>
> — "Toward Civilization: A Report on Arts Education"
> March 1988 National Endowment for the Arts

No consideration of the role of music in general education can ignore the implications of this indictment coming at a time when the attention of the nation is focused again on the critical need to improve education by strengthening "basics."

Support for our position that the arts are basic abounds in current statements such as: "The major argument for the arts in education is that since humans experience and give expression to their most deeply held values, beliefs, and images through the arts, there can be no adequate form of general education that does not include them."[1]

How to build a secure foundation on that consensus, if it does exist, has become crucial, for "if we maintain our present monolithic concentration on bands, orchestras, and choruses as the major ways to offer special musical opportunities, and if we continue to concentrate on performance-focused methodologies as the major way to provide general music education, then we may find ourselves left in history's dust."[2]

When Lowell Mason convinced the Boston School Committee in 1838 to include music in the public school curriculum as a required ("basic") subject, it was because music met the same criteria for inclusion as all subjects — intellectual, moral, and physical — plus added benefits in areas of recreation, worship, and discipline. Yet after nearly a century and a half of

191

spectacular lateral growth, with considerable emphasis on performance, Michael Mark reported that "music education, as a formal discipline within the public education structure, has not succeeded in making the United States a musical nation by producing an adult population that is musically literate, appreciative, and participatory."[3]

The story of the growth of music education was splendidly chronicled in the February 1988 special issue of the *Music Educators Journal:* "Music in Our Schools — the First 150 Years." One of the earliest recorded surveys on music education, a 1919 survey of 359 cities in thirty-six states prepared by a committee representing the National Education Association and the Music Supervisors National Conference, indicated that every high school in the sample had a mixed chorus, and two-thirds of these high schools offered separate boys' and girls' glee clubs. Three-fourths of the schools owned and lent orchestral instruments; band was offerend in one-fourth of the schools surveyed. Music credit could be earned in half of the high schools in theory (30 percent) and appreciation (35 percent), with credit for applied study outside of school recognized by one-third.[4]

The first of two NSSE yearbooks devoted to music education, published in 1936, opened with the editor's preface, which contained these words:

> There may be mentioned two distinct impressions gained while editing the material: first, that the presentation is eminently sane and practical — that, in other words, it is remarkably free from the emotional temperamentality that many persons persistently associate with the utterances of those professionally concerned with music; second . . . that the greater part of this yearbook can be read with distinct profit by superintendents of schools, curriculum supervisors, and other school administrators, even if they personally can't tell *Yankee Doodle* from *God Save the King*.[5]

It seems ironic that in attempting to be whimsical, editor Guy Whipple unwittingly juxtaposed the affective basis for aesthetic education with a major reason for our apparent inability to communicate this to those who make curricular decisions. It was so then; it is so today.

The rest of the 1936 Yearbook details a pattern for school music that must have been considered to be ideal for that time. James Mursell's guiding psychological principle was that the music program be an organized opportunity for aesthetic experience, defined as "one in which a person enjoys music." This requires three types of activity: listening, performing, and creating, which should give the pupil a vehicle of universal emotional expression.[6]

Lilla Pitts outlined typical musical activities of the school as (1) required general music (singing, music reading, listening); (2) elective extracurricular music (instrumental groups, vocal organizations, clubs, operettas); and (3) school assemblies.[7] Even then, Edgar Gordon was concerned that "with the endless crop of skillful performers who are being produced by the schools of America . . . we are faced with the necessity for a new orientation of objectives . . . away from the utilitarian and toward the cultural and avocational."[8]

The pattern of school music developed during the first century survived World War I without significant alteration, as depicted in the first *Music Education Source Book* published by MENC (Music Educators National Conference) in 1947. Recommendations for the future role of music in general education were contained in resolutions adopted by MENC in 1946:

> We commend highly the attention now being given to the glee clubs, choruses, choirs, orchestras and bands in the high schools. However, these elective subjects reach only a small percentage of high school students throughout the nation. To provide appropriate musical experiences for a larger portion of pupils we urgently recommend that more offerings in general music courses be included in the curriculum.[9]

Accordingly, eight years later, the second *Music Education Source Book* displayed growing concern of music teachers and general administrators about the role of music in education, and it documented the need for guiding principles — a philosophy of music education.[10] *Basic Concepts in Music Education, I,* was "designed to emphasize the emerging trend toward more effective orientation of instructional programs to accepted goals of formal education."[11] Fundamental concepts were drawn from selected major disciplines that were related to educational theory and practice in general and then to music education in particular. The result, though it may not have been a philosophy of music education, has been said to have provided guidelines for the development of such a philosophy.

In searching for guidelines at that time, we recognized that popular programs of school music activity existed in large numbers because of the universal appeal of music to young people, community approval of their efforts in public, and the undeniable enthusiasm of music educators who like children and like to work with them. In the face of such success, the need for new concepts may not have been apparent. Community demand for public performance could keep music programs going without them. Teachers were increasingly preoccupied with routine details of performance programs, insisting on higher standards because of the mounting pressure of professional performance from radio, TV, movies, and live concerts.[12]

193

One result has been an ever-widening gap between concepts/guide-lines/philosophy and school practice. The outward form of music education in 1958 had changed little from the pattern developed during the first hundred years. Elementary school general music, emphasizing singing and listening, seldom attained the desired minimum of 100 minutes per week taught by a music specialist. Secondary general music, usually limited to one or two junior high school years at most, was seldom required beyond the eighth grade. High school bands, orchestras, and choruses rarely involved more than 30 percent of the students in rehearsal classes in which the emphasis was usually on preparation of a limited repertoire for public performance. "To have won for music the voluntary support of the public stands out as the most magnificent accomplishment of American music education."[13]

The search for a philosophy continued from 1958 to the present, marked both by elaborate attempts of agencies outside of the music education profession to underscore the need for change and by apparent reluctance of those in music education to implement change even while acknowledging the need. One reason may be found in these words: "Music education, although created and nurtured by a popular love of music, has never-the-less always operated at a certain distance from the well-springs of American musical life, both popular and artistic. Music education in the United States has tended to create a world of its own with its own people, music, and thought pattern."[14]

The most ambitious of the attempts to effect change began rather modestly in 1959 as the Young Composers Project (YCP) funded by the Ford Foundation, which placed each of thirty-one young composers in a selected community school to write music for the performing groups there. In 1962 the Ford Foundation granted MENC $1.38 million to organize a Contemporary Music Project (CMP), which was to continue the YCP to 1968 with forty-six more composers and sponsor sixteen workshop/seminars plus six pilot projects in cooperating elementary and secondary schools.

In 1965 a CMP seminar held at Northwestern University defined "comprehensive musicianship" as a generating concept for planning music instruction in all areas and at every level, preschool through postgraduate. This was disseminated in six regional Institutes for Music in Contemporary Education, which then conducted experimental programs in thirty-six educational institutions.

In 1968 another Ford Foundation grant of $1.34 million, to which MENC added $50,000 annually, was used to administer the CMP for five more years. Three programs were continued:

1. Professionals in Residence — composers assigned to communities

rather than school systems
2. Teaching Contemporary Music — grants to teachers for experimental programs
3. Forums on Contemporary Music — to bring together representatives of all aspects of the music profession

The final invitational forum, held in January 1973, was cosponsored by CMP and Northwestern University. It brought together representatives of colleges and universities offering graduate study in music and of organizations concerned with the quality of such programs. The focus of this forum was the professional education of musicians. Himie Voxman asked: "What is new in graduate music education?" His answer: "In all candor, it must be said that to a great extent the winds of change and the ferment that has recently characterized undergraduate music education have pretty much by-passed the graduate area. . . . Certainly the implementation of the NASM Basic Musicianship Statement is going to require a breadth of training in the college instructor that we have not always provided in the past."[15]

Here, then, was combined a key guiding principle — comprehensive musicianship — with the need to reexamine the graduate education of those who will be the teachers of undergraduate music majors. If the implications of the NASM Basic [Comprehensive] Musicianship Statement are to be realized, the Forum recommended that graduate programs in music should require (1) a demonstrated understanding of the musical processes within a wide variety of music; (2) familiarity with a basic repertoire of music through performance, including performance practice, and analysis; and (3) fluency in making evaluative judgments about music and conceptualizing about it as an aesthetic experience. "Special emphasis was placed on the need for a demonstrated competence in the teaching of music as a significant aspect of every graduate program in music."[16]

In searching for guiding principles, we are always aware of exemplary music programs, "oases of excellence," which seem to successfully defy patterns of planning for popular performance. Invariably the catalyst seems to be an unusual teacher. Two such teachers have been featured in recent articles of the *Music Educators Journal*, Kenneth Phillips, who said, "The choir must become a vehicle for a comprehensive approach to music learnings if choral programs are to be a vital part of a student's music education," and Martin Bergee, who said, "To gain a more secure position for bands as a basic part of the over-all curriculum, we must first administer our programs as basic."[17]

Perhaps we have not been as concerned as we should be about the selection, education, and certification of music teachers. Most young musicians come to college with intensive precollege experience in solo and ensemble training and performance but with little knowledge of music theory, history, and literature, and with almost no basis for making aesthetic judgments in the fine arts. If their undergraduate education is fractionated among these elements, with continued emphasis on performance largely taught as error identification and correction ("show and tell") by teachers who are products of the same system, then the apparent resistance to change in music education can be understood but need not be accepted as inevitable.

Comprehensive musicianship is deceptively simple to describe: every music education class or activity, required or elective, should provide to some degree opportunities for performance, listening, composing, and analytical aesthetic judgment. In some, like band, orchestra, and choral classes, the emphasis will be on performance, but opportunities for student involvement in creating, listening, and evaluating as it relates to performance should be sought. Classes in theory, history, and literature can be combined and planned to include performance, listening, composing, analysis, and aesthetic evaluation in varying degrees.

A required high school general music course, first recommended by MENC in 1946, still appears in the curriculum of some of the high schools in the twenty-six states that as of March 1989 required a unit in the arts for graduation. In Illinois, one of the states in which music is included in the courses of study that a district must provide, a strong bid for a required music course appeared in the 1966 state guide:

> A high school which purports to provide a broad general education cannot logically avoid having a required music course. The required high school music course should be approached by both students and teachers as an opportunity for a serious study of the great music in the cultural heritage. The content of the course should be focused directly on developing the aesthetic sensitivity of students and on bringing about familiarity with the understanding of a representative portion of the great music of the world."[18]

Planned and taught comprehensively by teachers who were themselves comprehensively educated, such a course would be compatible with Reimer's projection for a music education program of the future:

1. Required general music (comprehensive music) to develop musical literacy
2. Elective performance
3. Elective composition

"A three-point program would, for the first time in history, truly represent in education the three major functions in the art of music as it exists in Western culture: listening, performing, and composing."[19]

Elective performance has borne the brunt of a great deal of criticism since the MENC resolution of 1946 that commenced bands, orchestras, and choruses but called for more general music courses in the curriculum. (See previous discussion in this chapter.) Any solution for this difficult dilemma must recognize several factors already mentioned in other connections:

1. Enthusiastic public support of high school performance
2. Universal appeal of music to young people
3. Performance-oriented education of music teachers
4. Increasing pressure to deny curricular status and financial support to any school-supported activity that is not considered "basic"

Performance was, is, and probably always will be the compelling motivation for school music activity. This is a given, not likely to be challenged. In an ideal situation, music educators should be responsible for three categories or levels of performance:

1. Performance used as a functional tool for promoting musical (aesthetic) growth in all classes at every level (comprehensive musicianship)
2. Public demonstrations of a refined portion of that process in concerts and recitals
3. Public entertainment probably not concerned primarily with educational values, but highly prized by students and community when done well

Where do we go wrong? We go wrong in ordering our priorities. Too often we have placed ourselves in indefensible positions as educators by giving highest priority to public entertainment in such matters as use of allotted resources, selection of only the most capable students, and choice of literature. When this becomes the total music program at the secondary level, there is no incentive to promote general music education.

Physical education faced a similar problem, but the solution was determined when it was found that children were leaving school physically incapable of coping with the demands of a highly industrialized nation at war. Physical education became a required basic for all children through high school, the first priority of the physical educator. Interschool athletic competition continues to flourish as an elective extracurricular activity, well supported by the community and usually coached by the teachers who also plan and teach the required classes designed to meet the physical needs of every child.

What are the needs of every child that music education purports to serve? How well are these needs being met? These questions are neither trivial nor rhetorical because "if music plays a considerable role in the lives of only a few individuals, or a trivial role in the lives of most individuals, it has no place in *general* education. . . . Formal general education includes only what (a) cannot be learned or learned well through informal means and (b) what is judged to be essential for all members of the community to know. . . . To say that music ought to be part of general education is to say that all of us ought to be musically literate."[20]

Musical literacy, implicit in reading, writing, singing, playing, knowing, and valuing, has been foremost in the stated objectives of general music since its inception. During the school years 1971 and 1972, these learnings were measured in a representative sample of children using instruments written and tested by music educators for the National Assessment of Educational Progress (NAEP). The results were reported to a special session of MENC meeting in Anaheim in 1974. They were so startling that they made TV news, and at least two of the major newsweeklies reported them. Not only were average scores extremely low, but when general music scores from schools with "exemplary" programs were compared statistically with those from schools having little general music education — skill scores held constant — there appeared to be no significant difference.

The first reaction of some music educators was to challenge the validity of the tests and reject the results. Others viewed them as needed documentation for strengthening required general music without devitalizing elective classes and activities. Ten years later, in 1984, MENC set three major goals for 1990 and beyond:

1. By 1990, every student, K–12, shall have access to music instruction in school. The curriculum of every elementary and secondary school, public or private, shall include a balanced, comprehensive, and sequential program of music instruction taught by qualified teachers.
2. By 1990, every high school shall require at least one Carnegie unit of credit in the arts for graduation. The arts shall be defined as music, visual arts, theater, and dance.
3. By 1990, every college and university shall require at least one Carnegie unit in the arts for admission.

As of November 1987, music was required in grades K–5 in thirty states; grades seven through eight in ten states; grade nine in one state; and music was not required for grades ten through twelve in any state.[21] These figures, disappointing as they must be to any music educator, may conceal far worse situations if Florida is any indicator. As reported by Bill Bouknecht, in 1987 music and art were no longer defined as basic subjects by Florida law; Florida's basic subjects are those that "shall be made available by the school districts to all students."[22]

A recent Florida Music Educators Association survey shows that in 38 percent of the schools reporting, students receive less than forty minutes of music instruction per week in grades K–3; in grades four through six only 4 percent receive instruction in general music three times a week; only 5 percent offer general music in grades seven through nine, and in these few the "exposure" can be as little as six to nine weeks during the three years.

According to the *Soundpost* survey, music in grades nine through twelve is offered as an elective in thirty-two states, with open admission required by law in twelve. In most communities this consists of instrumental and vocal performing groups, a few fine arts offerings including music, and very few high school general music classes.

Music educators have been curiously ambivalent about high school general music. Collectively we recognize the need, collectively we endorse repeated calls for action, but individually we are reluctant to offer general music unless required. We are certain that students will enroll in general music class only if it is required, yet we know that all of them share a nearly universal penchant for listening to popular music. If music is such a prominent part of their world without benefit of formal instruction, why persist in striving for what seems to be barely attainable? It is because what is immediately evident is such a small part of what is potentially there. And that is where our priorities must be.[23]

According to the *Soundpost* survey report, twenty-six states now have some type of arts requirement for graduation. Music is usually specified as one option for satisfying the requirement, but this offers little support for general music in most schools, where it is common practice to accumulate Carnegie units of credit through multiple or consecutive registrations in bands, orchestras, or vocal groups providing fractions of unit credit. The same can be said for the Goal 3 requirement of a unit in the arts for college/university admission now operative as state board policy in only seven states.

This leaves forty-one states in which "students can be given a high school diploma and called educated without any study in the arts."[24] In all fairness it must be noted that many of them also cannot read, write, or compute enough to meet the minimum requirements for helping us maintain national supremacy in today's high-tech world.

Will it help to point out that in primitive societies, where survival is the goal of education, the arts have always played an important role? This role seems to diminish in emerging societies that are busily engaged in learning how to create and maintain a surplus. What can we say about the need to educate for productive use of leisure time in our fully emerged technological society where more of the work is being done by fewer people in increasingly shorter units of time?

In 1780, in a letter to his wife, Abigail, President John Adams said: "I must study politics and war, that my sons may have liberty to study mathematics and philosophy. My sons ought to study mathematics and philosophy, geography, natural history, and naval architecture, navigation, commerce and agriculture in order to give their children a right [and the means] to study painting, poetry, music, and architecture." Adams predicted it would take three generations to go from education for survival to education for leisure. This was the amount of time that passed from when the first bill to establish a national arts council was proposed, which died in committee in 1877, to the first federal program in the arts, Federal Project #1, the WPA program that lasted from 1935 to 1943.

Twenty years of war and its aftermath were to pass before an Advisory Council on the Arts was created by executive order of President John F. Kennedy in June 1963. Yet, a few days before his assassination, he was able to say in a speech at Amherst College: "I see little of more importance to the future of our country and our civilization than full recognition of the place of the artist. I look forward to an America which will reward achievement in the arts as we reward achievement in business and statecraft." It is significant that this interest more than survived the tragedy in Dallas. In 1963, $15.5 million was allotted by Congress to build a John F. Kennedy Center for the Performing Arts in Washington; in 1964 the National Council on the Arts was created by executive order; in 1965 the National Foundation on the Arts and Humanities was passed, which provided $10 million per year to stimulate programs at all levels.

Can we afford anything like that today? The total budget for 1967 federal expenditures was $113 billion, of which $70 billion alone was earmarked for defense and war. In the words of the Honorable John Brademas of Indiana, cosponsor of the bill that established the National Foundation on the Arts and Humanities: "This less than one–ten thousandth for the arts pinches the federal budget as the purchase of a concert ticket pinches the president of General Motors."

Since 1968, if numbers are a valid indication, we still seem to be riding the crest of a cultural boom. Each year there have been more amateur musicians, more records sold, more people attending plays and concerts. It is unfortunate that we cannot say that the cultural level of today's society reflects this apparent proliferation in cultural activity. It requires neither a discriminating ear nor a discerning eye to deny this. Numbers alone won't do; quantity has never been enough. In the words of Richard Evans, commentator for an early Mormon Tabernacle Choir broadcast: "The outcome of a country depends on the quality of its idleness."

Can this be true today? Is it possible that our ultimate destiny as a nation will be determined more by what citizens do with their leisure time than by their productive efforts to solve the basic problems of continued existence in a hostile world? We find this hard to accept: "There are many who do not feel quite comfortable in the thought that music is an activity for leisure. . . . Leisure is now not only earned, it is now not only legitimate but is as legitimate as work. . . . Today it is as much a major assignment of education to supply the tools for leisure as it is to supply the tools for vocational activity."[25]

Another concept, closely related to the foregoing, was first noted in these words from the report of the Board of the Boston Academy of Music in 1836: "Now, the defect of our present system, admirable as that system is, is this, that it aims to develop the intellectual part of man's nature solely when, for all the true purposes of life, it is of more importance, a hundredfold, to feel rightly than to think profoundly."[26]

Our nation was recently engaged in war in the Persian Gulf, a war that could have escalated into a horrendous global conflict. As we agonized with the leaders of the civilized world who would make decisions, some of which involved the use of weapons capable of total destruction, these words supplied an urgency: "For in their emotions men are united, whereas the inevitable differences of intellect separate men from one another."[27] As we continue to grow in knowledge of ways in which music affects behavior, we can again affirm that "while music is not the only activity which relates directly to emotional growth and development, it does possess these unique qualities:

- Music is the most subtle, pervasive, and insistent of all the arts.
- It requires no intellectualization to work its effects.
- Its effects cannot be denied by the auditor. It is impossible to direct or divert the psycho-physical effects of the sheer potency of tone by an act of the will.
- Special abilities are not necessary. All can share in a response to music.

In the plainest language possible, we like music because it makes us feel good. Given proper guidance, that liking may be developed into refined aesthetic sensitivity. If the activities which foster that development continue to make us feel good, it cannot be anything but beneficial to our emotions. And, if the fun in being musical is not thwarted in the process, music will have made a significant contribution to general education."[28]

Do we need new concepts? It should be obvious that something should be changed if music education is ever to attain its major goals — the high hopes that have motivated succeeding generations of music educators for a century and a half. "Old" concepts should not be abandoned simply because they have not yet generated new methodologies, solved old problems, attracted loyal followers, or enjoyed instant public support. Neither should "new" concepts be embraced uncritically simply because they offer untried novelty. It could indeed turn out that what we welcome as new may not always be new, and it possibly did not work very well before.

A case in point could be required general music, K–6. New concepts are not needed as much as renewed commitment to old goals, seldom yet reached quantitatively and rarely productive of measurable attainments in basic musicianship. If school music is to make its maximum contribution to general education, the process must start here. Both the amount of class contact and the quality of the experience should be matters of concern to all music educators, their teachers of undergraduate music education majors, and their graduate music faculties.

Elementary music classes should be taught by music specialists. This does not rule out the possibility that a musically educated classroom teacher, alone or in combination with a music supervisor, can effectively teach the fundamentals of basic musicianship. It does place the emphasis where it belongs — on the quality of the experience.

Junior high school general music will continue to present problems as long as conflicting or shifting educational policies affect the curriculum. Is junior high school the culmination of elementary education? If so, should music be planned and taught by an elementary music specialist responsible for the sequence and balance in a comprehensive program? If junior high school is treated as the introduction to secondary education, can music retain its status as a required basic subject? If not, should general music become an elective among a plethora of band, orchestra, chorus, art, dramatics, and other similar courses introductory to high school electives? Should junior high school be replaced by a middle school with its own philosophy, curriculum, and teachers, geared to the adolescent needs of children in transition to adulthood?

In all this confusion, the common certainty remains that the quality of the experience will depend largely on the education, commitment, and motivation of individual teachers. Too often the junior high school general music class has been the dumping ground for students required to earn a music credit but unable or unwilling to elect band, orchestra, or chorus and for teachers of performance classes who are forced reluctantly to accept classes for which they have had inadequate education.

No simple solution seems evident at this time, but a "new" concept may provide guidance. If basic musicianship is ever to be required of all students for high school graduation, it would seem that there is no alternative to urging continuation of required general music through junior high school.

Should music be required in high school? The second MENC goal for the 1990's falls short of recommending it in specifying at least one Carnegie unit in the arts, wherein the definition of arts includes music. If credits earned in performance activities may be used to satisfy this requirement, it becomes, in a sense, self-defeating: "A high school music program consisting solely or largely of performance activities is deficient in at least two respects: students who do not perform receive no education in music; there is an inevitable gap between the performance level of any amateur performer and his potential for the aesthetic perception of music."[29]

If the intent of the second MENC goal is to mandate a required course in the arts, which can include music, a second anticipated weakness can be countered, namely, that of forcing the student to choose one among several fine arts courses.

Ideally, if every music course and every performance class were deliberately planned and taught so that students at every level (K–12) would have opportunities to sing, play, read music, write music, listen, criticize, and make aesthetic judgments about music, this whole discussion could become irrelevant (see the previous discussion of comprehensive musicianship in this chapter). I say "could" because this would happen only if music teachers were themselves educated comprehensively and were motivated, urged, and required to make the basic music education of all students their first priority.

The selection, education, and certification of music teachers has not changed fundamentally since 1936 when John W. Beattie asked: "Just what qualities should the administrator seek in selecting a music teacher? First of all, he should demand a reasonable degree of musicianship. By musicianship we mean thorough understanding of the theoretical and historical background of music, plus *considerable skill in its performance*."[30]

The first curriculum for the bachelor's degree with a major in music education was recommended in 1930 by the NASM. Of the 120 hours for graduation, thirty were to be in applied study (performance); thirty-six in music theory, history and conducting; twenty-six in professional education (including music education), eighteen in general academic subjects; and ten in electives. It was acknowledged that the 10 hours of electives would probably be needed to satisfy state certification requirements in academic subjects.

Although a certain amount of curriculum tinkering has altered the content and modes of teaching within each area, the pattern of one-fourth applied study (usually one-on-one), compartmentalized theory and history courses, and minimal liberal arts with scant room for any fine arts still prevails in most schools that offer a music education major.

High school students who have found great satisfaction in their school performing groups and who wish to major in music usually seek institutions where they can continue applied study and performance. Of this group, those who major in music education usually represent one of three categories:

1. Students who seek a career in teaching because they want to work with young people; they have chosen music because it brings them a joy that they want to share
2. Realists who want a career in music and recognize that for them teaching offers the best opportunity
3. Disappointed defeatists, bitter because they cannot succeed as professional performers

Most high school music teachers come from the second category. They bring to the classroom a love for music and a devotion to the art of performance that has been primarily responsible for the tremendous accomplishments of their bands, orchestras, and choruses. Paradoxically, the more successful their public demonstrations are judged to be by the community, the more difficult it becomes to find time, resources, and motivation to teach the basic musicianship needed by all high school students.

A music requirement could provide the support that high school music teachers need to help them order their priorities. In December 1987 the then-secretary of education, William J. Bennett, released his version of an ideal high school curriculum (see MENC *Soundpost,* Spring 1988). It included one year of art and music, required, at that time, in only fifteen states. Bennett said: "In an indelible and vivid way, they [the arts] give us insights into our heritage, our traditions, and our civilization. . . . They let us look at human nature through the eyes of master observers, and thus help us to see what we look at, hear what we listen to, and feel what we touch." Viewed out of context, such a course — half music, half art — might seem pitifully inadequate considering the enormity of the problem with which this chapter opened: that *basic arts education does not exist in the United States today.*

If, however, the required high school music/art course represented the capstone of a required "balanced, comprehensive and sequential program of music instruction taught by qualified teachers" (first MENC goal) it might well be that another generation of interested observers could look back at this time as a watershed in the development of music education. To accomplish this without destroying the truly remarkable edifice built largely on 150 years of skill development could be the greatest challenge any generation of music educators has been asked to face.

William Lepley, director of the Iowa Department of Education, has provided a projection of an ideal community school district for the year 2010. Some of its features (paraphrased) are the following:

1. Because education is continuous, spanning a person's lifetime, schools should permit citizens to enter at any time and never be forced to leave. In the process, students will move in and out smoothly without barriers such as district boundaries, grade levels, neighborhood locations, and regulatory restrictions.
2. In 2010, society will have realized that school is the single societal institution that can be at one and the same time an advocate, resource, and catalyst for children, families, and learners of all ages.
3. In addition to educational programs, the ideal school will house health, job, and human services agencies. It will be the senior citizen volunteer center, and educational opportunities will range from childbirth and parenting classes to preretirement planning.
4. Buildings will be open around the clock for adult and community education classes. The school year will not be limited to 180 five-and-a-half hour instructional days.
5. Students will be assessed not only on the work they complete, but also on the skills they master. Student advancement to grade levels will be based on abilities.
6. The ideal school will allow teachers to teach at their optimum. The typical teacher will spend about three hours daily in direct instruction by using new technological tools, paraprofessionals, volunteers, senior citizens, and parents. Flexible scheduling will allow time for planning, discussions with colleagues, and enhancing abilities through continued learning.
7. Preparatory programs for teachers will include college courses with internship or residency in a regional clinical school. The profession will attract highly qualified people, says Lepley, because we can improve the workplace for educators by recognizing differential roles and lengths of contracts, special skills and experience, and paying them based on performance.
8. In an ideal district the superintendent will function as a community leader responsible for coordinating children and family services. Lepley says, "While we have begun developmental efforts for teachers, we have ignored the development of the administrators who must make the new systems work."[31]

Will such new systems work? Lepley said, "Many of the initiatives that will result in the Ideal Community School District exist today in Iowa." In such functional/utilitarian systems, what will be the role of the arts? Again, Lepley affirms that the ideal school will aim to excel in two programs: science and fine arts.

One vexing problem in the arts has been the reconciliation of elitist, historically traditional aesthetic theories with socio-functional claims that the goodness of art resides wholly in its effect on the consumer and that art education should concern itself primarily with the creation, distribution, and consumption of art. This reconciliation has been made without sacrificing the integrity of either extreme and has resulted in an eclectic approach that recognizes both the traditional authority of value-centered theories and the reality of functional responses to musical stimuli. This approach endorses the teaching of comprehensive musicianship in which criticism has been added to creation (composing), distribution (performing), and consumption (listening).

We are aware of the insinuation of a counter mode of thought gaining strength in higher academic circles, where it is said to be spreading from its original source, literary criticism, with nihilistic implications for thinking about all of the arts and aesthetic education. "Deconstructionism" is labeled by its critics as an assault on Western notions, including thinking about history, criticism, and the teaching of literature.[32] It challenges those who place value on transmitting the cultural heritage, thereby undermining the authority of the cultural tradition and releasing the hold it has on teaching and learning. It rejects the traditional idea of liberal education, which claims that a human career is best shaped through the disciplined testing of a self against the best that has been thought and created.

Deconstructionism's principal thesis is that proposals of any kind that presume to match language with reality are forms of radical self-delusion. Consider the following in the light of that rationale. Given the prospect that Lepley's view of education tomorrow is desirable, feasible, and imminent, it becomes incumbent on all educators to ask themselves of their discipline: why and how. Philosophy and practicum, goals and implementation, concepts and their realization, rhetoric versus reality: however we verbalize it, the relations between what we say and what we do will become increasingly important as education continues to assume responsibility for community and life functions. Is this "radical self-delusion"?

The rift between rhetoric and reality began early in our history as a nation. The problems of both educating and training all of the children of all of our people in the same curriculum with the same tax dollars become almost insurmountable when compounded by the weakening roles of home and church and the consequent relegation of social problems to our overburdened schools. It is assumed that parents will have to pay an increasing share of the cost, with state and federal support given to those of greatest needs.

Cost is not our principal problem. The public has amply demonstrated willingness and ability to support those school activities that it deems to be important for young people, often without regard to their educational value. Two examples that are usually cited in this connection are football and marching band.

Our principal problem as music educators has been, and continues to be, one of clearly defining music as a basic core subject that must be required of all learners through their formative years. We have ample rhetoric for this. Our failure has been our unwillingness or inability to organize our priorities so that general music education of all learners becomes the *first* priority of those who educate music teachers, the *first* priority of those who organize music education curriculums, the *first* priority of those who determine how resources for music education shall be allotted, and — probably most important of all — the *first* priority of those who teach music in our schools — today and tomorrow.

Radical self-delusion? Only if we continue to fail to *reconcile rhetoric with reality.* Music will never make its maximum contribution to general education as long as there is wide disparity between what we say and what we do. The role of music in general education will only be fully realized when there is agreement that comprehensive musicianship (that is, musical literacy, aesthetic education) must be the primary goal of every class and activity deliberately designed to be designated as music education.

NOTES

1. Elliot Eisner, "Educating the Whole Person: Arts in the Curriculum," *Music Educators Journal,* April 1987.

2. Bennett Reimer, "Music Education as Aesthetic Education," *Music Educators Journal,* March 1987, p. 28.

3. Michael L. Mark, *Contemporary Music Education,* Schirmer, Macmillan, New York, 1978, p. 7.

4. Clifton Burmeister, "1929–1979, A Half-Century of Progress in Music Education," *Music Journal,* July–August 1979, p. 8.

5. Guy M. Whipple, ed., *The Thirty-Fifth Yearbook of the NSSE, Part II: Music Education.* Public School Publishing Co., Bloomington, Ill., 1936, p. x.

6. James Mursell, "Principles of Music Education," in Whipple, ed., *NSSE 35th Yearbook,* Chap. I.

7. Lilla Pitts, "Typical Musical Activities of the School," in Whipple, ed., *NSSE 35th Yearbook,* Chap. V.

8. Edgar Gordon, "A Program of Activities Outside the School," in Whipple, ed., *NSSE 35th Yearbook,* p. 187.

9. Hazel Morgan, ed., *Music Education Source Book.* MENC, Chicago, 1947.

10. Hazel Morgan, ed., *Music in American Education* (Source Book II), MENC, Washington, D.C., 1955. See Chap. I, "Music in General Education," and Chap. XVIII, "General Music Classes at the Secondary Level."

11. Nelson Henry, ed., *Basic Concepts in Music Education,* 57th Yearbook of the NSSE,

University of Chicago Press, Chicago, 1958.

12. Henry, *Basic Concepts,* Chap. 1.

13. Allen Britton, "Music Education: An American Specialty," in *Perspectives in Music Education,* Bonnie Kowall, ed. MENC, Washington, D.C., 1966, p. 27.

14. Britton, *Perspectives in Music Education,* p. 18.

15. Himie Voxman. "Current Status of Graduate Programs and the Need for More Versatility in Graduate Students," in Chappell White, ed., *The Graduate Education of College Music Teachers,* Northwestern University School of Music, Evanston, Ill., 1973, pp. 10-12.

16. Thomas Miller, "Summary," in White, ed., *The Graduate Education of College Music Teachers,* p. 28.

17. Kenneth Phillips, "Choral Music Comes of Age," *Music Educators Journal,* Dec. 1988, p. 22; and Martin Bergee, "Reform for the Band Program," *Music Educators Journal,* May 1989, p. 18.

18. *Music in the Secondary School,* Bulletin D-Eight, The Illinois Curriculum Program, Springfield, Ill. 1966, p. 29.

19. Bennett Reimer, "Music Education as Aesthetic Education: Toward the Future," *Music Educators Journal,* March 1989, p. 29.

20. Harry S. Broudy, "A Realistic Philosophy of Music Education," this volume, pp. 71, 83. See J. Terry Gates, ed., Music Education in the U.S.: Contemporary Issues, University Press, Tuscaloosa, Ala., 1988, for current philosophical trends that support Broudy's assertion, especially Chap. 5, "Of Conceptions, Misconceptions, and Aesthetic Commitment" (Abraham A. Schwadron); Chap. 6, "Aesthetics and Utility Reconciled" (Michael L. Mark); and Chap. 7, "Toward a Democratic Art" (Charles B. Fowler).

21. *MENC Soundpost,* Music Educators National Conference, Reston, Va., Vol. 4, No. 3, Spring 1988. "Status of MENC Goals" (Daniel Steinel), p. 8; and "Where Do We Stand on the MENC Goals?" (Linda Mercer), p. 9.

22. Bill Bouknecht, "Music as a Basic Subject," *Florida Music Director,* January 1989, p. 12.

23. See *Music Educators Journal,* March 1989, for articles with special focus on high school general music.

24. Charles Fowler, "Finding the Way to Be Basic: Music Education in the 1990's and Beyond," in this volume, p. 9.

25. John H. Mueller, "Music and Education: A Sociological Approach," In *Basic Concepts, I,* p. 110–111.

26. Edward Bailey Birge, *History of Public School Music in the United States,* Oliver Ditson, Co., Inc., Philadelphia, 1937, p. 47.

27. Robert Ulich, *History of Educational Thought,* American Book Co., New York, 1945, p. 348.

28. Clifton Burmeister, *Basic Concepts, I,* pp. 220–221.

29. Fishback, ed., *Music in the Secondary School,* 1966, p. 29.

30. John W. Beattie, "The Selection and Training of Teachers," in NSSE 35th Yearbook; *Music Education,* p. 207.

31. William L. Lepley, "How Iowa Can Create the 'Ideal Schools'," *The Des Moines Register,* December 28, 1989.

32. Ralph A. Smith, *The Sense of Art: A Study in Aesthetic Education,* Routeledge, New York, 1989, p. 170f.

10

Classicism Versus Individualism:
The Case For Changing Aesthetic Goals

Robert Ehle

Two areas in the arts today offer serious problems that are plausibly interrelated; the solution to either can help solve the others. The two areas are creativity and the area of arts education.

Problems in arts creativity revolve around who is creative, what is true creativity, and so forth. More specifically, in an era when artistic creativity has been institutionalized in colleges and universities, we have the situation where each would-be creator takes on a class of students and replicates him- or herself a thousandfold during the course of his or her career. The law of averages dictates that most of these students will not be able to make a significant creative contribution. The question that any creative individual, whether student or teacher, seeks to answer is if there are universal underlying principles of creativity that determine the significance of the activities of various artists.

The problem in the area of arts education would seem simple. It is, in fact, "What to teach?" The two answers commonly proposed are (1) "Teach classical culture" and (2) "Teach contemporary popular culture." Needless to say, neither of these two solutions is satisfactory to a large percentage of the professionals and students. The first solution, to teach classical culture, sounds elitist and ignores the students' own cultural background and heritage. The second solution, to teach contemporary popular culture, poses the question: "If it is popular already, what need is there to teach it?" The broader, implied question concerns the use in formal education of materials that can be completely understood and appreciated without any formal education. What reason is there to support such a process, if we consider how expensive formal education is?

This problem of teaching contemporary popular culture has come to the fore in contemporary, pluralistic, democratic, populist American culture. There has probably never before been a time or place when the content of the educational curriculum was determined by the popular will of the majority. The people of the United States today are asking themselves, "What is our culture?", "Where does our culture come from?", and "What do we wish to teach our children about our culture?" Recognizing that culture is replete with subliminal messages regarding nearly all aspects of life, decisions in this area are hotly debated.

A relationship between these two problem areas should now be clear. If one can determine what should be taught in the educational system regarding the arts, one can, in turn, give some guidance to would-be creative individuals as to how to make a significant contribution. These are two sides of the same coin.

This chapter was prompted by an idea that might help to resolve these two problems simultaneously: It is possible for anyone, of any cultural background, to make a significant artistic contribution simply by creating an image that has a unique identity, or in other words, a cultural image. A significant new cultural image is one that is uniquely and immediately identifiable. All cultures have and have always had cultural images, interesting and worthy of study. The thing that is significantly different in recent decades is the possibility that an individual might, almost single-handedly, create powerful and immediately recognizable cultural images. This possibility represents the height of individuality and has come to characterize the Western world in the twentieth century. We have national cultural images, corporate cultural images, and many sorts of institutional images, but we also have numerous individual images.

In the short term (decades or less), we identify these cultural images with public relations, promotions, fads, and "hype." That is in fact exactly what they usually are, but the value of cultural images may be greater than that; they may have true originality, true uniqueness, and lasting value. Conventional wisdom says that the test of time will separate the true values from the fictitious ones. There is, however, one test that can be made today — the test of identification. When confronted by a collection of objects that are said to embody a particular cultural image, how quickly and accurately is one able to identify that image? Such a test reveals whether or not that particular cultural image exists, how unambiguous it is, and how strong it is.

To create strong, unambiguous cultural images is not easy. The study of cultural images involves the subtlest aspects of materials, form, and, in particular, style. My claim is that the content of courses in the arts should be the study of style. Courses should investigate the materials, forms and styles, and how cultural images are created so that universal appreciation is fostered. Likewise, one should study the psychology of image making. In our modern societies, students desperately need to study the psychology of image making and fashion in order to learn that the quantity of objects does not correlate with the quantity or quality of styles and that unique and uniquely valuable styles might, in fact, be represented by a very few modest objects, or objects of great rarity.

Students must come to understand that to create is to create style; they must learn to dissect it and create it, certainly no simple task. Creative individuals may make useful contributions for numerous functional, utilitarian, practical purposes. But a significant contribution to art, as art, must be done in the area of style creation. Quantity of work is inadequate. Complexity of work is, by itself, inadequate. Novelty of work, too, is inadequate unless it contributes to a new style that is identifiable.

Whether such work must be taken by the culture as a cultural symbol — that is, whether or not it is adopted by the culture — is an open question. My belief is that every truly identifiable cultural image will make a place for itself; at first, perhaps, as a counterculture image, and later in the culture. The human need for cultural images is so great that, once presented to the public, any (valid) cultural object will achieve its potential. On the other hand, an object that fails to achieve cultural currency is simply not culturally unique, distinguished, or unreplicatable. Novelties soon cease being novel through imitation. Only if there is some ingredient not perceived by the imitators does the individuality of the image persist. Otherwise it blends into a much larger social image and loses its individuality.

INDIVIDUALITY: THE MODERN PARADIGM

Question: What is Beethoven's greatest creation? Is it his Ninth Symphony or is it *Fidelio*? How about the last string quartets, or the piano sonatas? I would make the suggestion that none of these is Beethoven's greatest creation. Beethoven's greatest creation is himself. That is, Beethoven's greatest creation is the almost mythological figure of the master composer that we know historically as Ludwig van Beethoven. The compositions are building blocks in this metaphor. Each of them is significant in itself but the totality of the Beethoven image and the Beethoven mystique is greater than the sum of its parts.

In his book *Art and Artist*, Otto Rank suggests that all art moves through three stages: (1) the collective archetypal, (2) the classical, and (3) the romantic.[1] The collective-archetypal stage defines the soul of the group and exalts the group ethos. The classical stage defines the highest form of the group ideal and usually derives from religion, and the third stage (the highest, as Rank describes it) exalts the individual. Rank suggests that the modern individual seeks self-actualization through many means but particularly through art. In Rank's definition and view, we have the "modern psychological type of artist" who seeks to define his or her individual identity through art. Beethoven, probably the first to do this in the field of music, has become the model for modern composers who seek self-definition and self-actualization through art.

Rank suggests, although never really states, that all three of these types can coexist and presently do so. For example, commercial art is collective archetypal because it exalts the norms and images of the group. Religious art is classical because it exalts the highest forms of idealistic groups of people. Modern art, on the other hand, is the most recent type because society had to pass through the previous stages to get to the level of individual self-expression. Today, many of the most acute struggles in art are concerned with which of these forms are to be pursued.

When it comes to individual self-expression and the modern artistic type, self-expression seems to mean "do your own thing" and "anything goes." The voice of modernism says, "Do the most unusual, original, radical, bizarre thing in art, and you have expressed yourself." The problem is, though, that it doesn't work. If you can do it, so can someone else. There is hardly anything in the avant-garde circles that hasn't been done and that won't be done many times. The solution is for the artist to do what Beethoven did: create himself. In other words, the artist has to create an original style that is immediately recognizable and so distinct that no one can copy it. You must do this if your goal is individual self-expression. If your goal is to create group-archetypal art or classical art, then you have to do other things, but in that case individual self-expression will not be your aim and will probably not be the result.

What is the key to achieving unique self-expression in art? Is not the answer to this question "style"? As everyone who purchases clothing or automobiles knows, "Style makes the world go 'round." The human race seems to be incredibly sensitive to the subtleties of style in all manner of things; why not also in art? This explains why the creation of himself was Beethoven's greatest achievement: the "Beethoven style" uniquely announced and identified its creator. The test of this accomplishment is simplicity itself. Can you identify the individual responsible for a work of art quickly, accurately, and repeatedly? If so, that artist has created a "self," an individual expression, that has the possibility of survival, intact, for a period of time.

Of course, not everyone welcomes this obsession with individual self-expression. The fundamentalist Christian philosopher Francis Schaeffer decries the obsession with individualism in modern art and calls for a return to the more universal styles of the past.[2] In essence he is calling for a return to the classical approach that exalts high, universal values. If Otto Rank is correct, however, individualism grew out of classicism and is a more advanced state of consciousness. It is not possible for one who has advanced to this state to go back. Rank himself, though, speaks of the sense of guilt connected with creation, guilt arising from the need to deny the group and group ideals.

How does one achieve individuality in art? It cannot be simple, or everyone would do it. The twentieth-century movement called "avant-garde" was characterized by the necessity to do something new. Artists also taught, and often said, that it was necessary to be first to utilize a new technique. Karlheinz Stockhausen, for instance, said that the invention of new techniques was a part of the creative process and that anyone who borrowed another's techniques was committing plagiarism just as much as if they had taken another's melodies or words.[3]

This notion is simplistic. Words and melodies are copyrighted only for commercial purposes, and being first to use style elements is a distinction soon forgotten. The key to achieving individuality in art is to assemble a cluster of style elements that, when taken together, create a unified image more powerful than the sum of the parts. That is what Beethoven achieved; everyone in the world, proverbially speaking, is aware of the Beethoven image, probably including some who have never heard a note of a Beethoven composition.

One step in achieving individuality in art is to limit one's materials. The overuse of diversity of resources is a major threat to stylistic unity, and stylistic unity is essential to individuality. Because of this fact, many modest artists achieve more than those with grander goals. Another step in achieving individuality is through the use of unifying techniques. There are two basic compositional techniques: repetition and variation. If it is clear to audience members that all of the shapes in a particular work are derived from a few basic ideas through repetition or variation, then a situation exists where identification can be made of (1) the work, (2) the style, (3) the creative artist, and (4) the embodied cultural image.

Yet all of the above is insufficient. Along with limiting the materials and using unifying techniques must come the third essential step that involves fundamental originality: something in the work must be new; that same thing must be present in a number of works in order to establish the style; and that same thing must characterize the work of one or a small group of creative artists in order to establish the cultural image. Very often this new thing will be represented by a name and will be associated with a cultural movement, but these features are secondary. The essential ingredient is technical. That is, the original feature must be a technical one in the artworks themselves; it must be perceptible to the audience; and it must be identifiable through analysis. In other words, it is a style element.

The use of style elements is critical in all art from all eras, but it is even more critical in modern, individualistic art because it is through technical ingredients that individual styles are made. The analysis of individuality in art is specifically the analysis of style. It is the presence of specific stylistic elements in an artist's work that makes that artist unique and establishes that artist's style and cultural image. Franz Liszt said that any new composition must contain at least one new chord.[4] Of course, new chords are just the beginning, but Liszt's attitude demonstrates the modern point of view clearly. Something in each work must be new in order to create an individual style and a new cultural image.

Now we can see the essence of the problem: *It is essential to do something new*. But one new chord does not make a new style. The new style must permeate the total work and, in fact, all of the works of the artist or group of artists who constitute the artistic movement. This is the nature of the gestalt that is more powerful in establishing a unifying image than the sum of its parts. In other words, *what is omitted or left out is as important as what is included*. It is just as important that the artist leave out all stylistic elements that would not contribute to the image as it is that the artist include certain new elements that do contribute. Hence, the usefulness of limiting one's materials; one automatically leaves out that which would confuse and disguise the style.

The analysis of style elements that are absent from an artistic style is particularly subtle. Normally it is approached historically, showing that something characteristic of one artistic period is omitted in the next. This step of paring away extraneous elements is the primary stumbling block for many would-be creative artists. It is also the defect in many early works of great composers. The process of clarification of vision must take place, a winnowing away of all that is foreign to the artistic vision. The process must be ruthless, allowing no sentimental attachment to the immediate past.

Many beginning artists do their best work by reacting against the past (which they see around them constantly) and by eliminating every element of this past style from their work. They use their present reality as a tool to forge a new reality by negation or reversal to arrive at a unique, identifiable personal style. Some artists who have been most successful in establishing their identities through unique styles include the French naive artist Henri Rousseau; the Russian Wassily Kandinsky; the Spaniard Pablo Picasso; the Italian Giorgio de Chirico; and the American Jackson Pollack. Among composers, the ones most easily and quickly identified include Igor Stravinsky, Arnold Schoenberg, and Béla Bartók. Also included, interestingly enough, are such "minor" masters as Edvard Grieg, Erik Satie, Anton Webern, Leoš Janácek, and Edgard Varèse. These latter composers are not known for their craft or for the size of their output, but simply for the individuality of their style and the purity of their vision. Among jazz musicians the same situation holds: certain composers, arrangers, and soloists are renowned and remembered for the individuality of their style. Included are Jelly Roll Morton, Duke Ellington, Miles Davis, Thelonius Monk, and Bill Evans.

We can infer from the preceeding list that size or complexity is not a criterion of individualism in art. It is not important that you compose nine symphonies or write scores for 300 players. Often the simplest works (such as many Franz Schubert songs) are the most perfect and convey the greatest individual utterance. The complete compositions of Webern and Varèse can fit on two CDs each. Most of Erik Satie's compositions are only a few minutes long. Edvard Grieg had problems with large forms and with orchestration, yet the individuality of his utterance is unmistakable. On the other hand, modest output is not a prerequisite here — witness Aaron Copland, Jean Sibelius, and Gustav Mahler.

It is clear to me as a music theorist that every original and individual effect in the arts springs from specific, identifiable techniques. Size and complexity are among these, as are simplicity and brevity. Without new techniques, there is no uniqueness of expression and thus no individuality. But uniqueness of technique may be found as a subtle variation on a commonly used element. Contemporary composers, for instance, often seek to juxtapose familiar style elements in various arbitrary ways simply to achieve novel sonic effects. Webern, for instance, juxtaposes atonality and serenity to achieve his style.

This search for style is a basic theme for humanity. Every social group desires images to express its identity. This was true for seventeenth-century Dutch patricians who hired Jan Vermeer and Sir Anthony Van Dyck to immortalize their organizations, and it is true for American teenagers today. Young Americans want to assert their individual and social identities, and they seek images and styles to do this. A teacher must be sensitive to this and recognize that the same universal force is present in classical European art and American popular art. But the question is, Who succeeds? That is, who achieves an indelible, ineradicable, individual image? This is the only criterion in today's art. It may be the graffiti artist who creates the most pregnant and powerful image in a particular society or generation.

What is forever rare and therefore valuable is individuality of utterance, wherever it arises, from whatever social, racial, or cultural group. Moreover, in today's world the striving for individuality is at the sacrifice of perfection. In the New World, a rough-hewn uniqueness is superior to any old-world perfection (Charles Ives's music is testimony to this fact).

What implications does all of this hold for the teacher in the arts classroom? What approach should be taken? Recognizing Rank's three categories, the teacher might use them to clarify works in the various arts. But if the teacher agrees that the modern actualization of individualism is today's legitimate artistic goal, the teacher has the obligation to seek out and respect individualism on whatever level or in whichever culture it occurs. This seems to solve the problem that has plagued so many teachers in our time, that of how to treat the popular culture. The solution is to discuss style elements and originality with the class. Which pieces of art or music exhibit original thinking? Which exhibit original style elements? How many have a unique style that makes their creators immediately identifiable in new or unknown works? Because most popular art is "copy-art," the point should be quickly made.

The value of Rank's theories as solutions to our educational problems can now be discussed. In the first place, Rank links art with psychology. As one of the members of the Freud circle in turn-of-the-century Vienna, Rank had opportunity to develop insights into the relations between art and personality development. Rank correlates the stages in artistic growth with stages of social development: the human race first developed group consciousness, then group ideals, and finally individual consciousness; his stages of artistic development correspond to these.

The implication for the teacher is that one should be prepared to address each of these stages. Classical culture may define the highest ideals of the human race, but the urge to individualism cannot be denied — so the teacher must deal with it, too. The urge to individualism is what motivates most of today's students; it is a different form of art, not inferior or superior, but different. Knowing this helps the teacher keep the objectives of the two forms separate.

As for the aspiring creator, Rank's theories may help an individual to define his or her goals and to understand why he or she fails to identify with classical goals or types. Further, a clear understanding of true stylistic originality will lead to the realization that not everyone who aspires to artistic self-expression will be successful; most, in fact, will fail to achieve it.

ART AND INDIVIDUALISM

Though every human being may harbor a secret creative urge, most are prevented from expressing themselves publicly by lack of education, lack of support, opportunity, confidence, and so forth. Public self-expression in the arts has been a controlled field, dominated by such institutions as the Ivy

League universities, New York publishers, the national radio and television networks, and a few other organizations most generally located on either coast. Other parts of the country are relegated to a "regional" or "local" status where little opportunity for public exposure arises. The situation is based on priorities, the Ivy League universities having been first in the arts in the country and the New York and Los Angeles media having been first in their respective fields.

While none of this is unknown or necessarily to be criticized, one should look for a backlash if the statement about a secret creative urge is true. In fact, the urge to create and to express oneself through an artistic medium may be seen as the next freedom to emerge in the world. In other words, once democracy has guaranteed life, liberty, and the pursuit of happiness to the citizens of a land, the next thing we might expect to see them seeking is freedom of artistic expression. Is this not exactly what we have been seeing in the United States through the rock 'n roll era? Though naive and created mostly by very young people, rock 'n roll may gain a greater sophistication as time passes. More than that, however, we should expect the young people in our schools to continue demanding that their right of self-expression through the arts be respected.

Examples of the creation of individual works of world impact should stimulate and guide the pursuit of self-expression. It is important to realize that all of the important images are not centuries old; many of them come from our own time. Ideas once within the purview of a very few individuals, such as Dada, Impressionism, Minimalism, and Expressionism, undergo a radical widening of spheres of influence until every individual in the world begins to participate in them. This is what we see happening on MTV, in New Age music, in rock concerts, in graffiti, and in other popular events.

Artistic domination is a subtle form of totalitarianism, based not on coercion but on subliminal messages of inferiority and superiority.[5] But all of this is changing. New technology has opened the world of self-expression to many who were formerly denied it. It can be said that the rock 'n roll explosion was made possible by electronic technology: microphones, amplifiers, electric guitars, and inexpensive recording equipment. Today, the home computer has made it possible for anyone to create a complete work of music, a novel, or a work of visual art and then to publish that work for distribution. The result, already beginning, will be a revolution in creative self-expression unlike anything ever seen. Students will expect to learn how to create, not merely to admire the creative work of individuals from the past.

In a sense, this is the biggest revolution to come from modernism or individualism in the arts. Admiration for great work will not cease, but the fact that individuals can attempt works of import, today, is sure to increase the pursuit of creative self-expression.

217

CASE STUDIES

THE VARÈSE PROBLEM

Edgard Varèse is often cited as one of the most important leaders in contemporary music. Joan Peyser included him with Stravinsky and Schoenberg in her book on modern music,[6] for example, and a Varèse piece seems to appear in every important anthology of twentieth-century music. Yet Varèse, in his entire lifetime, apparently composed fewer than twenty works, most of them short. Most are only one movement long, and many are ignored or have been lost. In fact, Varèse is well known for fewer than five works, all of which can be heard in two hours. Varèse is exactly the opposite of any good example of craftsmanship. In his electronic music, he is primitive simply because of the state of the technology with which he worked. How can Varèse be cited as one of the most important composers of our era?

Clearly Varèse is no classicist. He is hardly a good modernist because all of his innovations have been technically superceded. Varèse's unique contribution, it is becoming clear, is in the area of style. Two works in particular stand out: "Density 21.5" for unaccompanied flute and "Octandre" for chamber ensemble. Music theorists are just beginning to unravel the secrets of the Varèse sound, as exemplified in these two works that are seemingly simple yet very original.

Here we have a situation in a nutshell: no vast output, no particular craft or workmanship, no classical forms, no classical techniques, just unique sound. How is it achieved? So far no one knows and no one has succeeded in copying it. Varèse is a perfect example of Rank's "modern psychological type of artist" who does not need the trappings of classicism and who makes his way through style alone. His is a unique personal utterance, all the more valuable because it is so rare.

THE CHOPIN PROBLEM

For years, music critics have had unkind things to say about Frédéric Chopin's music. In the first place, the composer's limitations are so obvious: he wrote mostly music for piano, most of his pieces are only a single movement, and many of them are short. A good percentage of them are in popular dance forms such as the waltz and mazurka, and the technique of development is not in evidence in most of them. Many of his pieces are merely a page or two in length. Finally, he seems overenthusiastic about gymnastic pianistic technique. By these criteria, Chopin is a poor, second-rate composer.

So the argument goes. Actually what we have here is a case of the classicists criticizing one of the first of the "modern psychological type" of artists. Chopin's music has never fallen into disfavor with the public, however, and most people can recognize the Chopin style easily and quickly. Chopin's lyricism is never in doubt, either. It is clear that the supposed faults pointed out by the classicists are real enough. It is also clear that Chopin succeeds in his own way and does so in a manner that any modern artist could only dream of emulating.

The question here is one of style. Chopin avoids most of the classical forms and ideals and goes his own way, creating a unique, personal style. It is his unique style that is so valuable and constitutes such a considerable achievement. The teacher and student need to concentrate on understanding how this unique style is accomplished: understanding the Chopin style requires a very advanced understanding of chromatic harmony and it also requires a study of layer analysis as posited by Heinrich Schenker. Chopin's music functions in layers that are particularly subtle. Chopin achieved his unique style intuitively, and we can understand it that way, of course, but to define it requires the most subtle analytical tools available.

THE CASE OF NON-WESTERN ART

The primary thesis of this chapter is to extol the virtues of individual styles and to claim that a unique, recognizable style is the highest form of achievement in modern, individualistic art. What place could there be in such a scheme for non-Western art? After all, most non-Western art appears to be collective archetypal, at least to the eye or ear of a Westerner. It is an extremely rare situation when a work of art from a country outside of Europe and the Americas carries the name of its creator. Whether it be a sculpture, an ornament, or a piece of music, most will be created in age-old ancestral patterns by craftsmen trained in centuries-old ways by an oral tradition.

The interest that non-Western art can have for the contemporary artist is simply as a model for other ways of doing things. Because the objective in contemporary, individualistic art is to achieve an individual style, the styles of non-Western cultures, differing as they do from the conventions of the West, provide useful tools and examples. They offer different ways of thinking, different artistic goals, differing uses of materials, and, above all, differing ideas of what is beautiful. In other words, non-Western art can offer much to the individualistic artist.

For the student, non-Western arts are particularly useful because each one offers a new style and, taken together, they offer a useful range of styles. Likewise, they provide a useful example of how life styles and styles of art interrelate. The study of these subjects is extremely valuable for students and creative artists alike.

Robert Ehle

CLICHES

"Cliches are everywhere." This old cliche sets up an amusing paradox: the reductio ad absurdum of a circular definition. It also highlights the insidiousness of the problem of cliches. If it is true that every human being harbors a secret creative urge, it is just as true that, given half a chance, everyone will attempt self-expression by means of cliches. Cliches are the currency of group identification; self-expression requires new symbols. Self-expression requires that one distance oneself from the group and its symbols.

Schoenberg once wrote, "A new sound is an unconsciously sought symbol which an original person seeks for the purpose of self-expression."[7]

Of course the new sounds and new symbols will not have the power of the old cliches. They do not have the tradition behind them to give them power, but they are available to the individual. It is a matter of objectives. A person wishing to affirm the basic values and identity of the group will employ the group's cliches. In so doing, he or she will submerge his or her identity in that of the group. This behavior is highly encouraged and appreciated by society, which always likes to have its values and identity bolstered. This is a definition of Rank's category one, the collective archetypal. It is not always disastrous for the artist to do this, but to avoid disaster one must be very good. Charles Ives defined the situation when he said that "an artist has two choices—one is to do something that others have already done but to do it better than anyone else. The other is to do something new that no one has done."[8] The would-be artist who uses cliches in a naive manner is an embarrassment.

THE CASE OF VIVALDI

It has been said of Antonio Vivaldi that he composed one composition 600 times. He has often been accused of being repetitious, boring, and lacking in imagination. Yet Vivaldi is possibly the best loved of all baroque composers today. After falling into neglect for more than a century, Vivaldi's music has been resurrected by a public that finds great enjoyment in his work.

Vivaldi appears to be a composer whose music filled a different need when it was new than it does today. When new, Vivaldi's music was *Gebrauchsmusik* (music composed for a specific purpose), providing concerti for the student of his day to play. In our time, Vivaldi's simpler style, his repetition, and his colorful effects appear to be the most distinctive voice to come out of the baroque period. Coming from an era of general stylistic conformity, Vivaldi is appreciated for his individuality. Only the cynics continue to sneer at his melodiousness and his lack of intellectualism, complexity, and contrapuntal pretensions. His distinctive and highly individual style has won the day, another example of the triumph of individuality over classicism.

NOTES

1. Otto Rank, *Art and Artist,* Alfred A. Knopf, Inc., New York and London, 1939.

2. Francis A. Schaeffer, *Escape From Reason,* Intervarsity Press, Chicago, 1968. Especially see Chapter 5.

3. Karlheinz Stockhausen, record liner notes to *Momente* (Nonesuch Records 71157). Stockhausen states,

   I have given so detailed a listing of the instruments because their selection and combination belongs as much to the composition of "Momente" as what I have them play. The unique and nontransferable composition of one's sound materials is to my mind just as important today as for example the selection of themes, motives, and formal schemes was in earlier compositions, for the composition of timbres is indeed no longer the coloration of musical structure. . . . but is from the beginning fully equal to all other procedures that one employs in the production of a musical composition. I also feel, therefore, that the specific selection and combination of an instrumental force for a particular work should remain unrepeatable and uncopyable, both for myself and other composers.

4. Cited by Paul Griffiths in *Modern Music, A Concise History from Debussy to Boulez,* Thames and Hudson, New York, 1978.

5. Herschel B. Chipp, *Theories of Modern Art,* University of California Press, Berkeley, 1968. See particularly Chapter 8.

6. Joan Peyser, *The New Music, The Sense Behind the Sound,* Delta Books, Dell Publishing Co., New York, 1971.

7. Arnold Schoenberg, This quote appears first in his *Harmonielehre* and is translated into English on the dedication page of *The Technique of Electronic Music,* by Thomas Wells (Schirmer Books, New York, 1981).

8. Charles Edward Ives, "Essays Before a Sonata," in *Three Classics in the Aesthetics of Music,* Dover Publications, Inc., New York, 1962.

11

The Music Education of Exceptional Children

Richard M. Graham

E. Thayer Gaston entitled his chapter "Functional Music" in the 1958 NSSE Yearbook, *Basic Concepts in Music Education, I.* The philosophical positions taken in that writing were new to the profession of music education at that time but have since been incorporated into the thinking and writings of many in the field. Indeed, this very publication will reveal many of Gaston's points of view that are now commonplace. Because much of what appeared in Gaston's article is still highly relevant today, I will not attempt to revise or rewrite it. What will appear here is a current treatment of that section of the Gaston chapter given to music for handicapped children. I will treat this subject in response to the editor's questions to the contributors to the 1958 publication, which are as follows: (1) How has your thinking changed about the topic during the past three decades? (2) What influences have had a major impact upon your topic? and (3) If you were writing on that topic today, what changes would you make?

THIRTY YEARS OF INFLUENCES AND CHANGE

The thirty years since the publication of *Basic Concepts in Music Education, I,* have seen an enormous change, indeed a revolution, with respect to the music education of exceptional children. The revolution reflected the influence of the civil rights movement and court action in *Brown v. The Board of Education* (1954) as well as the Child's Right Movement started much earlier. It was in 1959, one year following the publication of *Basic Concepts, I,* that the United Nations General Assembly adopted the

Declaration of the Rights of the Child. Of particular interest from that declaration is Principle 5: "The child who is physically, mentally, or socially handicapped shall be given the special treatment, education, and care required by his/her particular condition." This attitude that imbued the areas of medicine, technology, government, and education led to a powerful movement for education of exceptional children throughout the country. The movement rapidly gained momentum in the 1960s, achieved landmark legal support in the 1970s, and continues to develop in the 1980s and 1990s. For music education the past thirty years have brought about conditions that the writers of the 1958 publication could not have envisaged at the time.

During the thirty-year period in question, there have been several court and statutory decisions that have markedly affected the education of exceptional children. The most important of these has been the enactment of Public Law 94-142, The Education of All Handicapped Children Act, which became law in 1975. An understanding of the basic features of PL 94-142 is central to understanding many of the practices and trends in music education of exceptional children today. The law provides (1) for a free, appropriate public education for all handicapped children; (2) that school systems must provide safeguards to protect the rights of handicapped children and their parents; (3) that handicapped children must be educated with nonhandicapped children to the maximum extent possible; (4) that an Individualized Education Program (IEP) must be developed and implemented for each handicapped child; and (5) parents of handicapped children are to play an active role in the process used to make any educational decision about their handicapped children. States that meet the requirements of PL 94-142 receive tax dollars to help offset the additional costs of providing special education services. Public Law 94-142 makes no mention of exceptional children who are gifted or talented but without specific handicapping conditions. Mitchell (1982) reports, however, that forty-eight states have programs for gifted and talented students but with funding far less than those for the handicapped.

EXCEPTIONAL CHILDREN

CHARACTERISTICS

The differences among most children are relatively small, enabling them to benefit from the general education program (namely, the general music program); exceptional children differ from the norm — either below or above — to such an extent that an individualized program of special

223

education is required to meet their needs. Thus the term *exceptional children* refers to children with learning problems, behavior disorders, and physical disabilities as well as to children who are intellectually gifted or talented. In spite of reactions against "labeling," exceptional children are usually grouped under the following nine categories:

1. Speech disorders
2. Mental retardation
3. Specific learning disabilities
4. Emotional disturbance (behavior disorders)
5. Orthopedic impairments (crippling)
6. Hearing impairments
7. Visual impairments
8. "Other" health impairments
9. Gifted and talented

The first eight of these are further categorized according to severity of the handicapping condition as "mild," "moderate," "severe," and "profound." The vast majority of exceptional children in music classes are "mildly handicapped." Gifted students have been divided into two categories: first-order gifted, for the highly gifted, and second-order gifted, for the remaining group of children and youth.

PREVALENCE

It is interesting to note that the number of exceptional children in the United States has not changed appreciably since the publication of the 1958 NSSE Yearbook, *Basic Concepts in Music Education*. There has been a great difference, however, in how many of these children are now found in America's schools. Government figures show that approximately 11 percent (over 4.3 million) of children and youth attending public schools have been identified as handicapped for special education purposes (U.S. Department of Education 1986, 4). Some have estimated the prevalence of gifted students in the public schools to be between 3 and 5 percent (Mitchell 1981; Sisk 1984). During fiscal year 1981, Mitchell (1981) reported that 909,437 children were served in programs for gifted and talented students. Because it is reported that between 1.45 and 2.42 million gifted children may require special education, it would appear that they are the most underserved group of exceptional children.

About twice as many males as females receive special education. Two-thirds of all children with handicaps receive at least part of their education in regular classrooms. The number is smaller for regular music classrooms because of the decreased number of handicapped children who study music in the upper grades. The three largest categories of children with handicaps are learning disabilities, speech and language impairment, and mental retardation. These three categories account for about 85 percent of all handicapped children who received special education of any kind (including music) in the public schools in the mid-1980s.

CONTEMPORARY INFLUENCES

MAINSTREAMING

Public Law 94-142 does not advocate the placement of all handicapped children in regular classes. In fact, the popularly used word to describe this process, *mainstreaming,* does not appear in the law. The law does, however, specifically call for special educators to cooperate with regular educators, including music educators, in providing an equal educational opportunity to the handicapped.

The major influence leading to current practices in music education of exceptional children and youth thirty years after the appearance of *Basic Concepts in Music Education, I,* has been mainstreaming. As already indicated, this is a popularized term that stemmed from frequently published and spoken remarks concerned with placing the exceptional child in "the mainstream of American education." The term may also be considered to be roughly equivalent to the "least restrictive environment" phrase that does appear in Public Law 94-142. Although it is interpreted in various ways, mainstreaming refers to the placing of exceptional children — particularly handicapped children — who were once educated in separate classrooms or schools (if, indeed, they received any education at all) into regular classrooms (which included music classrooms) for purposes of teaching and learning. In 1976 the Council for Exceptional Children offered the following definition of mainstreaming:

> Mainstreaming is a belief which involves an educational placement procedure and process for exceptional children, based on the conviction that each such child should be educated in the least restrictive environment in which his educational and related needs can be satisfactorily provided. This concept recognizes that exceptional children have a wide range of special educational needs, varying greatly in intensity and duration, that there is a recognized continuum of educational settings which may, at a given time, be appropriate for an individual child's needs; that to the maximum extent appropriate, exceptional children should be educated with nonexceptional children and that segregation should occur only when the intensity of the

child's special education and related needs is such that they cannot be satisfied in an environment including nonexceptional children, even with the provision of supplementary aids and services. (Reynolds 1976, 43)

With the advent of mainstreaming in the 1970s, it became evident that the typical music educator was not prepared to teach classes made up of handicapped and nonhandicapped children. The difficulties were more common in the lower grades but more marked in the traditional high school instrumental and vocal performance organizations. The 1970s and 1980s saw the development of special college methods classes to prepare prospective teachers of every subject discipline in education to deal with the exceptional child in mainstreamed and — in a few instances — in special or "resource" rooms for the handicapped. As part of or in addition to these special college methods courses, music education methods courses for prospective teachers of exceptional students have been developed. The best of these courses reflect the curriculum modifications that have been seen to work with exceptional students. It is not surprising that these curriculum modifications frequently come into conflict with many of the traditionally held concepts, values, and teaching procedures of music education that stem from the premainstreaming days.

Some of these traditionally held concepts, passed on through college music methods classes, curriculum guides, and published music education methods textbooks, which have probably impeded effective music education of handicapped children in contemporary mainstreamed music classes, are as follows:

1. All children at all ages love music and are highly motivated to study it.
2. All students are capable of, and desirous of, performing and listening to music in groups.
3. Music education means the development of music performance skills.
4. Music is to be taught to groups of children in twenty-minute periods in elementary school and in thirty- to sixty-minute periods in higher grades.
5. Elementary school music activities are planned around, and success is measured by, the acquired abilities to respond to musical sound in a linear (left to right) manner.
6. Comprehension of the generally accepted "basic concepts" and "rudiments" of Western European music is an essential prerequisite for aesthetic response to all music.
7. Music education at all levels must be directed toward "musical literacy" for the education experience to be of immediate and lasting value.

These concepts reflect much of what leaders of the discipline have always wanted of music education in a democratic society. Events of the past thirty years, however, have required music educators to look more realistically at what happens when a handicapped student undertakes to learn music with nonhandicapped peers, and empirical data have led to new rationales, new ways of knowing about music teaching and learning in American schools.

A PHILOSOPHY OF MUSIC EDUCATIO FOR THE EXCEPTIONAL CHILD

Elsewhere in this volume, the subject of a philosophy of music education has been treated brilliantly. I support these writings but suggest the need for an expanded or, perhaps, a different epistemology when considering the music education of many exceptional children. What emerges from this difference can be stated briefly as follows: The exceptional child, like all other members of society, must be provided an opportunity to develop fully his or her abilities. This philosophy requires that music education programs in public, tax-supported schools of the nation adjust or modify curricula, including teaching, and other offerings so as to meet a variety of needs.

Where this philosophy exists and policy is determined by it, one finds enlightened administrators and music educators striving to adhere to certain principles of methodology that permit effective music education of the exceptional child in mainstreamed and in "special" (homogeneous) classrooms. Some salient points of a music education philosophy expanded to consider the music needs of all of America's children would be as follows:

1. Individualized assessment, planning, instruction, and evaluation are absolutely essential and basic to any music education methodology with exceptional children.
2. Music education, use of the singing voice, and experience with high-quality instruments must be started as early as possible (that is, during the preschool years).
3. Music education should continue through high school or as long as the exceptional student remains in school.
4. Minority or low socioeconomic status and other aspects of culture may present an indelible effect upon the child's musical taste and motivation to pursue music in school settings.
5. Some handicapped children, particularly those with severe and profound irreversible disabilities, may be better served by music therapists in special environments for part or all of the school music experience.
6. Giftedness, talent, and creativity are not synonymous attributes and often do not exist at equal levels in otherwise brighter-than-average students in a music class.

Richard M. Graham

SPECIAL EDUCATION IN MUSIC

There are occasions when the manner of teaching employed by effective music educators of the handicapped or gifted can be differentiated from that employed by the regular music educator. One music educator may make use of such communication devices as the Braille music writer. Another may use sign language to accompany singing or listening activities. Still another music educator may use carefully structured procedures to control such things as teacher intensity or use visual prompts to bring about more effective subject presentation and delivery. For the most part, however, effective music educators of exceptional children employ the same set of fundamental teaching skills that all good music educators use. There are not two distinct sets of music education methods — one for use with exceptional children, the other for regular music students. Furthermore, there is no certain set of music teaching methods appropriate for exceptional students within a given category that differs significantly from the music teaching methods that are effective with students in another category. Indeed, there is considerable literature to support the position that specific teaching methods are not differently effective with learning-disabled, mildly mentally retarded, emotionally disturbed, and speech-impaired students, that is, the bulk of all handicapped students. Instead of attempting category-specific methodologies, music educators of exceptional children should be skilled in the procedures needed to *systematically design, implement, and evaluate music instruction.* Having become skilled in these procedures, music educators will then be able to apply the intervention strategies necessary to assist any child who has difficulty learning the various facets of music as an academic discipline.

Music education for the exceptional student is the individually planned and systematically monitored arrangement of physical settings, special equipment and materials, teaching procedures, and other interventions designed to help such students reach their highest possible individual levels of music performance, understanding, and appreciation. Such music education must begin with an unbiased assessment of the exceptional child as an initial step in planning the Individualized Education Program (IEP).

ASSESSMENT FOR SYSTEMATIC DESIGN OF MUSIC INSTRUCTION

The provision of an appropriate, individualized music education for handicapped students involves the use of assessment procedures to determine appropriate learning objectives and teaching strategies. The Music Educators National Conference (MENC) has taken the clear position that music educators should be involved in the placement of handicapped children into mainstreamed music classes (MENC 1986). Less clear, however, is the role that music educators should play in the assessment process, required by Public Law 94-142 and state and local statutes. Unless music educators are directly involved in assessment of what and how to teach music to the handicapped child, the MENC call for "involvement" in placement decisions is meaningless.

DEFINITION OF DOMAINS

When an exceptional student undergoes assessment for music study, the derived data are used to define the domains of the special education to be employed in music instruction. Whether norm-referenced instruments or more informal measures are used, the results of the assessments are employed to determine what to teach and how to teach the exceptional student in the music class. In the past, music educators and other educators attempted to design instruction to meet *all* skill deficits that might be revealed during an assessment (for example, tone-pitch discrimination problems, tonal memory difficulties, and general auditory perception problems); recent research, however, has brought about changes in thinking about what and how to teach.

ASSESSMENT OF WHAT TO TEACH

Music educators who have taught mainstreamed classes have learned that uneven patterns of skill development are more the rule than the exception for all students, including exceptional children. This knowledge has led practitioners to the realization that what is truly needed is an analysis of what the exceptional student in music needs to know (that is, what specific music skills and knowledge a particular handicapped child will need in order to master, adjust, and perform acceptably in a music class environment, whether a "special" or resource room or a less restrictive "mainstreamed" one at some future time). A combined use of formal norm-referenced and informal criterion-referenced assessment permits a data-based indentification of the curriculum domains for music in an individualized education program. Once the domains of music instruction have been identified, the music educator must place the exceptional student at the appropriate level within the music curriculum so that suitable instructional objectives can be developed (Graham 1989; Smith 1989).

When the assessment is done carefully, it can deeply influence the nature and appropriateness of the music education curricula provided to exceptional students. Having to make the decision of what to teach is the unique responsibility of the music educator, but it is the flexibility of specific objectives taught that makes the music experience for handicapped students individualized and special.

ASSESSMENT OF HOW TO TEACH

At the time of publication of *Basic Concepts, I*, in 1958, most special educators applied the aptitude-treatment interactions (ATI) model for teaching handicapped students. Assessment data would reveal strengths and weaknesses of the student, and the teacher would then design education to either compensate for student deficits by circumventing them or plan instruction to take advantage of student strengths. Music educators adopted this approach to planning curricula for exceptional children and were, thus, in step with special educators and other associated professionals. Indeed, music education literature over the past thirty years has presented many examples of differential methodologies that might be applied to student types (for example, auditory learners, visual learners, and kinesthetic learners). However, ATI procedures were initially, and remain largely, unsubstantiated as methods of choice for developing curricula for exceptional students. One reason for this is that assessment instruments currently available are not able to identify types of learners with any reliability or validity. With respect to the discipline of music education, ATI procedures remain unsubstantiated because music educators are just beginning to research and gain understanding of the the nature of effective instruction of all students, including those considered to be exceptional.

It would appear that a better way to approach teaching music to exceptional students would be to take a cue from the discipline of special education and to rely on effective instructional practices validated for all students (exceptional and nonexceptional alike) in the current research literature (Zigmond and Miller 1986). For example, during skill acquisition instruction, effective music educators model desired behavior (Moore and Mathenius 1987). They break a terminal goal into its component parts and teach each of the parts and their integration (Boardman 1989). They teach each music objective in a variety of music contexts with a variety of music and nonmusic materials to facilitate generalization (Nocera 1979). Effective music educators organize material to facilitate recall, using rehearsal strategies, overlearning, or distributive practice as necessary (Suzuki 1969; Peretz 1988; Rosenthal et al. 1988; Shehan 1987; and others). They introduce and consistently use motivators and interesting music tasks and materials (Greer 1981). The thinking reflected in this and other literature of music education has been shown over the years to engender even reluctant students with the will and motivation to study and learn music. Music education for individual exceptional children that employs these procedures may be thought of as a form of intervention — a term with special meaning for those who teach exceptional children.

MUSIC EDUCATION AS INTERVENTION

Intervention is a term borrowed from the health professions to describe all efforts made on behalf of handicapped persons. For years the profession of music therapy, closely akin to music education for the handicapped, has spoken of music experiences as intervention but, typically, with nonmusic goals in mind. The goal of any kind of intervention is to eliminate, or at least to reduce, the obstacles that keep a handicapped person from full and active participation in society. The music educator employs intervention strategies to permit full access of the handicapped child to music in all of its forms, styles, and uses.

There are three basic kinds of intervention efforts employed by effective music educators of the handicapped: *preventive* (keeping possible problems from becoming serious handicaps to music education); *remedial* (overcoming handicaps to music learning through training or education); and *compensatory* (giving the handicapped student new ways of dealing with his or her disability in music situations).

Preventive efforts with handicapped children are productive only when begun at a very early age. When *Basic Concepts, I,* appeared, the idea of any formal exposure of infants to music was little more than a topic of curious conversation. PL 94-142 called for teaching of handicapped children as early as age three, and a later law, PL 99-457, has focused a great deal of attention on the importance of identifying and serving infants and preschool children who may have disabilities.

Music activity has been a part of infant stimulation programs since the early 1970s. Although the effects of these programs have not been well reported because of relatively few adequate longitudinal studies, final reports and other kinds of summaries have yielded some interesting data. However, the results of some of the early or "preschool" studies have yielded conflicting, perhaps contradictory, results. Until more is understood about what facilitates and proscribes music learning to the very young, music educators of handicapped children must count on remedial and compensatory strategies to help students learn music to the fullest extent possible.

Remedial efforts with handicapped children, including those employed by effective music educators, are found in schools and in social agencies. The word *remediation* is primarily an educational term, whereas *rehabilitation* and *therapy* are terms more often used in social service and health agencies. All three terms have a common purpose — to teach the handicapped person

231

basic skills needed for independence. In music settings (classrooms and clinics), those skills are singing, playing instruments, music reading and writing, creative activity, and music-initiated body movement. Development of these skills leads to musical independence. In addition, many individual-ized music education experiences are designed to assist the handicapped student to learn certain basic academic and social tasks. Such an effort is part of the contemporary attitude of cooperation and interaction of all teachers from all subject matter areas with special education instructors for the good of the handicapped student.

The underlying assumption of both remedial music education and music therapy is that handicapped students need special help if they are to succeed in the study and learning of music and other skills. Whenever possible, this special help is designed to teach handicapped students the same skills that nonhandicapped students have, but through different or more intensive methods than nonhandicapped students employ.

Compensatory efforts in music education are employed to make up for a handicapped student's loss or disability by giving him or her a substitute skill or device on which to rely. An example of this kind of compensatory effort can be seen with physically impaired children. A child with cerebral palsy can be trained to make maximum use of his or her hands, but the use of weights on both forearms may make it possible for him or her to strike resonator bells on the beat with the remainder of the class (Clark and Chadwick 1979). Blind students can become effective members of marching bands by using heavy cord string to attach their belts to those of marching band members on either side of them. The point here is that compensatory efforts in music education are intended to give the handicapped student an asset that normal students do not need, whether it be arm weights for a cerebral-palsied child or mobility training for a seeing-impaired student. Compensatory music education when properly administered is one means to help bring about effective instruction for exceptional music students.

Within a framework of effective instruction, the question of how to teach music to exceptional children should be reinterpreted during the years to come as, "How can good music instruction be more responsive to individ-ual differences?" An a priori assessment of student characteristics (namely, learning styles, learning disabilities, and emotional disturbance) as the as-sessment of how to teach music to exceptional children will not answer that question.

EFFECTIVE INSTRUCTIONAL PRACTICES

Effective music instruction practices grow out of properly administered assessment. Heller, Holtzman, and Messick (1982) write directly to this point when they state that the "main purpose of assessment in education is to improve instruction and learning . . . [and] a significant portion of children who experience difficulties in the classroom can be treated effectively through improved instruction." In reference to a group of instructional practices that have been found to benefit a variety of students, the authors further state that "in planning instruction for the special child, primary attention should be directed to the specific features of the instructional treatments that have been identified as fostering academic progress in children with initial poor performance" (p. 88).

Elsewhere in this volume Zimmerman has touched upon theories of instruction that need not be repeated here. Some specific music teacher behaviors that have been reported from experimental teaching experiences will be touched upon briefly here because of what this recently gained knowledge lends to effective music instruction.

Madsen and his colleagues (1989) have investigated teacher intensity with prospective music educators. They report that this can be operationally defined, recognized, and taught. This kind of preparation is consistent with what the leaders of special education request for all educators of exceptional children. Meyen and Lehr (1980) and Lloyd (1984) argue that given the present state of formal knowledge, it makes more sense to organize instruction on the basis of "skills students need to be taught" and relevant kinds of (intensive) instruction to meet these needs, (rather) than on the basis of categorical labels. Yarbrough (1975) showed the positive effect of high magnitude of certain teacher behaviors. Sims (1986) showed differential effects of high and low teacher affect. A number of researchers have shown the positive effects of teacher praise and reinforcement on music learning and general classroom behavior of students (Bennett and Adams 1967; Madsen et al. 1989; Madsen 1982; Kuhn 1975; Greer et al. 1973; Murray 1972; Walker 1989).

Effective instruction research has shown that for music educators and others, exceptional children learn best under conditions of effective instruction. Factors such as diagnostic label or learning styles are far less important than once supposed. Music educators of exceptional children have come to know that if what is to be taught is clearly understood (from the assessment) then music educators can learn to teach with proper intensity the specific skills and knowledge that time and setting will permit. The effectiveness of this teaching can be shown by recurrent evaluation of student progress and teaching techniques. Such a systematic approach to music education makes for a more efficient use of time and effort and less time spent on spurious deficit skill domains that frequently appear when children are herded page by page through curriculum guides that are designed to teach "all things to all children."

Richard M. Graham

CONCLUSION

The thirty years since the appearance of *Basic Concepts, I,* has seen a revolution in the attitudes and practices related to the education of exceptional children. During this period of time, some 4.3 million children of school age have been accepted into the public and private schools of America. Of these children, approximately 90 percent of those considered to be mildly retarded have received music instruction in regular (mainstreamed) or separate (special or resource) rooms. Of the 2.42 million gifted and talented children, about 40 percent receive special education with only a miniscule number in specially developed music programs; this is the most poorly served group of exceptional children. Where it was once considered appropriate to match curriculum against assessed strengths and weaknesses or against diagnostic categories, the aptitude-treatment interactions model (ATI) is losing favor among curriculum planners. Effective teaching research strongly suggests shifting the focus away from learning style (handicapping categories) to analysis of student responsiveness to instruction. When students are found to be unresponsive, dimensions of the music instruction can be changed to facilitate greater learning.

REFERENCES

Bennett, L. and J. Adams. (1967) A comparative study of the effect of positive and negative reinforcements on the efficiency of musical learning. *Bulletin of the Council for Research in Music Education* 10, 39–46. Champaign, IL.

Boardman, E. (1989) The generative theory of musical learning. *General Music Today* 2:3, 11–16. MENC.

Clark, C. and D. Chadwick. (1979) *Clinically adapted instruments for the multiply handicapped: A sourcebook.* Modulations Company. Westford, MA.

Graham, R. M. (1989) Standardized tests as an aid to complete the complete student profile. *Georgia Music News* (Summer). Georgia Music Educators Association. Marietta, GA.

Greer, R. D. (1981) An operant approach to motivation and effect: Ten years of research in music learning. *Documentary report of the Ann Arbor symposium: Applications of psychology to the teaching and learning of music.* MENC. Reston, VA.

Greer et al. (1973) Adult approval and students' music selection behavior. *JRME* 2:4, 345–354. Reston, VA.

Heller, K. A., W. H. Holtzman, and S. Messick. (1982) *Placing children in special education: A strategy for equity.* National Academy Press. Washington, DC.

Henry, N. B. (ed.). *Basic concepts in music education, I.* (1958) NSSE. Chicago.

Kuhn, T. L. (1975) The effect of teacher approval and disapproval on attentions, musical achievement, and attitude of fifth-grade students. In Madsen et al., eds., *Research in music behavior: Modifying music behavior in the classroom.* Teachers College Press. New York. Pp. 40–48.

Lloyd, J. W. (1984) How shall we individualize instruction — or should we? *Remedial and Special Education,* 5:1, 7–15.

Madsen, C. K. (1982) The effect of contingent teacher approval and withholding music performance on improving attentiveness. In Proceedings of the Ninth International Seminar on Research in Music Education. *Psychology of Music,* special issue, 76–81.

Madsen, C. K., J. M. Standley, and J. W. Cassity. (1989) Demonstration and recognition of high and low contrasts in teacher intensity. *JRME* 37:2. Reston, VA.

MENC. (1986) *The school music program: Descriptions and standards.* Reston, VA, p. 25.

Meyen, E. L., and D. H. Lehr (1980) Least restrictive environments. *Focus on Exceptional Children* (March) 12:7, 1–8.

Mitchell, B. (1982) An update of gifted/talented education in the U.S. *Phi Delta Kappan* 64, 357–358.

Mitchell P. B. (1981) *A policy maker's guide to issues in gifted and talented education.* National Association of State Boards of Education. Washington, DC.

Moore, R., and L. Mathenius (1987) The effects of modeling, reinforcement, and tempo on imitative rhythmic responses of moderately retarded adolescents. *The Journal of Music Therapy* (Fall) 24:3, 160–169. The National Association for Music Therapy, Inc. Washington, DC.

Murray, K. C. (1972) The effect of teacher approval/disapproval on the musical performance, attentiveness, and attitude of high school choruses. Doctoral dissertation, Florida State University. Dissertation Abstracts International, 33/08A, 4459.

Nocera, S. D. (1979) *Reaching the special learner through music.* Silver Burdett Co. Morristown, N.J.

Peretz, M. A. (1988) Three time-saving tactics for rehearsals. *Music Educators Journal,* 29–31. Reston, VA.

Reynolds, M. (1976) Official actions of the delegate assembly. *Exceptional Children* (September). Council for Exceptional Children. Reston, VA.

Rosenthal, R. K., M. Wilson, M. Evans, and L. Greenwalt (1988) Effects on advanced instrumentalists' performance accuracy. *JRME* (Winter), 36:4, 250–257. MENC. Reston, VA.

Shehan, P. K. (1987) Effects of rote versus note presentations on rhythmic learning and retention. *JRME* 35:2, 117–126. MENC. Reston, VA.

Sims, W. L. (1986) The effect of high versus low teacher affect and passive versus active activity during music listening on preschool children's attention, piece performance, time spent listening, and piece recognition. *JRME* 34, 173–191. Reston, VA,

Sisk, D. (1984) A national survey of gifted programs. Presentation to the National Business Consortium for Gifted and Talented. Washington, DC.

Smith, D. (1989) Constructing effective teacher-made tests. *Georgia Music News.* Georgia Music Educators Association. Marietta, GA.

Suzuki, S. (1969) *Nurtured by love.* Exposition Press. New York.

U.S. Department of Education. (1986) Eighth annual report to Congress on the implementation of the Education of the Handicapped Act. Washington, D.C.

Walker, L. L. (1989) The effect of teacher approval and disapproval on musical performance, attentiveness, and attitude on seventh grade choral students. Unpublished doctoral dissertation. University of Georgia. Athens.

Yarbrough, C. (1975) The effect of magnitude of conductor behavior on performance, attentiveness, and attitude of students in selected mixed choruses. *JRME* 23, MENC. 134–146. Reston, VA.

Zigmond, N., and S. Miller (1986) Assessment for instructional planning. *Exceptional Children* (April) 53:6, 501–509. CEC, Reston, VA.

Zimmerman, M. P. (1990) Psychological theory and music learning. In this volume (Chapter 7).

12

Convergence: Music Technology and Education

G. David Peters

As readers in the 1990s are keenly aware, the rate of societal change continues to accelerate; advances in worldwide technology increasingly influence all areas of society — sociopolitical, economic, and most important, attitudes and values. Technology has served as a means to change attitudes and values, while it also shapes our approaches to problem solving and to expression. Many older, traditional means for expressing attitudes and emotions have been replaced or expanded by technological innovation.

Technological "expressive" tools have changed the very manner in which individuals and groups interact. Even as we benefit from speed of communication, rapid collection of data (information), and problem-solving processes, we recognize our inability to assess the validity of the information being communicated. This new problem affects the general public, as well as world leaders, on a daily basis.

While each new age brings new problems, many very exciting opportunities also emerge. To assess the opportunities that our microelectronic age is setting forth, one must consider the short history of change in technological tools and in music. The following technological advances help define a new history of music and music education, most of which has occurred since the 1958 publication of *Basic Concepts in Music Education, I*.

DEVELOPMENT OF THE TOOLS

Defining the various technological inventions and developments as tools is an important thesis. Three areas that have begun to converge and that

237

define a new music technology include "communications technology," "audio technology," and "computer technology." Each area offers a specific, requisite component to propel the learner forward.

COMMUNICATIONS TECHNOLOGY

When thinking of communication, we first think of telephones. Thousands of telephones network critical communication for every member of contemporary society. Within the past thirty years, the telephone has advanced from a rather primitive network of exchanges to a digital electronic communication network that allows the user to "direct-dial" worldwide. The improvement in the quality of telephone networking and voice transmission is an important cornerstone for interaction; other technologies rely heavily on telecommunication, including the transmission of valuable information for research and teaching.

Thirty years ago television was basically a two-dimensional black-and-white medium. Advances in television technology have ushered in high-quality color images, digital television images, and videocassette recorders (VCRs). The Electronic Industry Association reported that 56 percent of all U.S. households were equipped with VCRs in 1988. The ability to record color television images for home entertainment as well as for education has become commonplace. Television has also been greatly enhanced by the clarity and interactive nature of cable networking. Cable TV is the second largest communication network in the United States, reaching into more than 52 percent of U.S. homes. Although most cable television channels remain unused, the potential that "noncommercial" television holds for communicating music, arts, and education is well established; only leadership is needed to make full use of this important communication network.

Communication technology has been facilitated by the implementation and continued improvement of satellite transmission. We no longer know whether our telephone conversation or our television reception is being transmitted by satellite or by ground cabling. The obvious advantage of satellite communication is the international networking of information; from the Soviet Union to the United States, from Canada to Australia, and from Japan to Brazil, the satellites transmit their messages. This technology specifically has enhanced the scope, quality, and speed of our interactions.

AUDIO TECHNOLOGY

Another great advance was that which occurred in audio technology over the past thirty years. In the mid-to-late 1950s, recording technology moved from 78 rpm records to 45 rpm records, and in quick succession to 33 rpm, LP (long-play), recordings. "High-fidelity" was shortened to "hi-fi" as the quality of audio reproduction improved immensely. In very short order, stereophonic sound was developed as a recording technique and invaded the commercial market. Other improvements in sound reproduction included the short-lived 8-track audio tapes, which were immediately eclipsed by cassette tape recorders. The quality of recording materials and production facilities improved over the next several years. Experiments such as quadraphonic sound, direct-to-disc recordings, and digital recordings brought the listener closer to a "noise-free" reproduction of music performances.

The most recent development, already widely accepted, is the compact disc audio recording. The CD merges a digital sound reproduction technique with playback equipment to move the listener from an analog sound spectrum to a digital music environment. Recently available is the "digital-audio-tape," or DAT. This technology completes the previous cycle from 45 rpm records to cassette tapes.

As audio technology moved from early recording techniques of analog signals to the present digital world, sound synthesis has followed the same path. Synthesizers developed in the early 1960s were cumbersome, expensive electronic devices available to only a few composers. The most radical advance in audio technology is that of the digital synthesizer, through means of which the reduction in cost has allowed the general public to experiment with very inexpensive digital keyboards. Synthesized sounds now clutter the air, from the digital voice messages of cash registers to digital doorbell music.

Today, five musicians using digital technology can create or synthesize more sounds, more layers of sounds, and more complex music information than possible from a traditional "acoustic" symphony orchestra. This type of sound production now dominates background music for television and film. Digital sound synthesis as a technology allows a performer/composer to create music that can be stored in a computer memory or a computer disk as direct digital information. This information can easily be recalled and formatted into a CD audio disc for distribution. Further, resultant quality of sound is not degraded by any of the previous recording tape limitations. This level of audio technology now allows the teacher or the student musician to gain control of high-quality sound, sound manipulation, and sound reproduction.

COMPUTER TECHNOLOGY

A brief history of computer applications to music would include the following events. The first computer-generated music began to emerge approximately thirty years ago. Hiller's *Illiac Suite* (1958) was produced at the

University of Illinois as one of the first computer-generated pieces. It was not until the mid-1960s, however, that computers were used in attempts at music instruction. These early projects included work by Wolfgang Kuhn at Stanford University and the work of his students, including Reynold Allvin, Rebecca Herrold, and Rosemary Killiam. Ned Deihl at Pennsylvania State University used an IBM computer to teach instrumental materials as early as 1968. Earle Hultberg developed music fundamental drills, his research beginning in 1967 at the State University of New York–Potsdam. At the University of Illinois, I initiated a project on the PLATO system focused on pitch discrimination and music performance.

As the large mainframe computers improved in quality and speed, researchers in the early- to mid-1970s began to advance work in music theory and music education. Such research and development included work by Gary Wittlich (Indiana University), Fred Hofstetter (University of Delaware), Robert Placek (University of Georgia), Jack Taylor (Florida State University), and Ann Blombach (Ohio State University). With the exception of Blombach, these researchers implemented music instruction on the PLATO system on their various campuses, beginning their work in conjunction with the University of Illinois PLATO computer system.

"Minicomputers" emerged as a smaller classification of computers in the evolutionary process. Significant music projects were created on minicomputers, including the work of Marvin Thorsten (University of Iowa), John Appleton (Dartmouth College), and Rosemary Killiam at Stanford University and later at North Texas State University.

The minicomputer phase of software development was quickly eclipsed by the advent of microcomputers. As "home" computers appeared in the late 1970s, researchers and teachers alike quickly implemented music instruction on computers created by emerging corporations such as Apple, Atari, and Commodore. The miniaturization of electronic components, which continues even today, has tremendously enhanced the capabilities and flexibility of computer-based music instruction. The early "8-bit" microcomputers have been surpassed by 16- and 32-bit computers capable of supporting higher and higher quality music instruction. Current delivery systems include the networking of microcomputers and super microcomputers in local area networks. Given the evolution of faster, smaller, and less expensive computers, computer-based music instruction (CBMI) requires several essential components. Articles by myself (1977) and Hofstetter (1977) outline components deemed essential for high-quality music instruction. These components include:

1. computer graphics characters
2. computer-generated sound

3. random-access record/playback
4. analog-to-digital conversion
5. music keyboard

1. The graphics capabilities of computers have improved greatly since the first microcomputers were developed. Whereas the use of color is not essential, graphics characters are critical to display music notation and other educational icons. Without high-quality musical notation, most music instruction is not possible.

2. Computer-generated sound is closely allied to sound synthesis. Digital sound synthesis technologies have now been merged with computer programs to allow computers to generate high-quality music stimuli. These capabilities include merging synthesizer "chips" with computer components to create the capability of playing four, eight, or even sixteen voice sound examples for the student learner.

3. Random-access recording has been greatly enhanced by the creation of CD audio discs. The same technology that allows a CD player to search for specific music examples can be merged with microcomputer technology, thus allowing the music educator to play back, for example, orchestral passages or operatic selections totally under computer control. The great advantage to the random-access feature is to allow individual students to progress at their own rates of speed. Computer software has recently been developed to control such playback equipment using popular, powerful microcomputers.

4. A very important musical peripheral developed for sound sampling or conversion to digital information is that of the "analog-to-digital" converter. This device converts any music performance from sound into digital information. Once such a conversion is complete, a computer can quickly analyze the resultant digital information. My early research (1973) demonstrated the use of an analog-to-digital converter in judging trumpet performances. In the fifteen years since this research was initiated, several commercially available devices have been created for similar use. These devices offer the flexibility of judging music performances in a wide range of frequencies.

5. The most obvious component for the music instruction "work station" is that of a music keyboard. Many versions of keyboard peripheral devices were developed in the 1970s, but because of the numerous and varying approaches for attaching music keyboards to computers, little transfer of research or application software was possible. Only the development of MIDI (Musical Instrument Digital Interface) made possible the standardization of the manner in which keyboard peripherals can be used with computers. A growing number of instruction materials are now being developed using MIDI electronic keyboards as peripheral devices to microcomputers.

An important feature of MIDI synthesizers is that of digital performances. Using computers, the teacher or musician can generate data that can be converted into music performances using the MIDI keyboard. This two-way transmission of data allows for output of high-quality sound examples for education, plus the ability to assess student keyboard performances.

Advances in computer technology have also allowed for the merging of videodisc technology with music instruction. The use of color video examples available through videodisc greatly enhances the study of music through a combination of sound and motion. Students, for instance, can judge the conductor's precision or the pianist's hand position through viewing video performances.

Recent advances in computer graphics and printing capabilities have made possible the development of music-printing software. Like word processors, computers have the ability to facilitate the generation of high-quality printing. Music characters have been generated for music examples from single-line scores to full symphony orchestra manuscripts. More sophisticated music software allows the composer to create a music score, transpose each part to the appropriate key and clef, then print parts for each individual performer. The interaction between the music-printing software and music performance is direct. Several music-printing programs allow the composer to "play in" the music using a MIDI keyboard. These same programs will allow the composer to hear the completed full score using an "orchestra" of electronic, digital instruments. Nuances of slurs, dynamics, and articulations are included in the score printing and the score performance. Such "music-sequencing" is a powerful tool for the modern composer, teacher, and student.

IMPLEMENTATION OF THE TOOLS

With the merging of the three technologies — communications, audio, and computer — the teacher in the 1990s should be well equipped to transmit our modern musical culture as it emerges. In considering the computer as the appliance for classroom application of our music technology, one must critically review available software or courseware. All CBMI software development was initiated on college or university campuses. As CBMI software emerged at the various centers, each project reflected the interest of that college or university faculty. The University of Illinois focused early efforts on music performance judging and instrumental music methods. Florida State University focused its development efforts on the analysis of musical stimuli to be used in teaching listening skills. The University of Delaware has maintained a focus on music theory and ear training, and the University of Toronto focused early efforts on compositional environments. Each of these projects utilized large mainframe computers.

With the introduction of microcomputers, CBMI development multiplied to a level that was well-nigh impossible to assess. With easy access to computers, researchers and teachers developed a new body of software within the limitations of the new, smaller computers. Because fewer programming tools were available to these authors, they faced the formidable task of learning to create music application software in a rather primitive computer environment. The result of this initial microcomputer programming effort was a series of "first-generation" software that was lacking in depth, musical quality, or effectiveness. Ninety percent of this software was drill-and-practice in nature. Topics were easy-to-program areas such as cognitive, factual materials about music. Basic music theory was a first target for such programmers. The programs generally were linear in nature and simple in subject area. Note names, interval identification, key signatures, and chord structure are examples of these early efforts.

Learning topics have been expanded in recent years to cover broader areas in music education and music history. Applications in methods, pedagogy, learning theory, and classroom simulation are now appearing in software catalogs. A new series of music history topics focuses on composers, dates, periods, and events. The newer programs utilize CD audio performances of compositions rather than single-line computer-generated sounds.

As indicated earlier, new musical applications were created as microcomputers grew in size, power, and speed. Utility programs took precedence over instructional programs. The use of computers for music printing, desktop publishing, and digital recording of sequences became the primary focus for developers and users alike. The result in 1990 is the availability of numerous programs from a growing number of companies created to develop and sustain sound-based software. As is usually the case, the educational application of the technology has lagged behind commercial interests. Very few companies have developed a catalog of instructional music programs, even after nearly twenty years of research and development. Current interest, generated by professional musicians, continues to focus on sophisticated sound-control programs that are not readily appropriate for educational use.

The technology "tools" for CBMI are currently available. These very impressive computers, synthesizers, and videodiscs will make a difference in how we teach. The current situation must change, however, before we see new and more creative music programs developed for education. The cost of developing high-quality educational software exceeds the return. The result has been the development of only a small number of programs that surpass the basic drill-and-practice classification.

As evidence to support this view of inverted development, consider the number of CBMI music programs available on the Apple II computer, the IBM personal computer, and the Macintosh computer. Well over 600 CBMI programs have been developed for the Apple, whereas fewer than 200 CBMI programs exist for the IBM. At last count, fewer than twenty instructional music programs were available on the Macintosh computer. As the technology becomes more sophisticated, so should the instructional software. When reviewing software for the IBM or Macintosh computers, one does not find very innovative uses of the expanded memory, computing speed, or data storage.

Research efforts continue to demonstrate the effectiveness of using technology in teaching music. Examples of materials that should make their way into the CBMI market include interactive videodisc, interactive MIDI/computers, and the digital synthesis of sound. Digital manipulation of sound is the key innovation and common element among these applications. Through the use of these three tools, educators can approach teaching in exciting new ways. Timbre, intonation, tone quality, and expressive nuance can be presented in controlled instructional sequences by using digital control of video and audio.

CBMI software continues to improve in quality and quantity even though the number of companies creating such software has declined. Music lessons are being developed not only for school applications but also for the home learner. Music software is an established segment of computer-based instruction; leadership within the professional music associations recognizes the importance of the emerging technologies and of CBMI as a research and academic discipline.

EDUCATIONAL SOLUTIONS THROUGH TECHNOLOGY

After twenty years of CBMI development, we now find ourselves with easily available equipment. A growing interest in the music capabilities of computers is apparent. A large majority of high schools in the United States are now equipped with microcomputer labs to teach a number of different disciplines. CBMI, if improved in quality and increased in quantity, can enhance learning in several areas. In acquiring performance skills, compositional skills, or listening skills, students must still progress through sequenced instruction, trial and error, and supervised practice. CBMI can increase performance skills by improving students' ability to match pitches, recognize intervals, and judge intonation and by expanding their tonal memory. These performance skills can be applied to virtually any musical performance medium, vocal or instrumental. The direct application of MIDI keyboard and MIDI A-to-D conversion will allow students to assess their own abilities and improve their skills through immediate feedback and modeling.

Compositional skills can be improved through the use of computer tools. Using sophisticated sequencer computer programs, students can digitally record compositions and hear them played back immediately. The manipulation of digitally produced sounds has been greatly enhanced through the use of computers and computer software. With an expanded electronic sound pallet, composers, novice and professional alike, can greatly increase their control over this creative outcome.

Listening skills can be developed through directed listening activities. Now that CD audio can be merged with computer instruction, students have the ability to investigate works of art through individualized listening, to distort or manipulate any aspect of a music composition and hear the resultant performance. Through manipulating the very elements of a music composition, students can expand their listening skills far beyond the limitations set by earlier technologies. For instance, the listener can distort the balance of a piece, the tempo of a piece, the timbre of the melody, the registration of the soprano aria, or the very key of an entire composition. Through experimentation, students not only can study a composition as originally intended by the composer, but can also immediately learn the effects of other variations of the same piece.

Perhaps the most obvious educational problem that can be solved by the computer is that of instructional time. When students learn through self-guided individualized instruction, a great deal of instructional time is saved. With added pressures on school curricula from primary grades through college level, we must become more efficient in our teaching strategies. These technological tools can give us easy access to a much larger learning environment.

Through communications technology, learners will have access to a much richer arts environment than ever before. As educational networks mature, arts materials can be stored at a very rapid rate worldwide. The character of music can be transmitted from concert hall to classroom at the same time that sophisticated educational libraries are established. Video and audio materials of very high quality can assist in transmitting information for educational purposes.

The interactive nature of music can now be matched by opportunities for interactive learning. The use of the three technologies, communications technology, audio technology, and computer technology, can expand educational opportunities for all students involved in the music education curriculum.

REFERENCES

Deihl, Ned C. *Development and Evaluation of Computer-Assisted Instruction in Instrumental Music (Final Report).* University Park: Pennsylvania State University, 1969.

————. Computer-Assisted Instruction and Instrumental Music: Implications for Teaching and Research, *Journal of Research in Music Education* XIX (1971), 299–306.

Eddins, John M. Random Access Audio in Computer Assisted Music Instruction, *Journal of Computer Based Instruction* V, Nos. 1 and 2 (1978), 22–29.

Hofstetter, Fred P. Music Dream Machines: New Realities for Computer-Based Musical Instruction, *Creative Computing* III, No. 2 (1977), 50–54.

Kent, William P. Feasibility of Computer-Assisted Elementary Keyboard Music Instruction. Falls Church, Virginia: Systems Development Corporation, 1970 (Eric Document Reproduction Service no. ED 038 039).

Kuhn, Wolfgang. Computer-Assisted Instruction in Music: Drill and Practice in Dictation, *College Music Symposium* 14 (1974), 89–101.

Kuhn, Wolfgang, and Reynold Allvin. Computer-Assisted Teaching: A New Approach to Research in Music, *Journal of Research in Music Education* XV (1967), 305–315.

Peters, G. David. Feasibility of Computer-Assisted Instruction for Instrumental Music Education. Ed.D. dissertation, University of Illinois, 1974.

————. *The Complete Computer-Based Music System: A Teaching System — A Musician's Tool,* Proceedings of the 1977 Winter Conference of the Association for the Development of Computer-Based Instructional Systems (1977), 93–100.

————. Capabilities of Computer-Assisted Instruction in Music: The PLATO Music Project. Paper presented at the conference of the Association for the Development of Computer-Based Instructional Systems, Dallas, Texas, March 1, 1978.

Placek, Robert W. Design and Trial of a Computer-Assisted Lesson in Rhythm, Ed.D. dissertation, University of Illinois, 1972 (University Microfilms No. 73-17.362).

Williams, David B., and David L. Shrader. The Development of a Microcomputer-Based Music Instruction Lab. Paper presented at the Association for the Development of Computer-Based Instruction Systems, Arlington, Virginia, April 1980.

13

Evaluation

Richard J. Colwell

Charles Leonhard's opening statement in the evaluation chapter of the first *Basic Concepts in Music Education* book was that "evaluation is a rather new term."[1] Clearly, times have changed. In 1990 the evaluation of schools, students, programs, and community support and the comparison of test scores among schools, states, and even nations have become areas of public concern. This scrutiny goes on in music as well as every other aspect of public education. In 1982 I updated Leonhard's chapter on evaluation for the thirtieth anniversary of the University of Illinois doctoral program; that work itself is already woefully dated. Leonhard's chapter first discussed the measurement of student learning, then took up the subject of program evaluation. The present chapter will roughly follow the earlier format. But measurement and evaluation are tremendously more complex than in 1958; to give some order to that complexity, I will attempt a chronological tracing of the evolving ideas, theories, and events of the past forty years. Along the way some organizational coherence may be sacrificed in the interests of showing how new developments have arisen.

The controversy over ways and means to evaluate the musical experience has greatly increased in the recent past. Taxpayers and school administrators insist upon systematic evaluation of *all* school programs, with solid reasons for their demand. To operate schools is expensive, and the public appears reluctant to invest more heavily in education without valid data on past progress and evaluation of the prospects for the future. Expenditures for education have exceeded inflation, even as student enrollment has declined, while at the same time the schools are seen as less effective. In response to the charge of ineffectiveness, numerous accountability plans have been advanced by educators, research is being conducted on effective schools and effective teachers, and expensive technology has been added to the class-room. But the question is asked, "To what effect?", and the answers are not consistently positive or even optimistic.

Music teachers argue that much of what they teach cannot be evaluated, or they reject the evaluation techniques employed in other subject matter areas on the grounds that evaluation is an integral part of teaching performance skills and that these skills are constantly being demonstrated. This position rests on the narrowest of definitions of evaluation; such arguments stem from a failure to comprehend the extent of evaluative data being demanded of the schools. Contributing to the negative view held by the music teacher is the fact that evaluation is not a part of most college curricula, so few music educators comprehend the complexity of the discipline and the uses to which evaluation can and should be put.

Leonhard's chapter is historically significant today. The work was a landmark in 1958; the insights that the author had into the teaching and learning process are still applicable and, in fact, in many instances his suggestions have yet to be acted upon. In 1982 I identified three of Leonhard's points that had not stood the test of time: First, the sum of the parts no longer is thought of as equaling the whole; evaluating the various facets of music instruction and learning will not provide an accurate appraisal of the program. Second, program improvement can no longer occur primarily through action research conducted by the classroom teacher. The definition of program evaluation has expanded such that it is now a major undertaking. Third, the development of individual musical independence is seldom a priority of program evaluation even though such evaluation can bring about improvement in learning conditions. These three points are related to program evaluation, a subject that has had many ups and downs over the past thirty years. The frenetic activity in program evaluation has, however, changed our expectations of programs and made us aware of the important role that program organization and support plays in attaining educational ends. Leonhard's approach to evaluation was related to his *Foundations and Principles of Music Education* with Robert House, a book that although dated remains viable because its thrust so clearly describes at least one facet of today's music programs.[2]

Leonhard listed eight uses for evaluation in the school music program:

1. appraisal of student progress
2. guidance
3. motivation
4. improvement of instruction
5. improvement of programs
6. student selection

7. maintenance of standards
8. research

If broadly defined, these eight uses remain valid. For example, evaluation provides data on teacher effectiveness and the appropriateness of teaching materials, experiences, and activities — data that can contribute to improvement of instruction. Evaluation is also a form of instruction when accompanied by feedback such as with computer-assisted instruction and programmed learning. The relative emphasis and scope of the eight categories has changed as evaluation reflects the language of instruction and the objectives of music education today.

This chapter will cover three areas: first, a history of evaluation in music education; second, a description of present evaluation techniques and measurement; and in conclusion, a portrayal of the present status of student and program evaluation.

HISTORY

Distinguishing measurement from evaluation, relating objectives to evaluation, selecting appropriate measuring instruments, and properly interpreting the results of evaluation — these should come naturally to the student who has grown up with annual administrations of standardized tests and depended upon ACT or SAT scores to gain admittance to a university. However, the student seldom has this understanding. Our lives are surrounded by familiar devices that we do not understand; we cannot repair them and we don't know how they work. So it is with evaluation. Music teachers and teacher educators should ask themselves how much understanding they truly have of evaluation procedures in music — their validity, meaning, and interpretability. If one has not even read a basic book on tests and measurement, one's ability to select and use evaluation in teaching, understand the research in the field, and grasp the merits of various methods of instruction will be limited. Recognizing music teachers' lack of awareness, Leonhard laid out the principles of evaluation, which have not changed. For example, the value of any test relates to the purpose for which it is used. Administering a music aptitude test to all students has little value if selection of students for instruction on the basis of talent is not part of the school's philosophy. If the philosophy is that all students have the opportunity to take any offered course, the use of the aptitude test is not for selection but for motivation and guidance, and to provide data for improvement of instruction and for research. Thus there are numerous reasons for administering an aptitude test; the value of the test depends upon the intended purpose. Evaluative statements about tests are not feasible without knowledge of purpose. Therefore, in the review of tests that follows, only the most general comments will be made. Any single test might be essential or worthless depending upon interpretation of the data it produces. Aptitude tests are often given and the data seldom used — a waste of instructional time and resources.

Leonhard could not have predicted that by 1991 evaluation would become the most dynamic characteristic of American social science. No one writing in the 1950s envisioned the present range of social programs that depend upon education. These social programs have torn evaluation from its secure mooring in the classroom and catapulted it into the mainstream of twentieth-century social issues, bringing radical change, controversy, and complexity to the school. In theory the abiding school has faded, as have many of its most durable qualities. In practice, most educators remain conservative. When I began to teach in the public schools, the biggest school news of the year was the newspaper's annual publication of salaries. Today, no aspect of the school goes unquestioned and all events are newsworthy, from the cost of transporting students to the school to the average reading scores of Miss Appleby's class.

A serious problem for evaluation is the lack of consensus concerning the goals of education. The schools can serve society in many ways, and each way has its own constituency. Schools can teach values, indoctrinate, provide vocational training, promote liberal education, provide new experiences, and teach the basics. With this plethora of goals, evaluation procedures appropriate for the 1990s are only distantly related to those of the 1950s. In the midst of these changes, a major issue in evaluation is whether to focus on the education/achievement of the individual or to measure the school's success by its attainment of social goals.

MEASUREMENT

Over the past thirty-odd years, the publishing of tests for use in music education has been sporadic. A flurry of new editions occurred about 1958. The Gaston, Drake, and Seashore measures were each republished between 1957 and 1960; the *National Teacher Examination* appeared in 1957; and in 1962 James Aliferis (with John Stecklein) extended his college entrance examination to include a midpoint test. A second flurry occurred in the 1970s. The Conn music aptitude test was revised in 1976, the McCreery in 1970, and several other promotional tests that have no date were vigorously promoted. (Promotional tests are invariably atomistic and lacking in rigor but are better than no test for the purposes of student selection. Data from poor tests are not bad data, only inadequate.)

The *Gaston Test of Musicality,* recommended in the 1950s as the least atomistic of the talent tests, most recently was published by a music store (1957). The test contained several innovative techniques that still influence music educators. An important aspect was E. Thayer Gaston's belief that musicality is not dependent upon separate sensory abilities but upon the individual's interaction with musical items. Here are two examples: In Gaston's test a student hears a tone followed by a chord and is asked whether the tone occurred in the chord. In another section the student must indicate whether the missing last note of a melody should be higher, lower, or the same as the last note heard. Another valuable element in the test was his use of information about one's musical background to add to the total score points.

Herbert Wing's standardized *Tests of Musical Intelligence* were developed in England during the late 1950s, and Gaston and Wing may have influenced each other. Wing's requirement that the testee make judgments about the quality of the music is a departure from the straight sensory approach of Carl Seashore and his contemporaries. It is Wing's contribution to the field. Utilizing the innovations of Wing and Gaston, Edwin Gordon published his own measures of music aptitude in 1965, the *Musical Aptitude Profile.* Gordon's test constitutes a major effort to redefine aptitude and to break the hold maintained since 1919 by the Seashore *Measures of Musical Talent.* Gordon's test is comprised of two sections, an expanded judgmental section of three parts — phrase, balance, and style — and a section testing tonal and rhythmic memory.

Within a year of Gordon's test the English scholar Arnold Bentley published his *Measures of Musical Abilities* (1966), an attempt to measure aptitude in younger children. Bentley's efforts at establishing validity and reliability were more modest than Gordon's. The test has been widely accepted, with translation into a fifth language (Italian) occurring in 1990. Bentley returned to the sensory ideas of Seashore but gave the greatest weight to a test section that requires a student to identify the number of tones in a chord, an idea first used by Wing.

The publication of an aptitude test for primary grade children by Gordon in 1979 was followed in 1989 by his publication of *Audie,* a game (test) for preschool children. In his tests for younger children, Gordon has dropped the powerful preference section of his *Musical Aptitude Profile* and relies on recognition of same and different tonal and rhythmic patterns. In 1979, Ray Moyer published a music test, not systematically developed, designed to be an aptitude test.

Despite the energy of Edwin Gordon and his students in promoting the value of aptitude tests, the music profession continues to lack enthusiasm for testing; the most recent aptitude tests are recognized as interesting and well constructed, but teachers seem to have little use for knowledge about individual talent. Aptitude tests are not a powerful factor in curriculum construction or placement of students, nor are they frequently used as baseline data in the evaluation of programs, methods, and techniques. Research results indicate that the effectiveness of teaching methodology varies according to student ability and interest; the failure to use aptitude data is therefore surprising.

Measurement of music achievement has attracted researchers. Educational Testing Service (ETS) has emphasized college-level tools; however, it has influenced secondary school music education through its sponsorship of Advanced Placement theory and Advanced Placement history and literature. The music section of the ETS *Graduate Record Examination* (GRE) appeared in 1951–1953; the *National Teacher Examination* (NTE) followed in 1957. In many states the NTE is a barrier exam; to be certified to teach one must meet the state-established standard on the test. It is not surprising that ETS has focused its efforts in areas where standards are appealing, and its tests provide the best example in music of the potential of evaluation in the maintenance of standards.

Educational Testing Service has been challenged in the college market only by James Aliferis, whose 1954 *Aliferis Music Achievement Test: College Entrance Level* is designed for sectioning students into ability levels in music theory. Although the Aliferis test could be used as a barrier exam, it seldom has been used in this manner. Its chief use has been for placement in music theory classes. Aliferis capitalized on the belief that music theory is the basis of musicianship and that improvement in sight-singing and dictation is fundamental progress in music. Knowledge of music theory is so basic to musicianship that the Aliferis test does validly discriminate among students, making instruction more efficient. Students entering college with high Aliferis scores make substantially greater progress in music theory classes than those with low scores. In 1962 Aliferis with Stecklein published a college midpoint or posttest version of the *College Entrance Level* test. Based upon the concepts of the entrance examination, the midpoint test was designed to measure what had been learned in two years of music theory. It was the first test published since the 1930s that was exclusively a mastery test based on instructional objectives, whose data could be used both diagnostically and as a measure of achievement. Because near-consensus exists that theory skills are important, Aliferis was able to construct not only a fairly reliable measure but one with verifiable content validity. Aliferis made one additional attempt in the measurement field, a test to measure what had been learned at the undergraduate level and to set admission standards for the graduate level. It was not published, and today it is only of research interest.

In the 1960s, Newell Long formed a publishing company to distribute his revision of Kate Mueller's 1934 *Oregon Music Discrimination Test*. This unique test asked students to distinguish the original version of a piece of music from another version in which the melody, rhythm, or harmony had been changed, the underlying assumption being that the skilled student could recognize the "better" (original) music. Although high reliability was obtained in the United States, Australia, and Great Britain, no evidence of the validity of the test is available.

In the late 1960s Follett Publishing Company published my four *Music Achievement Tests,* the first test since the mid-1930s designed for use in the general music program. I based my tests on the written or implied objectives of current music series texts used in the elementary schools and texts used to teach the elementary music teacher. The four tests measure most of the objectives common to the texts consulted. Content validity of the tests was well established; I gave less attention to the tests' diagnostic capabilities. The decade of the 1960s ended with three authors publishing their own achievement tests. In 1967 William Knuth privately republished his 1936 test for three levels of music instruction. In 1968 Alice Snyder-Knuth published a test created ten years earlier as her doctoral dissertation. The Snyder-Knuth test remains today the only instrument designed to measure the music competencies of the elementary education student. (The *National Teacher Examination* has only two music questions on any version.) The third test author was Stephen Farnum, who added three sections to his earlier notation test. The sections contain adaptations or copies of questions from three extant measures — those of Seashore, Jacob Kwalwasser, and T. W. McQuerrie. Stephen Farnum published this test in 1969, the same year he added a string scale to his *Watkins-Farnum Performance Scales* (originally published in 1954). The 1969 Watkins-Farnum test remains useful today partly because it is the only published measure of instrumental performance but also because the exercises match the content of instrumental music instructional materials. The validity of the Watkins-Farnum test is especially remarkable in view of the fact that its musical material is based on cornet instructional materials published between 1900 and 1940. Content stability is a feature of many music tests, and their shelf life has been much longer than that of tests in other curricula.

Additional measurement tools were published during the 1970s. In 1979 Gordon's *Iowa Tests of Musical Literacy* were released. Begun as criterion devices for the validation studies of his *Musical Aptitude Profile*, these are a comprehensive battery of six tests, each measuring music literacy in terms of aural perception, reading recognition, and tonal and rhythmic notation. A major difference between these tests and my tests was that I identified the objectives by songbook series, giving the teacher the responsibility to decide which test or section of the test was appropriate. MAT contains norms for several grade levels for each test. Gordon, however, based his measures upon his own conception of appropriate objectives and a logically established progressive battery of six tests. Although no grade level is specified, level 1 is intended to be appropriate for fourth- or fifth-grade students where systematic music instruction exists, and the other five levels are to be used one each year, for six successive years of measurement.

In 1971 the Belwin Publishing Company issued the *Belwin-Mills Singing Achievement Test*, constructed as a commercial venture for the company. The test was not rigorously developed and no purpose is stated. In the mid-1970s two tests appeared in Australia: the Australian Council of Educational Research and the University of Melbourne's *Music Evaluation Kit* for secondary schools, and the *Australian Test for Advanced Music Studies*. The latter test, like the Aliferis test, is designed for the entering college music major. With a correlation of .70 with Aliferis and the use of interesting music, the test is attractive but three times as long as the Aliferis test. Neither of the Australian tests had wide usage in the United States.

The 1970s ended with the appearance of Richard Simon's *Measurements of Music Listening Skills for Young Children* (1976) and my 1979 eighteen-test battery entitled *Silver Burdett Music Competency Tests*. Simon's tests were based upon the objectives of a funded research project in Columbus, Georgia. They were designed to measure concepts such as loud and soft, faster and slower, same and different — concepts common to the primary grades and to several different teaching techniques. The Silver Burdett competency tests were the first effort to create music tests based on criterion-referenced principles. They expanded upon the "What Do You Hear" tests, part of the publication *Silver Burdett Music;* they are continued in an amateur version in the present series. The test items for SBMCT were selected from empirical results with students using the books and not on any ideal level. With reasonable instruction and instructional time, at least 80 percent of the students are expected to master the content measured by this device.

Three tests appeared in the 1980s. In addition to Gordon's *Audie,* Janet Mills from Great Britain published her *Group Tests of Musical Abilities,* Gordon also published an *Instrumental Timbre Test,* and James Froseth introduced instructional materials with accompanying tests: *Aural Skills Training Series, Instrumental and Choral Score Reading Tests,* and a visual *Diagnostic Skills Tests.*

The quantity of music tests published during the past thirty years does not indicate that music educators have a renewed interest in evaluation; rather, test authors were responding to the national interest in evaluation. Of U.S. tests, those presently available from commercial publishers include only the Watkins-Farnum and Seashore tests, Gordon's *Musical Aptitude Profile* and *Iowa Tests of Musical Literacy,* and those tests published by GIA and ETS. A wider range of aptitude tests is available, although when quality becomes a consideration even that choice is restricted. Evaluation in music education makes limited use of standardized measurements, and those tests that are available measure only a limited number of the objectives of a comprehensive K–16 music program.

The major measurement effort of this century in the United States was the National Assessment of Educational Progress (NAEP). Music was included in the first year of the testing program (1971–1972) when idealism was high and affective objectives were valued. The areas to be measured were typical of most programs — performance, knowledge, and appreciation. Reflecting the objectives then current, items included melodic, rhythmic, and harmonic improvisation. The test was well conceived although expensive — the performance items had to be individually administered and scored. The test results in music failed to have the impact upon education that test results had in mathematics, reading, and other subject areas. The reasons for this failure are unknown, other than the perception that music is less important than other curricular subjects. Music educators could have used the results in their research and curriculum planning, but the test and its outcomes have not become well known to music teachers or music teacher educators. One plausible explanation is that music teachers were already overextended and too involved in their work to give attention to the test data. Their viewpoint perhaps was that they could do no more with the time and resources allotted even if the test data revealed new insights. Music teachers never used the data to discover whether or not their efforts were correctly focused.

A second national assessment was conducted in 1978 and 1979, at which time the evaluation of performance objectives was dropped as an economy measure. The remaining music test items represented only a fraction of school music objectives. Further, the dissemination of information from the second assessment was cumbersome and the results unintelligible. Many of the questions from the first assessment had been retained, but the two sets of results were not easily compared; it was evident only that students were not improving on the questions asked. The results of the second assessment that caught attention were those dealing with attitude; the Education Commission of the States and the public learned what they already knew — that students preferred rock music to country and western.

The NAEP was mandated and paid for by funds external to local school districts. State testing programs have also been instituted with limited teacher involvement. Minnesota and Connecticut based their state evaluations on the national assessment model and used many of the NAEP-released questions. Michigan constructed its own test in 1974 and tested again with a revised instrument in 1982. Kansas developed an expensive battery of tests that were little used and are now unknown. Utah created a paper and pencil test; Illinois is presently developing paper and pencil tests. Indiana has piloted tests at fifth and sixth grade that test performance, creativity, and knowledge. West Virginia, with the aid of the National Endowment for the Arts (NEA), has constructed test items for students in first through fourth grade. Other states and local school districts are constructing test items under pressure from school boards and the public; these instruments range from adequate to good.

Two studies in therapy and a couple dozen research projects involving various published tests complete the miscellaneous picture of measurement research in music education. The focused effort of Gordon represents the only identifiable trend in measurement during the past three decades, and if quantity were a valid indicator, music educators are most interested in music aptitude.

EVALUATION

A case could be made for the importance of various types of evaluation based on an inspection of doctoral dissertations in music. Scores of authors have "evaluated" the impact of various treatments. Others have "observed" experts in action or "assessed" the worth of college programs; almost every component of the musical experience has been surveyed and/or evaluated in doctoral studies. As a rule, research in musical development and in psychophysical concepts uses author-constructed tests. Research findings are compared in ignorance of the great differences in difficulty that derive from subtle differences in musical stimuli (and thus content). Most doctoral researchers are inexperienced beginners in research. Often the investigator fails to distinguish between research and evaluation, applying techniques from each discipline at random; evaluation methodology is frequently shoddy and misses the mark of both research and evaluation. Questionnaires, opinionnaires, and other data-gathering devices are created that disregard both validity and reliability. The reader must distinguish between tradition, common sense, and systematic investigation, as all three are confused in the interpretation of results. Caveat emptor. A discussion of proper evaluation/research procedures is not appropriate here, but when evaluation principles are overshadowed by treatment, research design, and statistical manipulation, the results are not likely to be meaningful.

The paucity of interest in music education measurement can be seen by a quick review of doctoral studies over the past thirty years. Over 3,000 dissertations were completed during this time period, approximately forty in test development. Most of the forty studies focused on the development of a test to measure performance ability. They range in focus from Janet Montgomery's (1983) development of procedures for assessing the ability of preschoolers to discriminate melodic direction to Harold Jones's (1986) application of the facet-factorial approach to scale construction in the development of a rating scale for high school vocal solo performance. Also included are unpublished tests for pianists and flutists. Though some of the tests contain interesting ideas, few of them relate directly to the goals of the program being studied, and even fewer clearly define success or failure. In doctoral research, the predominant evaluation instruments continue to be rating scales and checklists, with some attention to observational measures; there is almost no interest in measurement.

Exploratory research has been initiated in the areas of attitude, recognition of musical style, and perception. The interest in student attitude toward music peaked about 1970 and quickly dropped. Three research studies are of special interest, however, because of the care with which they were conducted and the use of statistical techniques that may provide a more accurate measure of the response to music. Francis Hare's "The Identification of Dimensions Underlying Verbal and Exploratory Responses to Music Through Multidimensional Scaling," completed in 1975 at the University of Toronto, was a landmark. Robert Miller used a similar design in 1979 when he attempted to measure music perception. Walter Vispoel constructed the only adaptive test in the field when he applied item response theory to the assessment of musical ability. A popular but unpublished attitude test has been Dennis Darling's semantic differential scale designed to measure attitude toward selected styles of music.

OBJECTIVES

The lack of teacher interest in measurement research and development is consistent with teacher response to systematic procedures in other parts of the music education process. Teachers, publishers, and teachers of teachers show little interest in the formulation of aims, objectives, goals, methods, or procedures. Music education today is characterized by the absence of behavioral standards for the curricular goals of the profession. Excellent performing groups are common; these reflect the high musical standards of their conductors. But even these standards are not based on published curriculum guides. As long as there is no interest in student and grade-level standards, there will be no interest in improving evaluation procedures. Stated goals are usually fuzzy. If skill in matching pitch is a first-grade goal, the goals for second, third, and later grades will usually read "increased skill in matching pitch." Leonhard and House advocated the specification of behavioral objectives but, as philosophers, they did not attempt to prescribe the operational environment or the specifics of success.[3] Thus music teachers may cite Leonhard and House, but their old practices continue.

The opposite extreme exists concurrently. Curriculum guides are widely required, and impressive behavioral objectives appear in them. Many would be a challenge to Wynton Marsalis. The specific objectives are impressive, but to adopt them wholesale to any specific school situation would lead to failure or self-deception. Curriculum guides do not relate to individual teachers, students, or even materials; the objectives in most curriculum guides are unattainable because they describe the perfect musical world. Teachers may create their teaching plans in accord with these ideal objectives and then neglect to carefully evaluate student progress; they then falsely assume that their students are learning what is intended.

Avoidance of specific goals and standards is not the exclusive domain of music teachers. When office workers tire of fulfilling those routine behavioral objectives necessary to keep the office running, like typing and filing, they elect to "do about" — straightening the desktop or the drawers or watering the plants. Doing about feels good; one can avoid self-evaluation and any accompanying guilt; in doing about one is simply not accountable for how one's energy and time are spent. Doing about is pleasant, satisfying, and therapeutic, but a continual program of doing about in the music classroom does not contribute to the accomplishment of short- or long-range goals. Music provides many opportunities to do about, opportunities that should be recognized and avoided.

The rejection of specific standards by music teachers may be a reaction to the detailed programs of the 1920s and 1930s with their accompanying achievement tests that set the standards and controlled the program. During that period the musically educated person knew the names of the lines and spaces, the durational values of rhythm symbols, and the circle of fifths, and he or she could match the titles of compositions with their composers. This emphasis on knowledge fostered activities in the classroom like musical bingo, musical spelldowns, and easily constructed oral and written tests. Neglected were activities that nourished sensitivity and musical understanding. Although performance skills continued to receive emphasis, objectives in the affective domain were nonexistent. The knowledge emphasis created frustration in the music education profession; the good teachers found little time to teach "music" and the poor teachers were discouraged because their students did not achieve in either the cognitive or performance domains. As we look back upon that era, we do well to ask: Did the tests control the program or were they a result of the philosophy of the times?

It is interesting that teacher frustration was not a major factor in the movement away from cognition and performance. The music program simply followed other curriculum areas as humanism and discovery methods swept into the schools. With freedom in all curricula, teachers could discard the disliked cognitive objectives and select the replacement objectives with almost complete autonomy. The affective domain was an attractive framework because program objectives could be focused on the music (satisfying the better teachers) or on activities rather than goals (acceptable to the marginal teachers). Cognitive objectives rapidly disappeared from the general music curriculum; performance skills remained (mainly singing), but more often than not even singing skills frequently deteriorated under the rationale of limited time.

In this context the absence of achievement tests in the elementary school music classroom is understandable. Teacher-constructed tests were thought to be unnecessary; the students, if evaluated at all, were marked on participation or behavior in the music class. Few publishers cared to risk their capital on standardized tests, and those who did published tests emphasizing the safest and least controversial objectives. The professional organizations reacted in kind, supporting the new curricula and rejecting standards or age-level objectives as incompatible with the principles of musical development.

CHANGE IN OBJECTIVES

Once the apogee is reached, movement toward the middle begins. In music education, encouraged by the fascination with behavioral objectives, the ideas of B. F. Skinner, the challenge of *Sputnik,* and a general change in societal goals, Boardman and Bergethon[4] reintroduced the idea of grade-level objectives and experiences in 1963. Most publishers of music series followed their lead but handled the specification of behavioral objectives gingerly. Adoption of general aims was acceptable, but any idea of standards was rejected. Near-anarchy reigned in the general music program, the heart of the music education curriculum. Only through the stability of the musical culture itself and the goals of the performance programs was any semblance of program maintained.

The abandonment of evaluation in elementary general music strongly affected instrumental music. Instrumental music teachers found their beginning students illiterate. Rather than complain about the general music situation, instrumental teachers sought opportunities to teach recorder or other melodic instruments in the general music class before instrumental instruction was introduced. Their efforts were only partially successful; a change to simpler instrumental instruction books was necessitated, and books were selected that taught music fundamentals and moved at a slower pace. The instrumental teacher found that his or her program goals had a different focus from those of the general music teacher. Two distinct school music programs began to exist, one emphasizing skill, the other emphasizing method. This division became increasingly evident as the instrumental music teachers turned away and formed their own professional organizations, began to read periodicals based upon performance goals, and attended their own band and orchestra conference. Evaluation in music education, from aptitude to achievement, followed the instrumental music program and took on an instrumental hue. Instrumental music teachers had a continuing interest in identifying those students more likely to profit from specialized instruction; they had a strong interest in formal evaluation of progress: achievement, try-outs, contests, public performances, and even sight-reading.

THE PRESENT ROLE OF EVALUATION IN MUSIC EDUCATION

Fussing and kicking, all music educators have become involved in evaluation programs in the 1990s. Traditional testing, whether aptitude or achievement, may not be a major component in the overt activities, but student and program evaluation are affecting music programs. If music programs have been reduced in order to accommodate more reading or mathematics, this is partly because of evaluation data from reading and math that was convincing. If fiscal constraints have reduced music programs, evaluation data on budgets were used in the fiscal decision-making process. In order for music programs to retain their strength, the supportive data on goals and achievement must be as compelling as the data for the alternatives.

Education is a major function of state government, and much of the impetus for school evaluation has come from individual governors and/or the National Governors' Association. Music may be a stepchild in the school reform movement, but no leader has suggested that music and the arts are not important school subjects. In the National Governors' Association's *Results in Education: 1989*, the arts are specifically mentioned in the Foreword.[5] Governors are leading the effort toward higher levels of learning in

260

mathematics, science, geography, history, communications, world languages, *and the arts*. Ample references to accountability systems are provided in the governors' report: how to set and achieve high student performance standards; the use of quality and effectiveness indicators; and ways to build outcome assessments into ongoing processes, for example, use of program review, planning, and budgeting.

Recognizing the breadth of the problem, the governors' document addresses curriculum restructuring, teacher salaries, at-risk students, physical facilities, and college programs that include teacher education. The main thrust of the document is the selection of strategic educational goals that will become national education goals for the year 2000. A comment from the report on curriculum illustrates the emphasis on evaluation: "One way to insure that curricula are adequately focussed on in-depth understanding and higher order thinking skills is to set appropriate learner outcome goals."[6]

If individual state governors, legislatures, and departments of education require an outcomes-driven school, then where the arts are an important component of the curriculum, a strong emphasis on evaluation will be required in the arts as elsewhere in the curriculum. If all subjects are considered important, common expectations in curriculum development and evaluation must exist. Only if music teachers successfully argue that the outcomes of music instruction are different from those of all other school subjects, or that music is a cocurricular or extracurricular subject, will unique evaluation programs be feasible. It is doubtful that any rationale for the program can be created that will permit the absence of evaluation. Performance will be judged, and resources for other program objectives must be justified. We cannot justify the music program as unique and cocurricular and also argue for music as part of general education offerings; we cannot have it both ways.

Music educators who avoid or criticize evaluation do so on the grounds that measurement issues are inappropriate and that measurement tools in music are weak. Measurement is only a small part of an evaluation program in music. Where there are critical knowledges and skills to be mastered, tests are essential for diagnostic and assessment decisions. Measurement is an important technique in teaching and learning. However, to rely completely on measurement would indicate a failure to fully understand the relationship among objectives, the curriculum, and evaluation. Evaluation is a many-faceted undertaking; no single component is adequate for decision making.

One important component of evaluation is minimum competency testing, the primary function of which is the establishment of standards in a subject for all enrolled students. Presently there are no procedures for establishing minimum competencies in the several areas of music education — it is a judgment call. Mandating minimum competencies is usually more reactive than active and will not *by itself* cause education to improve. Test results can only inform about the extent of the inadequacies. State and national minimum standards are presently being proposed to aid in ensuring that everyone can read and write and make simple calculations. However, minimum standards may put pressure on the poorest students to drop out of school, and emphasis on minimum accomplishments cheats the better students, creating ennui, sloppiness, and a lack of respect for the subject and the teacher.

On the positive side, minimum standards improve the public's perception of the effectiveness of the schools, motivate many students, provide assurance to teachers of student readiness for additional learning, give meaning to diplomas, encourage school personnel and the public to identify essential competencies for all, and may encourage clearer expectations of the schools. Minimum competency testing is not the whole answer to the school's problems, but it can be part of the answer.

Accountability is another approach to evaluation. Although accountability has for the public become the favorite word in evaluating the schools, it is a highly restrictive concept. Accountability assumes a direct relationship between goals, means, and ends. It focuses on the methods, techniques, or inputs and ignores a concern for improving teaching and learning; attention is on who or what is responsible for the relationship that exists between goals and outcomes rather than on the value of the outcomes.

With respect to student accountability, the accountability movement crested in 1981. In the years that followed, the emphasis shifted from holding the student responsible for failure to looking at total school reform. The school reform movement that began in 1983 was propelled by comparisons of students with those in other countries, by comparison and standardized test results with those from previous years, and by data on the amount of time students spent in school and in doing homework.

By 1986 the accountability movement had focused on the teacher as well as the student as a cause of the schools' failure. Teachers were characterized as overpaid, underworked, and poorly prepared. Once finger pointing became the accepted procedure for improving education, the finger traveled the complete circle: colleges and their teacher education programs were added to the list of culprits, the concerns including lack of well-planned field experiences and failure to teach higher-order thinking, problem solving, or application of knowledge.

Accountability required data. Some schools were all-inclusive in their data gathering, instituting student tests in music and evaluating music teacher competence. But neither the NAEP data nor the data from student or teacher tests have materially changed music teaching practices or music teacher preparation. The reasons are several. Music is not a priority subject comparable to reading or mathematics. Music performance programs, subjectively evaluated, are generally satisfactory. In those instances where performance standards do not meet expectations, the individual teacher rather than the teacher training program is faulted. Where students or individual teachers fail, the failure is not seen as a reason for systematic change. Professional organizations of music teachers and teacher training institutions believe in the present adequacy of teachers and methods; low standards are a result of lack of resources — the public's failure to support the programs.

By 1988 the accountability movement had dwindled. Educational reformers realized that support and cooperation from teachers were essential and that finding fault with the instructional staff would not bring about improvement of the schools. New ideas such as teacher empowerment, site-based management, and choice reduced the pressure on teachers to pursue extensive evaluation. Music teachers also felt the reduced pressure, although they had never wholeheartedly joined the evaluation movement. Their lack of involvement had not been completely caused by negligence or lack of interest. There were few measurement or evaluation tools that could be easily used, nor was there consensus on minimum musical competencies for living the good life in American society. No statement existed on the level of skill, knowledge, or understanding in music that is essential for all citizens. Ample historical evidence shows that the arts are valued and that participation in music as listener or performer is part of the human experience, but the goals of arts education were an exception to the economic model of the good life that provided the impetus for the educational reform movement.

Without minimum standards or requirements, the role of evaluation is less clear. Evaluation depends upon philosophy and goals. If the goal is simply to improve, with no minimums, the degree of improvement is measured. If no mandated degree of improvement exists to use as an indicator of success or failure, both instruction and evaluation lack focus and direction. Furthermore, establishing a recommended degree of gain (for example, from one grade level to the next) is more difficult than suggesting minimum standards (for each grade level). The issues of evaluation in music education are complex, especially in multigrade performing ensembles: What is the "minimum level" for orchestra concertmaster? Or for the third violin? How do we pinpoint achievement goals for percussionists as opposed to trumpeters? The music teacher has good reason to be cautious about making evaluation commitments that could have instructional consequences.

If the accountability model were systematically applied to the general music program, school administrators would encounter difficulties: they would find themselves advocating program goals for music that would be impossible with the resources of time and personnel allocated to the tasks. The present program in music education could not exist without the private music teacher, parental support, and the many music opportunities available outside the school day. Impressive goals have been accepted because some students can attain them. Further, a little-recognized fact is that the failures of inadequate music programs become the responsibility of the parent rather than the school system. If a student is not learning enough in general music to be accepted into the band, pressure is not applied to the general music teacher but, instead, a private instructor is found to teach the student the instrument of his or her choice.

Measurement, minimum competency, and accountability are all pieces in the evaluation puzzle. Writing in 1958, Leonhard saw a direct connection between objectives and outcomes.[7] That connection is still crucial, but in 1991 much evaluation may be conducted without knowledge of the objectives. Students learn many things in school never intended by the teacher, and these learnings are not limited to trivia. These important unintended accomplishments are seldom identifiable through multiple-choice tests; to discover them requires comprehensive procedures, sometimes labeled as responsive evaluation. In such an evaluation, the task is not to judge the extent to which the goals of the school are being accomplished but to determine what the students are learning, how well they are learning, and the cause and reasons for the learning and then to relate this information to the objectives of the student, parent, or community. Hence the term *responsive*. Different evaluation strategies are necessary because of the lack of consensus on the objectives for the music program. The expectations of the school board for the music program are often quite different from those of the music teacher; further, the expectations of the participating students would vary from each other, from those of the teacher, and from those of the school board.

Evaluation techniques can flourish in either a competitive or a cooperative environment, and the music program is an admirable mixture of both environments. Competition has long been a healthy component of musical performance, dating as far back as the Olympics. Individuals compete not only against their peers but also against their own earlier performances and accomplishments. Musicians accept try-outs, chair placements, and auditions for acceptance into ensembles in the school and into all-city and all-state groups as valid competitions with their peers. Musical performance also requires cooperation. Participants follow the conductor and must continually be aware of blend, balance, tempo, and style. Performers value group accomplishments at least as much as individual accomplishments, and noncompetitive evaluation plays an important role in group improvement.

All sorts of musical groups look forward to being evaluated, whether a major symphony in Carnegie Hall or a high school group at a district contest.

CHANGES IN EVALUATION

Evaluation has expanded beyond student and program to include teachers, resources, inputs and outputs, community pressures, and more; the scope of any evaluation has become a matter of philosophical, sociological, and political importance. George Bush has declared himself to be the education president. An unprecedented conference of the state governors and the president's cabinet met in 1989 to discuss education policy: education is valued both for its economic importance and as a solution to health problems, crime, the environment, social justice, the work ethic and moral and value issues. The states spent $160 billion in 1988 on education, a third of their revenues. Once the fiefdom of the Democratic party, education has become a tool for both political parties. Educational successes and failures have become partisan issues as priorities for funding are established by legislatures and governors. Political success is judged both by inputs (amounts of money given to the schools) and outputs — the percentage of high school graduates, the average ACT or SAT score, increasing or decreasing ACT/SAT scores, the attitude of industry toward the schools, college admission rates, as well as student achievement on local, state, and national examinations. States have committed themselves to statewide evaluation programs, beginning teacher assistance programs, licensing standards, alternative programs for at-risk students, and technical assistance or management advice for school systems falling below minimum standards.

Positive and negative evaluation data are equally powerful in justifying expenditure in the previously listed. These evaluation data determine priorities within school programs and priorities among the school districts eligible for additional state funds. Evaluation data within a school influence support for the various programs. A successful band program as evaluated by contest ratings and marching band trophies seldom is a candidate for reduced support.

Test data also influence course offerings. If students can be shown to have higher gain scores in course A than in course B, students will be encouraged to take course A. Parents and taxpayers approve of adopting charts like those used by business that show gains in sales, productivity, and profits. More than one state legislature has mandated that colleges and public schools evaluate their worth in terms of student gain scores from pretest to posttest. Not only will those courses be offered that can show the most gain, but tests that focus on readily taught concepts will replace tests that are based on course goals. Where teachers are rewarded on the basis of student gain scores, course goals will come to reflect those areas most amenable to student growth.

Although "accountability" in its original sense of holding one group (teachers) responsible has faded, the broader idea of accountability has become an important part of school evaluation. As this has occurred, the *means* of evaluation have become the focus of legislators and bureaucrats in governing bodies, individuals often naive about evaluation. Evaluation entrepreneurs each have a product to sell. The National Center for Fair and Open Testing was initiated as a response to the manipulation of education by these entrepreneurs, who often work through political bodies. In 1990 Fairtesting released a statement about testing of kindergarten through third grade children in the center's publication, *Fair Test Examiner:* "Testing encourages emphasis on a developmentally inappropriate curriculum for young children. This undermines quality education and may turn young children off to schooling altogether."[8] When administrators believe that the state or some influential external body favors an activity like evaluation, no stone is left unturned in an effort to comply. If a little is good, more must be better. To comply is to be judged by the state as a superior school system. To curb this tendency, legislatures have had to provide additional instructions to school systems. For example, complying with the Illinois legislature's 1985 reform package would require that all students be tested in all basic subjects (six) each year, seven to ten hours of state assessment plus any locally mandated evaluation. In 1989 the Illinois legislature was forced to pass a bill limiting to five hours per student per year the amount of time devoted to state-mandated standardized testing, and as a part of the bill each district is required to report the amount of time spent per year on the state student assessment testing and the total amount of time spent per pupil on local student assessment testing. Tennessee has also had to reduce the amount of time allowed for testing; the Arizona superintendent of public instruction called for alternatives to standardized testing. Oklahoma, on the other hand, has just expanded its state testing program, and so on down the roll call of the states. States overreact in both directions. California, which restricted IQ testing because of a supposed cultural bias in the test, now finds that the restrictive legislation also deprives minorities of demonstrating potential for special opportunities.

When music is designated one of the basic subjects, the mandates for testing and evaluation of basic subjects apply precisely as they do for evaluating attainment in mathematics, reading, and science. The stance that music achievement can be validly evaluated in the same way as mathematics may be a political concept rather than an educational one, but the outcome is the same: test scores that are objectively obtained. Such testing may strengthen the rule of music as a basic, but no state assessment instrument presently available would be a valid measure of student achievement in music. Either the students will do poorly on the test or the test will not discriminate between good and poor programs.

The public would like to believe that music education has a sociological basis and that refined taste is a reasonable objective of music education. A common music curriculum goal is to change (improve) student preferences and attitudes, to have graduates attending concerts and supporting the arts. Such an objective for school music may be infeasible. Television programming, including that of PBS, follows the public's taste rather than helps to form it. Music television (MTV) and similar programs provide a strong counter to the work of the schools. Programs similar to the 1950s educational series of Leonard Bernstein on the symphony orchestra have been replaced by the Boston Pops, whose programming is increasingly pops and decreasingly classical. American culture is quantitatively based and market driven. If audience development for the arts is a legitimate function of the school, the challenge of audience development is greatest for music. But is it fair to judge the worth of music programs on the degree of graduates' continued participation in music? Should a community with an excellent school music program expect its graduates to support all serious music endeavors in the community? To what extent are values education and artistic literacy goals of the music program? What evaluation measures (for example, attendance at concerts, purchase of CDs, and television viewing) are valid indicators of goal attainment?

PRESENT PROGRAMS

Evaluation is directly related to philosophy of education; thus the critical need for a coherent philosophy. Functionally the 1990 school music program is the performance program; general music in the elementary grades or at the secondary level is not part of the public's notion of school music. Defined thus, the program operates on an elitist philosophy, providing talented students the opportunity to develop that talent. Aptitude tests are given to identify students with potential, and the program organization of grades K–12 is primarily one of sifting and screening students through classes and experiences in a search for talent. The emphasis on selection has been so extreme that few adults believe children can learn much from music courses unless they are talented. This belief has reduced the pressure on

267

school music programs to be accountable, a fact that has not been lost on the music education profession. Failure in music can be attributed to a bunch of untalented kids, not to a failure in teaching or materials. Talented students are recommended for private instruction outside the school; the untalented are encouraged to drop out or to participate in music classes having primarily nonmusical goals. In the elementary schools, students are screened by tests and by teacher judgment for possible talent. The talented are encouraged to study instrumental music — strings and winds — or to participate in a school chorus. At middle school the most talented students study instrumental music including keyboard, while the less talented enroll in general music. In middle school the idea of first and second choruses and first and second bands reinforces the talented/less talented organization of instruction. With music elective at the senior high school, there is a talent hierarchy among orchestra, band, and choir. Other music offerings — keyboard, listening, general — each have their own place on the scale, a scale characterized by the perception of talent. Within the performing organizations, talent and ability determine membership in jazz bands, madrigals, string quartets, and girls' glee club. Interest alone will not secure membership in the vocal/jazz ensemble.

Given the above, it can be seen that administering a music achievement test to all students of the same grade or age would be philosophically unsound. The goals of the various music offerings differ, school music courses are elective. There are few common objectives for band and chorus: the literature differs, and the literature influences goals and goal attainment. The importance of the ability to read music, to know about Ludwig van Beethoven and Ned Rorem, differs not only by type of musical organization but by performing level. The music used by the fifteen-member madrigal group differs from that of the sixty-voice girls' glee club. Any identifiable core of common goals for high school or middle school music is so small that it is immaterial in making most evaluation decisions. Common examinations, such as those proposed by state and local curriculum guides and evaluation plans, would be absent of content validity.

Because tests influence what is taught, those who contemplate standardized tests in music should consider the large mix of nonmusical goals that has been a consistent and positive characteristic of performance programs. This mix is not a weakness but is a strength, and it is not exclusive to music. English teachers teach more than the elements of English and literature. They have goals of neatness, responsibility for assignments, punctuality, and respect for the work of all students and authors. The value of musical organizations includes many nonmusical learnings. Music courses have successfully shared, even led, in attaining the goals of the school in a democratic culture. If cooperation and self-discipline are important, if respect for quality of work is stressed and effort rewarded, evaluation must reflect the importance of the elements to the instructor, administration, and parents, if not the students. Robert Stake has suggested in his Responsive Evaluation Model that different audiences have different expectations of the schools.[9] For example, we have learned that creativity is not valued by most audiences, but playing the right notes is. If a goal such as creativity cannot be promoted within the educational community or included in the philosophy and goals, introducing it into the curriculum through evaluation destroys much of the credibility of evaluation. Policymakers have turned to evaluation as a means of ensuring that the arts are offered and taught; the present emphasis on school evaluation is seen by arts educators as an opportunity to secure their agenda. But the evaluation must be carefully designed to include all of the goals and at the same time reflect the uniqueness of the various parts of the music program.

Differentiation and individualization within the music programs extend as low as fourth grade, and with different experiences there should be different outcomes. The belief that different experiences can lead to core goals is optimistic, because transfer of learning is not well developed in music education. Grades K–3 do have a common core of experiences across most school systems, with most outcomes related to student attitude toward music. However, the evaluation of attitude at any grade level is not adequately represented in most evaluation schema.

The philosophy of Foster McMurray, presented in Chapter 2, would dictate an evaluation program that would not emphasize unique goals or differentiated learnings. For McMurray the purposes of education are democratic and require a common core of knowledge and aural skills that would serve as cultural equalizers, providing equal opportunities for all students. According to his philosophy, music would be a basic course for all students and would have grade-level expectations and sequentially presented experiences. In McMurray's approach, program evaluation becomes more relevant than student evaluation, as educational programs exist because of their value to society and the cultural fabric of the community.

EVALUATION OPTIONS

Measurement tools were described earlier in the chapter as part of the chronological history of measurement in music. Evaluation in the broader sense cannot be adequately traced through descriptions of the devices used, for many of these devices were transitory — part of a single research project or a short-term endeavor.

Richard J. Colwell

One important means of evaluation is observation, which seems to have been used since the days of Lowell Mason. Student groups were brought to professional meetings to perform, and classroom visitation by school administrators, parents, and lay individuals was common. At the organizational meeting of the Music Supervisors National Conference in Keokuk, Iowa (1907), supervisors observed Phillip C. Hayden's successful teaching methods in the Keokuk schools, a practice continued at the national meetings for many years. Visits to the host schools in convention cities are less common today, but demonstration groups and performing ensembles remain an important aspect of meetings of professional music educators. An opportunity for the host city to perform is usually extended. Systematic or rated observation is a part of contests and festivals, events that began in the 1920s. Observations of performing ensembles are accompanied by a list of elements to be evaluated. The first contests were marked by an arbitrary number of points assigned for attacks and releases, appearance, intonation, and the like; the reliabilities of these observations were remarkably high. The categories to observe remain basically the same today.

Observation, whether of a class or a formal concert, remains the most common evaluation technique for musical performance. The data obtained are informative but generally not useful diagnostically for either students, teachers, or the curriculum. If qualified observers were used, the data could be very valuable. Rating scales and checklists that accompany an observation add little validity if the observer (rater) is not trained in their use. The first systematic observation of music *teachers* was part of doctoral research done by Kenneth Snapp (1953), followed by Robert Erbes (1972) and others. These observations recorded the verbal patterns of teachers and students using the categories of Ned Flanders (1970). More recent observational studies have focused on conducting gestures of instrumental and vocal teachers, but these gestural scales have not had sufficient use to be considered valid.

The attainment of specified skills is one of the most important goals of music instruction, and evaluation of skill levels is best accomplished through the use of measurement techniques. The rating scales for band, choir, and individual instruments that are derived from aural observations have been investigated with the facet-factorial technique. Begun by Harold Abeles with clarinet performance, the research has continued with choir by John Cooksey, band by Charles D'Camp, and on individual instruments by Martha Bergee, Harold Jones, and others.

The critical incidents test has had limited use in music but can be informative to instructors about the memorable events of a rehearsal or concert. Critical incidents measures should be researched for their potential

270

in evaluating the general music outcomes or those of specific instructional ventures. Teachers can gain insights by asking students a single question such as "What was the best thing about yesterday's rehearsal?" or "What composer do you remember from last week's concert?" or "What was the biggest flaw in last Sunday's concert?" Because critical incidents tests have not been widely used in music, and because the nature of the experiences in music are different from those in other classes, this promising technique needs to be researched for its potential in evaluative procedures.

Unobtrusive observation is part of the evaluation package. Goals of habit and attitude are especially amenable to unobtrusive evaluation, as is appreciation. One's practice habits, listening habits, and other musical behaviors that are "habitual" can be measured through data on the use of practice rooms; library listening rooms; record purchases; ticket sales; behavior at concerts; use of program notes; wear on instruments, cases, and needles; marking of music; and much more. Unobtrusive measures are limited only by one's imagination; the goals of music instruction are so broad that a wide range of "clues" can be helpful in determining progress toward the goals.

Listening and perception objectives are best evaluated with standardized tests. Classroom teachers rarely have the resources necessary to develop valid instruments in these areas.

PROGRAM EVALUATION

As implied earlier, program evaluation is not presently emphasized in music education. Precise scores of what an American child knows about music do not reveal data about the quality of the program. Musical competence along with musical incompetence is found in school programs of any quality. The Music Educators National Conference has supported development of program evaluation for several years and, in 1990, had a pilot version of a complex and thorough program evaluation instrument.[10] Separate assessment instruments have been developed by MENC to assess (1) goals and objectives, (2) leadership, (3) staffing, (4) curriculum and scheduling, (5) instructional materials, (6) equipment, (7) facilities, and (8) outcomes. A separate instrument exists for use by school principals, and there are on-site assessment instruments for classroom instruction and large ensemble rehearsals. Completing the program evaluation package are instruments for required music instruction and elective music instruction. In program evaluation the focus is on the adequacy of the seven supportive areas (previously listed) and the relationship of each area to individual and student outcomes. Student achievement is important only in the general or class outcomes; the concern is for the adequacy of the means of delivery.

A move away from the emphasis on behavioral objectives in program evaluation was taken in the late 1960s when Elliot Eisner advocated consideration of expressive objectives.[11] He suggested that students need to have educational encounters as well as attain the isomorphic behavioral objectives. For example, analyzing the structure of the Mozart G Minor Symphony can provide an opportunity for students and teachers to interact, to probe, to discuss, and to explore the many facets of this great work. The outcome of such an educational encounter cannot be predicted in advance but that fact does not diminish the importance of the event. At times the discussion might go nowhere, one or two students may take the lead, or the discussion may shift to the movie *Amadeus* instead of remaining focused on the music. Such encounters must be planned for in the program, and it is not impossible to evaluate what the students have learned from the encounter — but it is impossible to specify what the outcomes will be.

Eisner was joined by Robert Stake in this fresh look at program evaluation; each of them suggested that additional desirable outcomes may be impossible to evaluate. Students should attend a band concert, view an entire opera, or make an oboe reed. Schools should provide experiences that are part of the discipline being studied. Even though there are no common outcomes for students attending a symphony orchestra concert, for example, a program providing this experience would be greatly enriched. These objectives, of high value but with outcomes difficult to evaluate, are called expressive or experiential objectives to differentiate them from the objectives characteristic of accountability programs. To figure in program evaluation, experiential objectives must be planned for and systematically introduced into the program. A program based on a series of loosely planned experiences is no program at all; to justify ex post facto a teaching period when nothing happened as perhaps providing some "experiences" is to totally misuse this important and valuable idea. Too great an emphasis on experiences can be as barren as focusing solely on behavioral objectives. A place should be found on the program evaluation checklist to describe the desired experiences and to portray student and teacher responses to them.

Formal programs usually contain a strong evaluation component. However, these formal programs, such as Suzuki, Orff, Kodaly, Rolland, Manhattanville, and CMP, have focused very little on program evaluation. Better examples of the beginning of program evaluation in music are the Greater Cleveland Arts Program and Interdisciplinary Model Program in the Arts for Children and Teachers (Project IMPACT). Accrediting agencies, in their reports on schools and colleges, also offer initial models that can be expanded into thorough program evaluation schema. Evaluation centers such as Eva Baker's at UCLA and Robert Stake's at Illinois have excellent examples of program evaluation conducted in school subject areas other than music.

Related to program evaluation are goal-free and responsive evaluation. The authors of these ideas advocate that standards not be preordained, that the determination of success or failure be made while recognizing local conditions. Goal-free evaluation makes use of an expert or connoisseur who scrutinizes the program, judges the worth of the effort, and determines the extent to which students have learned. The expert describes the quality of the program in narrative terms rather than in tables of test data. The interpretation of the data then falls heavily on the user.

Goal-free and responsive evaluation tend to blur the traditional distinction between formative and summative evaluation. Summative evaluation judges the worth of a program and may be a complete evaluation of cognitive, psychomotor, and affective domains — a summing up. Student demographics and other variables are considered. Formative evaluation is that which has the potential to change a program — to shape and form it. When the teacher makes an assessment of how things are going and changes his or her plans and goals based on that assessment, formative evaluation has occurred. The goals can change in formative evaluation based on an assessment of student abilities, interests, the opportunities available, and more. Goal-free or responsive evaluation shares some of this informality. Diagnostic (formative) evaluation is possible with either individual or program evaluation. With diagnostic evaluation, strengths and weaknesses are identified that can improve learning or teaching. Goals, however, are not changed.

Use of responsive evaluation for creative experiences makes sense. But use of responsive evaluation to avoid establishing knowledges and competencies for a given grade is irresponsible. Tests wrongly used can have bad effects: they can restrict the curriculum, place students in inappropriate ability groups, and promote unhealthy competition. Also, responsive measures inappropriately used can evaluate setting rather than focus, people instead of material, and actions rather than outcomes. Use of responsive evaluation does not improve decision making. Responsive evaluation increases the amount of information and thus can contribute to decision making, but harder data are needed for decisions concerning whether and where the program should be strengthened, whether the students are performing as well as expected, and whether the program is receiving an appropriate share of the resources.

Ernest House, in *Evaluating With Validity,* has identified eight major approaches to program evaluation.[12] Behavioral objectives, goal-free, art criticism (connoisseur), and professional review have been discussed. In addition, House lists systems analysis (the McNamara Ford Motor and Pentagon efficiency models), decision making (arriving at general goals through surveys), quasi-legal (a jury basis of arguments for and against the program), and case study. These approaches are valuable for music educators to consider in selecting the kinds of questions that should be asked and the data to be gathered.

Evaluation in music education has not been limited to the reactive (quantitative assessment) model; music educators have been interested in qualitative questions and the qualitative outcomes of the program. It does not seem necessary to present the arguments for qualitative and quantitative evaluation or those for proactive and reactive evaluation, as they parallel the distinctions made between formative and summative evaluation. Assessment as differentiated from evaluation should be clarified, however. State legislators have indicated faint interest in what college students are learning and in public school curricular offerings, but they have concerned themselves primarily with gains in subject matter competence and noncognitive areas such as values, citizenship, self-esteem, and interests. Student-focused testing and measurement such as that mandated by the curriculum fall under the heading of assessment; evaluation data are derived from program-focused activities. The difficulty of providing unencumbered data for either assessment or evaluation may be one reason why interest in assessing college students seems to be waning and why the distinction between assessment and evaluation made by legislators is blurred.

MUSIC EDUCATION ACTIVITIES

Music education literature indicates that music educators are becoming more favorably inclined toward evaluation than they have been toward measurement because of the development of new techniques in evaluation. This favorable attitude must show itself in the commitment of resources to make evaluation data useful, and also in some consensus on music education goals. Music educators must be concerned with both program evaluation and student assessment. Program evaluation would illuminate the program's strengths and weaknesses; for example, whether students encounter music of many cultures, avant-garde music, and country and western. Student assessment would determine students' strengths and weaknesses — how well they have developed those core skills and knowledges that make experiences in music possible and meaningful. Evaluation must be diagnostic for the improvement of learning.

An interesting endeavor in student assessment is Arts Propel, a project in assessment that provides the musician with data on his or her performance similar to data in a portfolio of the visual artist. In Arts Propel, student musicians periodically record their performance, either solo or with the ensemble. The teacher and/or the student can then evaluate the execution dimensions of performance, including: pitch production, rhythm/tempo production, articulation, dynamics, hand or finger control, and general considerations. Higher-order dimensions of performance include expressivity and style in musical phrasing, evidence of grasp of musical structure in phrasing, balance and voicing, performance proficiency, and, when applicable, ensemble performance. The student reflects on the taped performance and is judged on whether he or she can be specific about good and poor aspects of the performance, have a critical perspective on the performance, and suggest appropriate revisions.

Students are also asked to make comparative observations of their performance or that of the ensemble over a period of time. Here too the student is still expected to be specific, to have a perspective, and to suggest revisions. In the comparison mode, there are two levels: "How I sound within the ensemble," and "Remarks concerning how the ensemble sounds." The constructive comments are directed both to oneself and to how the ensemble could be improved.

The assessment and the process in Arts Propel are both instructional. There is also value in having the student make his or her comments public to the rest of the ensemble, a process requiring still more instructional time. The technique is useful in class lessons as well as large ensembles and may be more feasible there. The need to balance priorities for instruction and evaluation is obvious, as student time is limited.

Students in music do more than perform, and some assessment goals may emphasize thinking about and understanding the music. Teachers may wish to evaluate how students acquire musical knowledge, chunk it, and connect it to existing knowledge, restructure it for deeper understanding, and apply that knowledge to new performances. Course goals may include the ability to reason, to make musical decisions on style, and to accurately judge quality of music and quality of performance. Evaluating these abilities is complex, as thinking about music is affected by one's preconceptions, experiences, and attitudes.

Sophisticated assessment can take place if sufficient time is allotted. Music educators will need to adapt for music the cognitive and conative strategies being developed to assess general learning. The tasks will involve requiring students to generate explanations, recognize symbols, solve musical problems, and assemble skilled performances. Three approaches appear promising: Case-Bereiter, which is a new Piagetian approach; the neo-Vygotskian approach of Campione-Brown; and a free response personality inventory by the Belgians Claeys, DeBoeck, and others.

The computer has changed evaluation possibilities in performing, listening, and cognition. Use of the computer to present musical elements has been available for a decade and is now common in college music theory instruction. As opposed to the timed listening tests, with their disadvantages for the student who falls behind or needs additional hearings, musical stimuli produced by the computer can be controlled by the student for number of repetitions and length of time between hearings, providing to the instructor realistic data on the student's ability given enough time. The computer can also offer help defining terms and other test prerequisites. Test restrictions, such as a limited number of hearings, can be programmed when desired.

Another technical innovation, interactive audio, is the connection of a compact disk to a computer; this innovation offers high potential for both evaluation and instruction. The drawback is, of course, that more than a pencil is required — each student must have access to a properly equipped computer.

Micro-evaluation is another behavioristic approach that fosters evaluation in terms of clearly established objectives. Although there is some validity to this approach, it is not really evaluation; it is another form of measurement. Program evaluation is not a combination of micro-evaluations. No sum or set of measurements can add up to an evaluation, because results from tests merely reinforce the attainment of old objectives. Program evaluation moves the profession forward. Although use of tests is necessary in the improvement of instruction, facilitating the learning processes, and attaining critical goals, no battery of tests of any length would validly sample the music education program.

Evaluation in music education must consider the political, sociological, and educational constituency while remaining above all three, for the purpose of evaluation is not to reinforce either the present educational system or present research procedures. The evaluator must be able to gather from the three constituencies, from observations (often biased), and from incomplete data enough clues and evidence to allow him or her to make accurate inferences and formulate new programs and policies. Gordon Munro pointed out in 1977[13] that the evaluation used in the Eight-Year Study of thirty high schools in the late 1930s[14] was the only program evaluation that still commands respect. (The results of the study itself, in a summative sense, were relatively unimportant, although it was interesting that students from unconventional high school programs did equally well in college, and that the Carnegie unit need not be sacred.) The real residue from this project was that from these exiguous results the evaluators were able to make inferences that encouraged new thinking about the ends and means of education. If that experimental program had been judged solely upon student achievement scores, the Eight-Year Study would have been soon forgotten, but Ralph Tyler's evaluative schemata focused on general college readiness rather than on the effects of the separate programs and courses studied. In 1990 the results of the Eight-Year Study are being reevaluated and republished for their insights and relevance to school reform. World War II had prevented the education community from giving proper attention to the results of the study at the time of its completion. The interpretation of those half-century–old data should provide an interesting exercise for all evaluators.

True evaluation does not provide data to support immediate reform, and evaluation data are not an appropriate basis for on-the-spot changes; evaluation data and their subsequent interpretation have their greatest potential when the evaluation is independent of current policy. Good evaluation incorporates the time required to consider more than situational successes and failures. If public policy for music education is to be questioned, the answers should come from an independent evaluation format created by individuals not in the service of the present bureaucracy.

In 1980 Lee Cronbach abandoned his 1963 position that the purpose of evaluation was to assess objectives.[15] He now believes that evaluation is to illuminate emerging questions rather than to pass down a verdict on what happened last year. Evaluators must provide focus, and they must portray both the present status of music education and the conditions and forces that have brought it about. Put another way, the role of the evaluator is as much to formulate new questions as to answer the old. This role has been missing in music education evaluation, where few questions have been adequately framed.

Music education evaluation can flourish without consensus on program goals. The influence of Robert Mager and the behaviorists has restricted our thinking. More clarity is needed in defining expected student competencies.

Evaluation remains the primary hope of those who want to bring about change and improve present practices in education. The numbers and statistics that often go with evaluation programs are important, even critical, in raising public awareness to the "flash point" where change is possible. The statistics on the number of functional illiterates who are graduates of American high schools, the statistics on declining SAT scores, and the data from the National Assessment for Educational Progress have heightened the public's concern for quality education; it is this concern that has made possible new programs and increased resources for reading, science, and mathematics. Evaluation reinforces excellent music programs and structures the new.

NOTES

1. Charles Leonhard (1958). Evaluation in Music Education. In Henry Nelson (ed.), *Basic Concepts in Music Education. The 57th Yearbook of the NSSE, Part I* (pp. 310–338). Chicago: University of Chicago Press.

2. Charles Leonhard and Robert House (1959, 1972). *Foundations and Principles of Music Education.* New York: McGraw-Hill.

3. Leonard and House. *Foundations and Principles.*

4. Eunice Boardman and Bjornor Bergethon (1963). *Musical Growth in the Elementary School.* New York: Holt, Rinehart & Winston, Inc.

5. National Governors' Association (1989). *Results in Education: 1989* (p. 9). Washington, DC: National Governors' Association.

6. National Governors Association. *Results in Education: 1989.*

7. Leonard. Evaluation in Music Education.

8. *Fair Test Examiner,* Vol. 4, No.1, p. 4. Winter 1989–1990.

9. Robert Stake (1975). To Evaluate an Arts Program. In Robert Stake (ed.), *Evaluating the Arts in Education* (pp. 12–31). Columbus, OH: Merrill.

10. Music Educators National Conference (1988, 1990). *Program Evaluation Project,* working draft. Reston, VA: Musical Educators National Conference.

11. Elliot Eisner (1969). Instructional and Expressive Objectives, Their Formulation and Use in Curriculum. In Popham et al. (eds.), *Instructional Objectives,* AERA Monograph #3 (pp. 1–31). Chicago: Rand McNally.

12. Ernest R. House (1980). *Evaluating With Validity.* Beverly Hills, CA: Sage.

13. Gordon Munro (1977). Adolescent Values. *Adolescence* 12 (47), 329–337.

14. Ralph Tyler, E. R. Smith, and the Evaluation Staff (1942). Purposes and Procedures of the Evaluation Staff: Appraising and Recording Student Progress. *Adventure in American Education, Volume III.* New York: Harper & Brothers.

15. Lee J. Cronbach and Associates (1980). *Toward Reform of Program Evaluation.* San Francisco: Jossey-Bass.

14

A Message for the Teacher of Teachers

Eunice Boardman

The purpose of this book, as I see it, is to review progress in light of the recommendations presented thirty years ago in *Basic Concepts of Music Education, I*, and, in response to that evaluation, offer new concepts to guide our paths over the next thirty years. My comparison of the chapters being prepared for the current volume with the corresponding chapters found in the 1958 edition quickly confirmed my suspicions — that the *basic* concepts have not changed: our belief in the value of music as an avenue to aesthetic awareness and our conviction that music should therefore play an integral role in the schooling of all youth remain constant.

So why the need for a new look at music education? The answer to that question lies in the facts and opinions found in articles and books written during the thirty-year interim for both the professional and the lay reader as to the status of music and arts education in the schools of the 1990s. The depressing similarity between the concerns expressed in 1958 and those expressed in 1991 force us to recognize that, for the most part, we are no further toward our goal of helping *all students* become knowledgeable enough in the arts for that knowledge to make a difference in their lives than we were thirty years ago. I will not take time to quote the sources that force me to accept that conclusion but, in the remainder of this chapter, consider issues that will — if we can solve them — perhaps help us avoid having to look back in 2021 and admit that we are still fighting the same windmills.

In 1958 the concept that the value of music lay in its ability to provide the individual with a medium for expressing deeply held feelings and ideas that no other symbol system could convey was a relatively new idea, one to which only a few music educators had been introduced. Granted, Susanne Langer's "key" to grasping the significance of music as conveying the "form

279

of feeling" had been in the bookstores for nearly twenty years, but its significance for music educators, and for molding the direction of music education, had to wait for others to serve as interpreters. Charles Leonhard and Robert House fulfilled that role by demonstrating the potential of Langer's theory as a basis of planning music instruction in *Foundations and Principles of Music Education* published in 1959 one year after *Basic Concepts, I*). Since that time the assumption that the primary purpose of music education is to educate the feelings — to enable individuals to live lives enlightened by the aesthetic experience — has become a common slogan, stated (with variations) ad infinitum in every curriculum guide, music education methods book, and statement of purpose offered by various professional organizations. Rationales for the validity of this assumption have been offered by individuals from our own field (including Bennett Reimer [1989]) as well as from the fields of psychology and philosophy (Goodman 1984; Gardner 1985). Certainly, by now, we have a firm basis for the development and implementation of curricular and instructional practices that will provide for the education of the aesthetic potential inherent in every individual.

Yet perusal of the same body of published works referred to earlier, which avers the importance of music as the source of aesthetic experience, suggests that the translation of belief into practice has not occurred. Research journals are replete with reports of investigations on "the uncertain singer," "a comparison of three ways to teach rhythmic reading," "the history of the ocarina," "attitudes of middle school children toward music listening," and so on. Professional magazines headline, "Your Marching Band Can Win Contests!", "The Place of the Swing Choir in the Elementary School Curriculum," and "How to Make Johnny Behave in Music Class." If there are articles purporting to focus on application of aesthetic principles to music instruction, the reader is usually drawn to the uneasy conclusion that "aesthetic experience" is or should be confined to classes in appreciation or something called "allied/integrated/related arts." The equation "aesthetics = 'appreciation' " becomes the basis for educational planning.

Such a simplistic, and erroneous, conclusion has its roots in the same misinterpretations that inspired a similar equation in the 1970s: "teaching concepts = teaching theory." The response to the assertion that the development of "musical concepts" should be the focus of the curriculum resulted in a "sixfold curriculum" (or sevenfold, depending on who was making the list!) — singing, playing, moving, listening, reading (creating), and conceptualizing. In both cases the outcome of the acceptance of false equations was the same: "helping students to grasp concepts or develop aesthetic sensitivity is something extra, to be added on, when we have time, after the 'basics' have been covered. Then we'll work on concepts, or have an aesthetic experience — sort of like playing rock records on Friday to reward the kids for having been good during the previous week!" (Goodman 1976). Bennett Reimer, in his chapter titled "Music Education Philosophy and Psychology After Mursell," speaks also to these miscomprehensions and suggests ways that, in the Mursellian tradition, the principles of contemporary cognitive psychology can provide guidance in the redirection of music educational practices to a more wholistic conception of learning and teaching.

IMPROVEMENT OF INSTRUCTION REQUIRES
IMPROVEMENT OF INSTRUCTION

The purpose of this somewhat lengthy introduction is simply to set the scene for the main intention of this chapter: to speak to the teachers of teachers (hereafter identified as the "teacher educator") about their responsibility for the current chasm that exists between the "ideal" — our declaration of the value of music as embedded in the aesthetic experience — and the actuality of what happens in most music classrooms on most days. In previous writings (Meske 1985) I have spoken to the need to break the vicious circle of mediocrity by seeking ways to improve the preparation of teachers. Examination of current practices in undergraduate music education has forced me to the conclusion that such improvement cannot occur until we address the preparation of the teacher educator. In spite of the many calls for reform and suggestions for ways to implement change, it takes only a few minutes to compare college catalogs from the 1960s and the 1990s and conclude that any differences that appear in undergraduate music education requirements are basically cosmetic.

It is a truism that teachers tend to teach not as they have been taught to teach, but as they were taught. This is not only true of the public school music educator; it is equally true of the teacher educator. Regardless of that individual's dissatisfaction with his or her preparation, the courses that he or she offers today are likely to be more similar to, than different from, those personally experienced as an undergraduate. At least part of the reason for this can be traced to the fact that individuals directing doctoral programs in music education (from which most present-day teacher educators are drawn) make little attempt to intervene — to provide the future teacher educator with experiences powerful enough to use as a basis for the creation of new models that define appropriate content, experiences, and objectives for music education classes.

It is long past time that the profession pay at least as much attention to the improvement of the education of teacher educators as we have claimed to pay to the improvement of public school music instruction by calling for change in undergraduate music education instruction. Perhaps we should begin by considering the same issues that are frequently the focus of attempts at reform in undergraduate education.

RECRUITMENT AND RETENTION

In *Music Teacher Education: Partnership and Process* (Olson 1987), a number of recommendations regarding the establishment of procedures for recruitment, admission, retention, and evaluation designed to attract and retain the best young musician educators were made. Such a call is an echo of many such recommendations presented by the profession for many years. Some of these calls for reform continue with lists of preferred personal, intellectual, musical, and instructional teacher attributes such as that offered by Lehman at the Symposium on Music Teacher Education, Arizona State University (Lehman 1986). Should we not be asking the same questions, and making similar recommendations for recruitment, admission, retention, and evaluation of the teacher educator? What personal, intellectual, musical, and instructional qualities should that individual possess? To my knowledge, there is no research, or even published speculation, that seeks to answer these questions. Yet, until we undertake procedures that ensure that the very best possible cadre of teacher educators are guiding the undergraduate music education programs throughout the country, we cannot hope to break the vicious circle. We cannot aspire to solving the equation: music education = aesthetic education.

Although perhaps not measurable, or teachable, certainly one quality to be considered must be what Foster McMurray calls "passion." In his "Variations on a Pragmatic Theme" in this volume, McMurray maintains that teachers must be "clear in their own minds about what that role [of music education] is and be *passionately* devoted to it" (p. 60). Certainly this basic commitment must be as strong in the teacher educator as in the public school music educator. Only to the extent that the teacher educator is "clear to the role of (music) education and passionately devoted to it" can that individual construct the kind of undergraduate music education experiences that will help future teachers implement a truly *musical* education for *their* future students.

Such a teacher educator cannot be one who chose to enter a doctoral program and eventually seek a position as a college music educator because he or she was dissatisfied, bored, or frustrated with his or her current public school music teaching assignment (or couldn't find one, so decided to go back to school). Further, I find it difficult to believe that this individual could be someone who has had minimal public school experience. It *will* be someone who is so passionately committed to helping young people become aesthetically sensitive human beings that leaving those youth will be seen as a sacrifice. One would assume further that, in actuality, the teacher educator will never completely leave the precollege classroom. Teaching in a pre-college setting on a fairly regular basis will be an indispensable part of every teacher educator's instructional and/or research activity. By continuing to work in such a capacity, the teacher educator serves as a model of passionate commitment, retains credibility, and continues to grow in his or her own understanding of the complex dimensions of the teaching act.

The future teacher educator must also grasp, and demonstrate, the relationship between theory and practice as well as between belief in music goals and actualization of those goals within the classroom. Probably the most consistent complaint of teachers in the field (not only music teachers) is that their undergraduate education was "theoretical," "irrelevant," "impractical." Too often, their complaints are valid because their experience consisted of classes where lectures on aesthetic meaning, or cognitive psychology, were interspersed with instrumental technique labs and demonstrations on how to teach "sol-fa." Theory was presented in a vacuum, with the problem of translation into practice left to the individual least able to make that translation — the music education student.

It is the responsibility of the teacher educator to possess, first, the knowledge of those theories that have the potential for improving instructional practice; second, the skill to demonstrate how those theories inform practice. He or she must be able to illustrate the "if-then" equation (*if* research tells us X, *then* this is how we use that knowledge to improve instructional practice).

Finally, teacher educators must possess the intellectual curiosity and the desire for constant growth that cause them to stay abreast of current research findings and adjust their instructional practices accordingly. In other words, the teacher educator must be able to avoid the "yellowed paper" syndrome, where the references, reading lists, musical examples and personal anecdotes offered in todays' classroom are identical to those used thirty years ago.

Until the personnel of existing doctoral music education programs are willing to consider potential for successful college teaching as characterized by the triarchy of commitment, knowledge, and skill as at least one of the criteria for admission into these doctoral programs from which the next generation of teacher educators will emerge, it is difficult to see how truly significant changes in undergraduate music education programs can occur.

CONTENT OF THE CURRICULUM

When considering improvement of undergraduate music education instruction, a second task that reformers undertake is identification of essential content. What does the future music teacher need to know? What skills must be acquired? What kinds of experiences will most effectively ensure acquisition of desired knowledge and skill? To answer these questions, reformers usually begin by looking at successful music teachers and/or music programs or by designing hypothetical situations, which can then be analyzed. Answers to these same questions must be sought by those concerned with the preparation of the future teacher educator. We may wish to begin by considering the attributes of the ideal undergraduate curriculum.

What would such a curriculum emphasize? This chapter opened with a plea for implementing the goal our profession has defined — to develop a music education curriculum that is truly aesthetic, that is designed to help all (precollege) students reach their aesthetic potential. If this is our goal, then teacher educators must be able to design an undergraduate curriculum insuring that undergraduate music education students (1) have experienced the power of music to speak to and for them in ways no other symbolic form can and (2) be able, because of educative experiences they are currently having *within their own teacher education curriculum,* to organize experiences that are truly and wholistically aesthetic for their future students.

For the moment, let us bypass those aspects of the undergraduate music education curriculum that deal with "liberal" or "general" studies as well as those that are focused on developing musicianship (that is, theory, history, performance, ensemble). We will concentrate on that dimension of the total curriculum for which we, as teachers of teachers, have primary responsibility — "introduction to music education" courses, methods classes, field experiences including student teaching, and the like. Is it possible to make such experiences "aesthetic experiences"? Can we organize instruction so that the student teacher leaves each class having engaged in a potentially "aesthetic" experience on one level and, on a second level, understanding how the environment had been organized to provide that potential?

If we accept cognitive theories of learning, such as that espoused by Bruner (1986), we are aware that learning (and thereby instruction) cannot be separated into discrete dimensions of action, cognition, and emotion. We recognize that these three aspects of human behavior are an indivisible network that functions *only* as a whole because each persuades the other, leaving indelible imprints, no matter which of the three may be supposedly emphasized within the instructional context. We are also aware that cognitive activity resulting in the formation of concepts that subsequently control action is initially based in observation and participation in concrete events. Such events serve as models for internalized schemata of appropriate actions. Recognizing this, the teacher of teachers must apply that knowledge to the structuring of experiences for the student teacher that reflect the kind of action-cognition-emotion gestalt we expect them to create for their future pupils. Such settings then become the model from which future teachers create their schemata of appropriate music classroom experiences.

A methods class that is aesthetically based? How could that be? It *could* be one where the focus is on discovering how *music* carries meaning (emotion), intertwined with examination of what one needs to understand (cognition) in order to ascertain musical meaning, and culminating in rehearsals (action) of classroom instruction where the potential for this triptych could be repeated with endless variations.

Yes, information regarding specific methodologies and techniques probably needs to be shared, but only in the context of its value as a route to discovering the aesthetic potential that resides within any valid musical experience. If a method focuses purely on "action" — in the form of how best to teach fingerings, or on the sequence for introducing tonal syllables — it may not be worth spending time on in a methods class. Such out-of-context emphases will not help student teachers understand how to teach toward musical meaning. Time spent on providing students with specific "knowledge," such as lists of pentatonic songs, will also be wasted if such knowledge is not enlightened with consideration of musical value.

Perhaps one needs to spend time talking about scheduling and preparing programs and classroom management and public relations and budget and teacher rights and all the other topics that form the typical music education course outline, but just possibly, if the primary focus of such courses is on helping student teachers find ways to make each music class a truly aesthetic experience, many of the concerns implied by these topics may disappear. For example, classroom management takes care of itself in a music classroom where the students know that something truly *magical* is likely to happen because the heart of the day will be on music of meaning, for the students will then "manage themselves." Scheduling problems will gradually disappear because the administrators who determine scheduling know the importance of providing ample time for music because they, as they pass by the classroom, have seen for themselves the value of such experiences for the entire school population.

If the previous description suggests an appealing picture of appropriate undergraduate teacher education experiences, then it is time to return to the question posed at the beginning of this section: what should be the content of the doctoral programs from which come most teacher educators? As an initial answer, let me suggest that it should include some of the same kinds of integrative, wholistic experiences that we have described as essential to successful undergraduate programs: courses based on the recognition that knowledge-action-emotion are indivisible; rehearsals of appropriate undergraduate classroom situations; and observation and analysis of undergraduate teacher education activities. All of these experiences must be integrated with opportunities to acquire knowledge essential to effective undergraduate teaching, such as knowledge of the psychology of the college student combined with immediate consideration of implications for instruction (application of the "if-then" hypothesis).

Is it possible to offer such an educational environment within the doctoral program without weakening the research component that is considered the core of most current doctoral programs? If we recognize the validity of the proposal that the role of the teacher educator is to present meaningful ways of translating theory into practice, then it seems that the design proposed is exactly that which must become the content of the doctoral program. Just as action-cognition-emotion is an indivisible whole, so must research-instruction be seen as inextricably intertwined. That this fails to be the common practice can be easily documented by perusal of required and recommended courses in most music education doctoral programs as well as through examination of topics chosen for research by the graduates of our doctoral programs. *The Handbook for Research in Teacher Education* contains a chapter on research in music teacher education (Boardman 1990) that ends with the conclusion that research directed toward consideration of teacher education concerns is minimal, sporadic, and fragmented. Surely research into issues of learning, curriculum, and instruction that should influence the structure of teacher education programs is as valid a research topic as research into how those same issues affect the structure of pre-college music education programs. It is evidently not considered so if the number of studies can be considered one measure of level of concern. The teacher education practices currently found in most colleges and universities have not been subjected to the type of stringent evaluation that well-structured research might provide. For example, requirements for hours spent in field experience (frequently defined as experience in school situations preceding student teaching) have increased *n*-fold over the past forty years, yet no one has made even the most casual attempt to determine whether increase of hours in the music classroom results in improved teaching, or what variables might influence the quality of that experience. The only aspect of undergraduate music education that has been researched fairly consistently over the years (although the focus of this collection of studies is so fragmented that little guidance can be gained) has been into courses designed for classroom teachers. Are we so sure, as a profession, that traditional practices are best or that outside pressures preclude change, that we see no need for research? Or is it that the problems of designing meaningful research are simply too overwhelming? Or that by conducting research we are admitting weakness — admitting that we do not have "all the answers" — an admission our ego cannot permit? Whatever the reason, it seems the ultimate of irony that those who direct research, and speak to its value, fail to use research as a tool for improvement of their own instruction.

Although the music education profession has not aggressively pursued research as a means of improving curricular practices and instructional strategies, there is an extensive body of research and writing in related fields that offers direction for change. Examination of music education undergraduate programs, methods, books, and conference reports makes it difficult to ignore the conclusion that this body of information is also frequently neglected.

Writers in numerous fields have brought to our attention a new world view based on recognition that all effective systems, whether human, humanly constructed, or natural, are synergetic — gestalts that, while composed of parts, compose a whole that is greater than the simple summation of those parts. Despite the existence of this new body of knowledge, we continue to develop curricula, plan programs, and develop instructional strategies that "act" as though the reductionist theories of Isaac Newton (most strongly reflected in American behaviorism) still serve as convincing models for educational practice. Jerome Bruner decries "the habit of drawing conceptual boundaries between thought, action and emotion as 'regions' of the mind, then later being forced to construct conceptual bridges to connect what should never have been put to sunder" (Bruner 1986, 106); Goodman, as cited by Zimmerman (this volume), posits the existence of systems, interactive from birth, that combine sensorimotor actions and perceptions with affective reactions. This recognition that the individual is a system where thought, feeling, and action are both interdependent and indivisible has not only been hypothesized but has also been well documented.

It would seem time, then, that those of us in music education, at all levels, move to erase artificial conceptual boundaries and begin to construct models of learning and teaching that are founded in such synergetic concepts. Unless we do so, I fear that the future may simply be a repetition of the past, and that in 2021 my successors will once again echo the pleas for implementation of truly aesthetic-based music education curricula that were first voiced in 1958.

REFERENCES

Boardman, E. (1990). Music teacher education. In W.R. Houston, ed., *Handbook of Research on Teacher Education*. New York: Association of Teacher Educators and Macmillan.

Bruner, J. (1986). *Actual minds, possible worlds*. Cambridge, MA: Harvard University Press.

Gardner, H. (1985). *The mind's new science: A history of the cognitive revolution*. New York: Basic Books.

Goodman, N. (1976). *Languages of art*. Indianapolis, Ind.: Hockett Publishing Company.

———. (1984). *Of mind and other matters*. Cambridge, MA: Harvard University Press.

Lehman, P. (1986). Teaching music in the 1990's. *Dialogue in Instrumental Music Education* 10(1), 3–18.

Leonhard, C., and R. House (1959, 1972). *Foundations and principles of music education*. New York: McGraw-Hill.

Meske, E. (1985). Teacher education: A wedding of theory and practise. *Bulletin of the Council for Research in Music Education* 81, 65–73.

Olson, G. (ed.) (1987). *Music teacher education: Partnership and process*. Reston, VA: Music Educators National Conference.

Reimer, B. (1989). *A philosophy of music education*. (2d ed.) Englewood Cliffs, NJ: Prentice-Hall.

Index

289

Index